THE DEVELOPMENT OF CHILDREN'S
IMAGINATIVE WRITING

The Development of Children's Imaginative Writing

Edited by Helen Cowie

ST. MARTIN'S PRESS
New York

Library of Congress Cataloging in Publication Data
Main entry under title:

The Development of children's imaginative writing.

    Includes bibliographical references and index.
    1. English language — Composition and exercises — Study
and teaching — Addresses, essays, lectures. 2. Creative
writing — Study and teaching — Addresses, essays, lectures.
3. Imagination in children — Addresses, essays, lectures.
4. Children as authors — Addresses, essays, lectures.
I. Cowie, Helen.
PE1404.D4   1983   808'.042'088054   83-13970
ISBN 0-312-19743-8

CONTENTS

ACKNOWLEDGEMENTS

I would like to record my thanks to the people who have made this book possible:

for permission to reprint articles:
Chapter 6: Judy Ollington[1] and 'Aspects of Education', *Journal of the Institute of Education*, 28, University of Hull, Autumn 1982 for this revised and expanded version of 'Images for Life?';

Chapter 7: Peter C. Wason and *Visible Language*, vol. XIV, no. 4, 1980, Box 1972 CMA, Cleveland, OH 44106 for this revised version of 'Conformity and Commitment in Writing';

Chapter 8: Donald H. Graves and Donald M. Murray, and the *Journal of Education*, Boston University, vol. 162, no. 2, 1980;

Chapter 12: Donald H. Graves and the Primary English Teaching Association, PO Box 167, Rozelle NSW 2039 for this article which appeared in R.D. Walshe (ed.), *Donald Graves in Australia* (1981), Bridge Printery Pty. Ltd, 29-35 Dunning Avenue, Rosebery, NSW.

For permission to reprint 'Time' by Velma Sylvan, Chapter 3: Velma Sylvan whose poem was originally published in P. Ashton (ed.), *Side by Side: Writing from London Schools for the International Year of Disabled People* (1982) Trade Printing Company, Cowcross Street, London SW1.

For permission to reproduce Figure 11.3, Chapter 11: *Junior Education*, October 1981, p. 23, Scholastic Publications (Magazines) Ltd, 141-3 Drury Lane, London WC2B 5TG.

To all the contributors for their enthusiastic commitment to the task.

To the staff and children of St Mary's and St Peter's School, Church Road, Teddington, Middx for their interest in writing processes and their unfailing support;

to Aidan Warlow, Heather Hanrott and the children of Form 1, Ibstock Place School, Clarence Lane, London SW15 5PJ, for their willingness to share the experience of a writing community;

to the Roehampton Institute of Higher Education for generous financial support which enabled me to participate in the University of New Hampshire Summer Writing Programme, 1982, directed by Donald H. Graves;

to Phil Salmon, Department of Child Development and Educational Psychology, University of London Institute of Education, London, for her friendship and guidance.

[1] Sadly, Judy Ollington died while this book was in press. Her warmth and friendship are greatly missed.

LIST OF CONTRIBUTORS

Chris M. Anson, graduate student, Department of English, Ballantine Hall, Indiana University, Bloomington, Indiana 47405, USA

Clive Butler, deputy head, Collis Junior School, Teddington, Middx

Helen Cowie, senior lecturer, Department of Psychology, Froebel Institute College, Roehampton Institute of Higher Education, Roehampton Lane, London SW15 5PJ

Dilys Davies, clinical psychologist, Psychology Department, Carlton Hayes Hospital, Narborough, Leicester LE9 5ES

Donald H. Graves, Director, Writing Process Laboratory, Department of Education, Morrill Hall, University of New Hampshire, Durham NH 03824, USA

Heather Hanrott, teacher, Ibstock Place School, Clarence Lane, London SW15 5PJ

Barry M. Kroll, Associate Professor, Department of English, Ballantine Hall, Indiana University, Bloomington, Indiana 47405, USA

Donald M. Murray, Professor, Department of English, University of New Hampshire, Durham NH 03824, USA

Judy Ollington, senior lecturer, Department of Religious Studies, Whitelands College, Roehampton Institute of Higher Education, West Hill, London SW15 3SN

Linda Pollock, Research Fellow, Churchill College, University of Cambridge, Cambridge

Peter K. Smith, senior lecturer, Department of Psychology, University of Sheffield, Sheffield S10 2TN

Joan Tamburrini, principal lecturer, Department of Education, Froebel Institute College, Roehampton Institute of Higher Education, Roehampton Lane, London SW15 5PJ

Peter C. Wason, Reader, Department of Phonetics and Linguistics, Annexe Wolfson House, 4 Stephenson Way, London NW1 2HE

James Willig, principal lecturer, Department of Education, Froebel Institute of Higher Education, Roehampton Lane, London SW15 5PJ

To Julian and Anna
and to Peter
for their inspiration

PREFACE

Helen Cowie

At a recent seminar in which I was discussing the difficulties involved in evaluating pieces of writing by children, a learned colleague asked, 'Why don't you use quantitative measures for the analysis of the stories? You could, for example, calculate mean sentence length or estimate the proportion of verbs to total word count.' On hearing this story, a friend who is a great admirer of Tolstoy commented, 'Imagine if I asked you what you thought of *The Kreutzer Sonata* and you replied that you were impressed by the number of verbs per sentence. I would think that you had answered a different question.'

Of course, the quantitative approach to the analysis of written language is a perfectly valid one, but it is not, on the whole, one which is adopted in this book. In fact, the book arose in part out of the dissatisfaction which I felt at my original attempts to evaluate stories written by children simply as end-products. I soon discovered that the more I knew about the young writers, the more I had observed them as they wrote, discussed the process of composing with them, and talked to them about the sources of their ideas and the problems which they encountered in capturing their thoughts, the greater was my understanding of what these children were trying to do. As an English teacher, I realised how important it was to establish a context in which children had enough trust in their audience to share the stories which they had written and to seek help, where necessary, with problems of style, structure of plots, credibility of settings and events and, in general, with writing blocks. In addition, where the writing was very personal, it was important to listen with sensitivity to the voice which was trying to be heard and to see the potential in the most unpromising first drafts. Later, when I went into St Mary's and St Peter's School, Teddington, as an observer in the class room, I found an atmosphere which was highly conducive to the development of imaginative writing. This was illustrated by the children's eagerness to talk about their writing, which grew, I felt sure, from their trust in the teachers and from their frequent and happy experiences of reading, writing and talking together. The children in the top junior class would often stay in at play-time to finish a piece or to rehearse a play which a group was writing; stories would

1

be taken home voluntarily to be completed and shared with family and friends. At the time I concluded that, rather than viewing the child's writing in isolation, there was value in considering it as part of a dynamic relationship between child and teacher, child and home, child and peers, and child in a particular class room with a certain audience in mind. Some of the complexity of the process emerged in my interviews with the children. Writing, as far as they were concerned, seemed to be a strongly personal matter, a way of expressing the self. At times the ideas were so personal that they could not be shared with anyone; when they were shared, the presence of a sensitive reader, usually the teacher, was crucial. At the same time, the children were evolving in their own minds a sense of what made good writing. Getting it right with the *topic* – the form and content of a story, the development of a character, the reality and credibility of a plot – and getting it right with the *self* – expressing their own meaning, capturing their own experiences and emotions – seemed to be factors which preoccupied many of them, from the most to the least articulate. The 'indwelling of reader in writer' seemed also to be a factor, whether this grew out of the child's own experience of reading and hearing stories or from the knowledge that the writing was in some ways directed towards others. Of course, this was one group of children, aged between 11 and 12, in one particular context, and it would be rash to conclude that this could be a universal experience. However, the observations did point to the importance of the environment where the writing mostly took place – the classroom – and suggested that where there was an on-going concern for talk, reading, drama, listening, and an interest by the teacher in the children and the issues which preoccupy and move them, then this was the climate in which the development of writing abilities could flourish.

Later still I became aware of the work which was being done by Donald Graves in the Writing Research Laboratory at the University of New Hampshire. During our correspondence and subsequent meetings I learned about his concern for process and his view that it was revision, redrafting and rewriting which created real writing. He argued that the young child, like the accomplished author, should learn to view a piece as a draft which can be worked on and improved. The key to this was 'ownership'; the child should feel that he or she had control over the writing, and that the voice which was being expressed was an authentic, personal one. From this it followed that, where possible, the child should be encouraged to write about topics of interest to him or her, not themes imposed by the teacher. The concept of the 'conference', which appears over and over in his writing, refers to the short interview between teacher and children where sensitive, concerned questions are asked and where the young writers are enabled to express more effectively the meanings which they intend to convey. The process which I had observed in 11-year-olds is, Graves claims, evident in first school children who often come to school believing that they can write. (Vygotsky's claim that writing grows out of the young child's discovery that he or she can not only draw things but also words is relevant here.) Through the one-to-one meetings or conferences between teacher and child, where the teacher is in the role of learner about the information which the writer wishes to impart, the young author discovers how to value what he or she knows and how to express it effectively in his or her own voice. The conference too is the place where the mechanics of writing can be most efficiently taught — as the need for punctuation, accurate spelling, readable handwriting is felt by the writers themselves.

In 1982 I participated in the Summer Writing Programme directed by Donald Graves at the University of New Hampshire. There I experienced at first hand his message that teachers should write themselves if they are to foster writing ability in their pupils, since it is by doing this that they rediscover how difficult the process is. In addition, they can experience the variability of their own writing capacity from day to day, and their own vulnerability as they share writing with an audience. During the three-week course, the teachers learned ways of overcoming writer's block, strategies for free writing, revision and editing; they worked on leads and effective endings; they shared their writing in the small conference groups which they were encouraged to form and discovered the importance of 'finding a voice', that is, finding what *they* wanted to say and how to express it well. Each week culminated in a public reading of the pieces which had been composed with such intensity during the previous four days. In addition, they attended lectures on Donald Graves's action research in the New Hampshire schools. We all gained from the experience of being part of a writing community; 'finding a voice' and learning not to put 'fingerprints' on another person's piece — the recurring themes of the course — were ideas which could usefully be put into practice at any level by teachers who were concerned to foster writing abilities. The issues are explored in the present book.

Another source of influence on my thinking about writing came from the symposium on the subject which I organised at the British Psychological Society Annual Conference at the University of York in 1982. The speakers from various disciplines — psychology, education, English, linguistics — opened up new perspectives on the writing process.

Barry Kroll analysed the effect of audience on the style and content of children's persuasive writing; Peter Wason's paper focused on the experience of writing, and subsequent discussion showed its relevance to a variety of contexts – the academic writing for a learned journal, the novelist, the child writing for a teacher; Alex McLeod showed how it was possible to study children in the midst of the composing process through the use of video; my own paper indicated developmental trends in the expression of emotion by junior school children. Comments from the audience at the time and correspondence afterwards suggested a number of lines of enquiry. Research in the field of social cognition, especially work on social role-taking and its part in the child's growing sensitivity to others, seemed to be relevant to the writer's sense of audience on the one hand, and the developing ability to enter into the experiences and feelings of characters in stories on the other. In addition, it seemed plausible to argue that imaginative story-writing might grow out of episodes which had been enacted in play at an earlier age. This could all be seen as part of an interacting process of development through which the child gained an increasing understanding of the social world. Again, a useful line of enquiry came from the study of highly personal writing, the diaries of children and adolescents from the past which gave unusual insights into how these writers saw themselves and others at a particular point in history, and how their sensitivity to feelings increased over time. Finally, work on children's religious thinking suggested ways in which, through writing, children might come to terms with spiritual and emotional issues in their own lives.

The book falls into four main sections. Part 1 presents a theoretical introduction which analyses some of the processes which underlie the world of the imagination. Part 2 explores children's growing awareness of themselves and others, for example in their perceptions of sex-roles, their ways of dealing with issues like illness and death, fear and separation, and emotions of religious awe and wonder, and their understanding of the social world across time. Part 3 examines the writing process and draws parallels between the adult and the child writer; the growing complexity of the structures inherent in children's stories is analysed. Finally, in Part 4, we look at children's own perceptions of writing, see one writing community in the class room in action and discuss how far children can have control over the writing process.

It is worth ending with words written by Froebel (1887):

Writing in pictures and in symbols assumes an overflowing richness of life in thought and experience. This richness gave rise to writing and only in virtue of it does the child develop a real need to write. Parents and teachers must, therefore, take care to make the life of their children's minds as rich as possible, not so much in diversity as in activity and meaning. If this is not done and if writing and learning to write are not connected with some inner need, the mother tongue becomes something extraneous, alien and lifeless, as it is now for so many people.

Reference

Froebel, F. (1887) *The Education of Man*, translated by W.N. Hailman, Appleton and Co., New York

Part One: FANTASY AND IMAGINATION:
A DEVELOPMENTAL PERSPECTIVE

INTRODUCTION

Helen Cowie

Britton (1982) reminds us of Vygotsky's (1978, p. 116) perception of the links to be made between writing and other forms of symbolic representation, such as make-believe play and drawing, which he saw as 'different moments in an essentially unified process of development of written language'. Although many aspects of the process through which children make the transition from speech, drawing and play to written language are still far from being fully understood, the contributors to this first section of the book indicate some of the findings which researchers have made through their observations of children's imaginative activities. We see how children may progress to imaginative writing, with all the new opportunities which it offers them, from their earlier experiences of make-believe play, talking and listening to stories, and drawing.

Peter Smith, considering possible connections between the fantasy and socio-dramatic play of young children and written-language development, draws parallels between the themes and narrative structures which emerge in play and those which later appear in children's stories. He points out the dangers of drawing premature conclusions from the evidence available so far; my own view, which I develop in Chapter 3, is that the learning which occurs as children take on a variety of roles in play may continue as they find out that through the creation of characters in narratives they can capture familiar experiences, have adventures which take them beyond their normal environments, express emotions and experiment with different modes of behaviour. In his discussion Peter Smith also stresses the crucial effect which adult involvement has on the facilitation of fantasy play in young children. Do these play experiences contribute directly to later writing skills? I would suggest that there are connections to be made between this work and the research by Britton on the child's sense of audience, and by Graves on the role of the teacher in establishing a writing community in the classroom. Again, are these influences specific or general? Does the fantasy play provide practice for the elaboration of particular themes in stories, or does it relate in a wider sense to the development of social perspective-taking skills?

This is one of the issues explored by Joan Tamburrini in her developmental analysis of three uses of the imagination — the 'as if' type of thinking which is involved in make-believe, the 'if then' type of thinking in which ideas are extended, and the ability to take on the perspective of another person. She discusses children's capacity for understanding other people's points of view in terms of the growth of distancing. In her review of the literature on story-telling and story-writing, she shows too how, with age, children develop greater distancing abilities — spatially as they place the events of their narratives in increasingly unfamiliar settings, and psychologically as they give the characters that people their stories experiences and feelings distanced from their own. Thus, she indicates the part which imaginative role-taking can play in children's ability to put themselves at the points of view of the characters about whom they write. Increased distancing in imagination in the role-taking sense also characterises the development of the ability to identify the reader's point of view. Parallel to this runs the increasing complexity of the structure of children's stories and a growing awareness of possible underlying meanings. This point is further illustrated in the third chapter where we see examples of children's reflections on their own writing processes. I argue that there are developmental trends in the ability to express feeling, to analyse intention and to understand the motives which underlie actions. I also suggest that there is a growth with age in young writers' self-awareness and capacity for entering into the experience of others.

The three chapters in this section provide some support for the argument that not only are imaginative activities intrinsically valuable to children, but that they also help them to develop social skills, sensitivity to others and a deepening understanding of themselves.

We can return to Britton (1982) when he writes:

It remains for me to point out that make-believe play (embracing the social environment children construct with their play-things), story-telling, listening to stories, pictorial representation and the talk that complements it, story-reading and story-writing — these are all activities in the role of spectator. As I have suggested, I believe it is this characteristic that develops a need for the written language in young children and the intention to master it. In such activities children are sorting themselves out, progressively distinguishing what is from what seems, strengthening their hold on reality by a consideration of alternatives'. (pp. 164-5)

References

Britton, J. (1982) 'Spectator Role and the Beginnings of Writing' in M. Nystrand
    (ed.), *What Writers Know*, Academic Press, New York and London
Vygotsky, L.S. (1978) *Mind in Society*, edited by M. Cole, V. John-Steiner, S.
    Scribner and E. Souberman, Harvard University Press, Cambridge, Mass.

1 THE RELEVANCE OF FANTASY PLAY FOR DEVELOPMENT IN YOUNG CHILDREN

Peter K. Smith

It is a morning late in March, and some twenty children, 3 to 4 years old, are nearing the end of the morning session of their preschool playgroup. There has been a lot of fantasy play, recorded by an observer watching unobtrusively. Two girls have been playing 'mother and baby', one wheeling the other around in a pram. Several of the older boys have been chasing each other, being 'monsters', and pretending to shoot each other with outstretched arms and fingers. At one point they besiege the Wendy House which the girls are in. Later, Simon pretends to be a captain on a boat (a long chair at the end of the room). To attract attention, he yells 'I'm a dead captain – I've got an arrow in there', pulling up his vest and poking his tummy. 'Let's take the arrow out', says Christopher; 'Let's leave him – till he gets better', says Mark. However, Simon does not like being left alone, and announces he is a shark. More chasing play, but then they set up some stools in a row and turn it into a 'chair-train', pushing the chairs backwards along the floor (until stopped by the playgroup supervisor) and making train noises.

Jane has joined in some of the monster play and is on a chair making monster noises. Kate runs up to join her: 'I know you're a monster, Jane, but I'm a monster. Those two boys and those two girls, we'll make them scream and they'll run away from us, we'll be monsters.' They run and chase some other children, then crawl under a table together. 'I know what, I'll be a witch', says Jane. 'Yes', says Kate, 'put my hat on.' She pretends to put a hat on her head. 'I'll get my stick', says Jane. 'Oh yes, my stick', says Kate. They pretend to get on imaginary broomsticks and ride off on them, developing into a chase with both girls yelling 'We are witches, we are witches! We will spell you!' (Another girl, Emma, watches and runs off by herself, muttering 'We are witches.') Jane runs up to Mary and clasps her with her arms: 'We've got you, we are witches!' Mary says 'No!', but Kate pretends to wind string round her, 'I've tied her up'. They run off to a book corner. Kate says, 'These are special witch books, you know! Set them out like this', putting half a dozen books in a row. Jane fetches more books. 'We are witches, we are witches, we will turn you into a monster', Jane shouts to Mary. 'We are turning, we are turning you into a nasty monster', Kate shouts to Stephen, adding 'No, you're not having these books', as he grabs at them. The play is ended by the arrival of parents at the end of the morning.

These examples of fantasy and sociodramatic play are fairly characteristic of young children in our society. They are characterised by pretence, imagination and drama. It is pretend play, as the girls are not really witches, they do not have real hats or spells. The term *imaginative play*, often used synonymously with pretend, fantasy or symbolic play, refers to the imaginative use children can put ordinary objects such as chairs and books to, and to how they can imagine absent objects as well. And clearly, there is drama in the action. At an age before they have learnt to read or write, these children are making up and acting out little adventures, many of them prosaic imitations of home life, some more removed from domestic reality. When children are acting out roles together, this is referred to as *sociodramatic play*.

In some important respects the fantasy and sociodramatic play of children can be thought of as the precursors of later imaginative story-writing or telling. There are structural similarities, and some psychologists have suggested more direct links. In this chapter I shall review what we know about these forms of play, highlighting links to language, creativity and writing skills where appropriate. For recent general reviews on play, see Rubin (1980a), Pepler and Rubin (1982), and Rubin, Fein and Vandenberg (in press); on fantasy play, see also Fein (1981).

The Developmental Sequence of Fantasy and Sociodramatic Play

Fantasy play seems to develop in a fairly regular way as children get older. Piaget (1951) was one of the first psychologists to describe this in detail, and since then several other investigators have described the changes which occur up to 2½ or 3 years of age. A useful summary of these studies is provided by McCune-Nicolich (1981).

The earliest pretence behaviours are generally seen around 15 months of age. These are typically self-directed behaviours — for example, Piaget observed his daughter Jacqueline at this age lie down with her head on a cloth, suck her thumb and blink her eyes (as if going to sleep) — and smile. By 2 years of age other-directed actions are more common, such as putting a doll or teddy-bear to sleep.

Another clear developmental trend is the lessening dependence on realistic objects for fantasy. Up to 2 or 3 years, children most easily fantasise with the aid of miniature items such as toy cups, combs, dolls, etc. As they get older, they are more able to make fantasy use of un-structured materials such as boxes, sticks and so on, transforming them in play into such things as boats or guns. The more such transforma-tions are simultaneously involved, the more difficult for the child. One experimental study showed that at 20 to 26 months of age, 93 per cent of children would imitate making a detailed horse model 'drink' from a plastic cup. Only 33 per cent would imitate making a horsey shape 'drink' from a clam shell. If the horse alone or the cup alone was real-istic, the figures were 79 per cent and 61 per cent respectively (Fein, 1975).

Pretence sometimes involves imagining an object when no substitute object is present (for example, the witch's hat, and the string, in the opening example). This is possible for 3 and 4-year-olds, but is easier still in middle childhood. For example, when asked to pretend to brush their teeth or comb their hair, most 3 or 4-year-olds use a substitute body part such as a finger; whereas most 6 or 8-year-olds imagine the toothbrush or comb in their hand (Overton and Jackson, 1973).

Pretence-play episodes also involve more combinations as children get older — combining a number of objects in play, or different actions on the same object (for example, bathing, dressing and feeding a doll). As such combinations and sequences develop, we can talk of role play, with a child acting out a role such as 'mother'. When two or more children role play together — either similar roles, such as the 'witches' example, or different roles such as 'mother' and 'baby' — then socio-dramatic play develops.

There has not been such intensive study of developmental changes in fantasy play after 3 years, but it is fairly clear that sociodramatic play increases in occurrence at least up to 5 years of age. Older children engage in more role play than object-fantasy play, and in more socially interactive pretend play (Field, De Stefano and Koewler, 1982). How-ever, after the age of 6 or 7 years, symbolic play generally becomes less frequent as children engage more in rule-governed games such as hop-scotch, tag and football.

Symbolic Play and the Acquisition of Language

Both early words and early pretence substitutions in play are thought by many cognitive psychologists such as Piaget to be reflections of a general capacity for symbolic representation (see also Fischer, 1980).

The ability to pretend that a doll is a baby may be linked to the ability to 'pretend' that the word 'baby' refers to a baby; both seem to imply a symbolic concept of what a baby is, going beyond just a sensorimotor response to an actual baby, such as smiling or touching.

Several psychologists have attempted to draw closer parallels between the development of pretend play and the development of early language. One of these is McCune-Nicolich (1981), who suggests there are parallels between the two domains first in presymbolic behaviours; then in initial pretending and first referential words; then in the emergence of combinatorial behaviours in both domains; and finally in the hierarchical organisation of symbolic play and language.

For example, the sorts of combinations in symbolic play which were mentioned earlier have been found to occur at about the same time as two-word language combinations, such as 'baby bath'. However, as McCune-Nicolich states, additional research is needed to confirm how close and how invariant these parallels are.

Further evidence for such a link between symbolic play and language has been reported by Corrigan (1982). She showed 2-year-old children certain play behaviours, such as making a doll walk across the floor saying, 'I'm dirty. Now I'm going to take a bath.' They were then asked to imitate the same actions. Corrigan also got the children to imitate sentences such as 'The mummy is giving the baby a bath.' In their imitations the children seemed to go through a similar developmental sequence of increasing complexity in imitating the play actions and the spoken sentences.

Several other studies have found parallels between the development of symbolic play and the development of language. For example, Ungerer and Sigman (1981) found that autistic children showed similar impairments in both their symbolic use of play objects and in language comprehension. However, it is important to remember that these parallels do not necessarily mean that symbolic play and language influence each other *directly*; it could be that they are both aspects of a general symbolic or cognitive development. Also, one longitudinal study of Canadian infants (Russell and Russnaik, 1981) found that symbolic-play measures did not correlate with language (although measures of the latter were restricted to utterance length and vocabulary). A recent review of this area is by McCune-Nicolich and Bruskin (1982).

Structure and Conventions in Symbolic Play Episodes

Whatever the link between symbolic play and language production or comprehension, there is another parallel with written, narrative language. Fantasy and sociodramatic play episodes are themselves acted-out narratives or stories. Several psychologists and linguists have discussed the narrative-like features of fantasy play, the conventions governing sociodramatic play, and the fantasy/reality distinction. These analyses have usually been based on audiotaped or videotaped interactions in nursery or laboratory playroom settings.

The simple forms of symbolic play seen up to 2 years of age do not often tell any sustained story, or have a plot. Wolf and Grollman (1982), working with the Harvard 'Project Zero' research on the development of children's symbolic abilities, have constructed a developmental scale for levels of narrative organisation in play. At the *scheme level*, a child just performs a simple action or brief series of actions; for example, feeding a doll with a spoon. At the *event script level*, a child performs at least two schemes which are part of the same process or part of achieving the same goal; for example, pouring a 'drink' into a cup, adding 'sugar', and offering it to drink. At the *episode level*, a child performs at least two script events aimed at achieving a particular goal; for example, first stirring some 'food' and 'cooking' it; then serving out the 'meal' on plates at a table. Wolf and Grollman looked in very great detail at a small sample of only four children, who reached episode-level play at round about 2 years of age. In this and previous work, these researchers also distinguish between *styles* of play. They hypothesise that *patterners* primarily explore the uses and properties of objects, whereas *dramatists* more often imagine non-present objects, events or persons, and use objects as props in social interaction.

While solitary fantasy play may have quite a complex narrative structure, the latter becomes particularly obvious when one child plays with another, or with an adult; the play episode needs first to be initiated, and then continued along a plan, often with the participants adopting certain roles in sociodramatic play (Sachs, 1980).

Some of the ways in which 4-year-old children initiate fantasy play have been described by Matthews (1977). She observed six main ways of introducing a transformation from reality to fantasy:

Substitution. A child directly gives a new identity to an object; for example, picking up a stick and saying 'This is my space gun.'
Attribution of function. A child ascribes a pretend function to an object;

for example saying 'Don't shoot me' when another child picks up a stick.

Animation. A child attributes animate characteristics to an object; for example tucking a teddy under a cushion saying 'Go to sleep, baby.'

Insubstantial material attribution. A child refers to non-existent objects; for example picking up an empty box saying 'I've got some presents in here for you.'

Insubstantial situation attribution. A child refers to a non-existent situation; for example announcing 'Come on, let's go to the party!'

Character attribution. A child directly adopts (or gives to another child) a role; for example saying 'I'll be mummy, okay? You be daddy.'

The first three modes of initiation Matthews calls *material*, and the latter three *ideational* (apparently corresponding to the *patterners* and *dramatists* of Wolf and Grollman, 1982). Matthews found more ideational initiations amongst girls than boys (though her sample of 16 subjects is really rather small for such comparisons). She also found that they became more common with increasing familiarity between play partners.

When a fantasy episode is initiated, how do the participants know what to do next? If it is to continue, some theme, plan or narrative must be followed. This has been most thoroughly discussed by Garvey (1977). She suggests that fantasy themes are generally built around certain plans, the popular ones being 'averting threat', 'telephoning', 'packing', 'taking a trip', 'shopping', 'cooking', 'dining', 'treating/healing' and 'building/repairing'.

Garvey suggests that each of these plans has a basic structure; for example, 'averting threat' has the three-sequenced components: identification of threat or danger/defence/outcome. The threat might be another child running up saying 'I am a witch', the defence might be running away, and the outcome that the first child is caught and 'tied up' (see episode at beginning of this chapter). As another example, 'telephoning' involves initiating a call/greeting/body of call/closing. Within a plan, one or more components might be omitted; not all pretend telephone calls have a greeting, for example – or some might *just* be a greeting! Also, there are many possible transformations within a component; a threat might be a snake, a fire, a bomb, etc.

The most common roles adopted, according to both Garvey and Matthews, are *relational* ones, such as parent-child, or wife-husband. These can of course be fitted into a number of plans, such as 'shopping' or 'dining'. Garvey also distinguishes *functional* roles, defined around actions such as driver/passenger; and *character* roles, stereotyped or fictional, such as cowboys or Santa Claus. Finally, *peripheral* roles are just referred to by the child; imaginary friends, for example.

These roles can be enacted using knowledge the child has, either directly in the family (relational roles), through wider experience (functional roles), or TV or stories (character roles). Garvey found that the youngest children were confined to relational roles; and even in older children, it is these relational roles which often have the most detailed repertoire of narrative plans.

Roles may be exchanged between children, for example, two children might exchange the role of 'mummy' and 'baby' after a while. Most roles remain sex-appropriate, with a girl being 'mummy'. According to Matthews (Brooks-Gunn and Matthews, 1979), girls more often adopt relational roles in domestic-type plans such as 'cooking' and 'dining'; almost three-quarters of the time in her observations. Boys engaged more in a wider variety of plans, such as 'taking a trip', or 'averting threat', or in more unusual plans such as 'firework displays' or 'marching bands'.

Watching role adoptions and portrayals in 3 and 4-year-olds reveals their sex-role perceptions in a very clear way. For example, in one episode observed by Matthews, 'mummy' doesn't mend a broken ironing board because 'when daddy comes home, he'll fix it'. Sometimes there are disagreements though; later on when 'daddy' arrives and mends the ironing board, he grasps the toy iron and starts to do some 'ironing'. 'Mummy' quickly grabs the iron, saying 'No, no, daddies don't iron.' 'Daddy' thinks for a bit, then says 'But when mommies are gone, they iron.' 'When, when mommies are gone, daddies iron?' stutters 'mummy' incredulously. 'Yeah', says 'daddy'. 'Oh', says 'mummy' and goes back to the 'cooking'.

During negotiations of roles, and disagreements over action, the 'fantasy' nature of an episode may be momentarily suspended. In her study, Matthews (1978) found that 21 per cent of interactive fantasy play was taken up with interruptions; these were caused by wandering attention, disagreements, distraction by other objects, exchanging real-life information, intervention by others, or 'real' discussion of how to continue or elaborate the fantasy.

Such breaks and resumptions of the fantasy show that the children are fully aware of the fantasy/reality distinction, and are able to negotiate their way in and out of it without great difficulty. Indeed, fantasy episodes can sometimes call upon or reveal a great deal of social skill. The example below, adapted from Garvey's (1977) work, shows how a

3-year-old girl is both acting out the 'baby' role, and directing the 'caretaker' role, coming in and out of the fantasy as necessary.

The girl (aged 3 years 3 months) initiates a baby/caretaker sequence with a boy (aged 2 years 9 months) and carries it through twelve exchanges before a 'real-life' query ends it.

Girl	Boy
Say 'Go to sleep now'	
	Go sleep now
Why? (whining)	
	Baby . . .
Why?	
	Because
No, say 'Because' (emphatically)	
	Because! (emphatically)
Why? Because why?	
	Not good. You bad.
Why?	
	'Cause you spill your milk
No, 'cause I bit somebody	
	Yes, you did.
Say 'Go to sleep. Put your head down' (sternly).	
	Put your head down (sternly)
No	
	Yes
No	
	Yes. Okay I will spank you. Bad boy (spanks her).
My head's up (giggles). I want my teddy bear (petulant voice).	
	No, your teddy bear go away (sternly).
Why?	
	'Cause he does (walks off with teddy bear).
Are you going to pack your teddy bear?	

The Role of the Adult in Narrative Structure

On the one hand some aspects of children's fantasy episodes can seem remarkably sophisticated. On the other hand many episodes are mundane or even dull; a high proportion of actions are simple imitations of domestic tasks, tucking in baby, washing dishes, eating food.

Potentially, an adult can do much to enrich a child's fantasy. This is true both for the early episodes of 1½ to 2-year-olds, the sociodramatic play of 3 and 4-year-olds, and the thematic fantasy play and sociodrama of older children.

The role the adult can have in extending the fantasy play of younger children is described by Sachs (1980), enlivened by transcriptions of play between her, or her husband, and their daughter Naomi when she was aged between 21 and 25 months. In the earlier episodes the adult is mainly suggesting actions to the child, for example, 'Get the baby and bring him to bed', or 'Can you feed Georgie with the spoon?' The separate components or building blocks for later narratives or plans are being suggested, but as yet Naomi does not provide this integration. A few months later, however, Naomi begins to be able to establish a storyline in her play when helped by an adult. Now, the adults' comments help Naomi move from one action to the next, e.g. Naomi (putting dolls in sitting position): 'Baby sit there'; adult: 'Do they want something to eat?' Quite possibly, the prompts provided by an adult (or older sibling, perhaps) when a child is only 2 years old help the child to create his or her own plans in sociodramatic play a year or so later (see later section on individual differences).

In the 3 to 5-year age range it is by now well established that adults can encourage sociodramatic play in children who do not engage in it spontaneously to a very great extent. This *play tutoring* was pioneered by Smilansky (1968) in Israel. She was concerned at the low levels of sociodramatic play which she observed in immigrant children in Israeli kindergartens, and examined a number of ways of facilitating it. Taking the children on visits (e.g. to zoos, hospitals) and providing appropriate props helped, but most effective was if an adult suggested themes to the children and/or helped sustain the narrative. This technique has since been employed widely in the USA, UK and elsewhere. Follow-ups show that play tutoring does facilitate the subsequent spontaneous sociodramatic play of the children. What other benefits it may have will be reviewed in a later section.

With older preschool children, another possibility for adult involvement is via *thematic fantasy play* (Saltz and Johnson, 1974). Here, children are helped to act a story whose plot is already sketched out; for example, folk tales or fairy tales such as The Three Billy Goats Gruff, Hansel and Gretel, Little Red Riding Hood. It is argued that thematic fantasy play demands more of the children than much sociodramatic play, since the roles and behaviours acted out are further removed from ordinary experience.

With older children still, forms of dramatic play or role-playing can be employed in the curriculum. For example, Iannotti (1978) asked 6 and 9-year-old boys to act out short stories or skits, sometimes switching roles, in an attempt to encourage altruism and empathy. Hartshorn and Brantley (1973) organised 8 and 9-year-olds in dramatic play in a child-size city they constructed, as a way of increasing problem-solving skills and social responsibility. Chandler (1973) asked delinquent and non-delinquent 11 to 13-year-old boys to participate in film/drama workshops to improve role-taking ability and decrease anti-social behaviour. These latter researches are closer to work on role-playing in adults (Moreno, 1946), and it is outside the scope of this chapter to consider them more fully.

Individual Differences in Fantasy Play

Children differ very greatly in the amount and complexity of fantasy play which they spontaneously engage in. For example, in two pre-school playgroups in which I made observations (Smith and Connolly, 1980), I recorded incidents of fantasy play over a total period of 6 hours; a couple of children were seen in fantasy play for a total of only 2 or 3 minutes; whereas another, in the same environment, spent over 2½ of the 6 hours in fantasy activities.

Social class and cultural differences have both been implicated in the causation of such differences. Observations in nursery schools, and interviews with parents, suggest that children from lower socioeconomic backgrounds engage in less fantasy and sociodramatic play, and receive less encouragement from parents to do so. For example, Newson and Newson (1968) found that in their sample of 4-year-olds there was a large social-class difference in the extent to which children talked about fantasies or imaginary companions to their mothers, and also the extent to which mothers participated in the children's play. Smilansky (1968) and others have reported subcultural differences too. Such conclusions have been criticised by McLoyd (1982) on a number of methodological criteria; for example, social-class differences found in nursery schools might not be observed in streets or playgrounds.

Rather than simply stating that social class is an important variable, it is necessary to try and find out exactly what environmental factors are important. We have seen that the kinds of toys young children are provided with may or may not facilitate fantasy. Also the encouragement of parents may or may not serve both to scaffold early fantasy narratives, and allow, or forbid, the expression of the child's imagination.

Two quotes from mothers in the Newsons' (1968) study — both from working-class backgrounds — express these different parental attitudes. Encouragement: 'Oh yes, I always play house — he plays house, and he's the mummy and I'm the auntie and come to visit him.' Discouragement: 'I've said to him, you know, "That's never happened, you're imagining things!" I've told him, I've said, "Now that's *wrong* — you've got a vivid imagination".'

The role of adults is also important in considering the effects of different preschool or infant school curricula. Adult tutoring of fantasy play in the preschool can have considerable impact. Such adult tutoring seems to have more direct impact than either simple or mediated use of television films (Singer and Singer, 1976). The effects of the mass media on fantasy are complex; many of the role adoptions in sociodramatic play are taken from TV serials, but most studies find that watching a great deal of television correlates with less imaginative or fantasy play (Rubin, Fein and Vandenberg, in press).

Singer (1973) has written about 'high-fantasy' (HF) and 'low-fantasy' (LF) disposition in children. He assessed this by asking children about the kinds of games they liked, whether they ever had pictures in their head, and whether they had make-believe friends or imaginary companions. He found that 6 to 9-year-olds of HF disposition, when asked to tell stories to a suggested topic (e.g. a mother and son; they look worried), produced stories which were rated as more creative or imaginative. Pulaski (1973) confirmed that in a sample of 5 to 7-year-olds, HF predicted to a much higher level of observed fantasy play with objects than did LF disposition. In this study the experimenter asked the child to make up a fantasy story with the materials available. HF children produced more imaginary details in their stories, which were better organised, less anchored to everyday reality, and showed a greater variety of themes.

Similarly, Lieberman (1977) has argued that children vary on a general playfulness factor. She, and others, have found some evidence that playfulness, and a disposition for pretend play, correlate with creativity. However, there are problems with concluding too directly from their work that playfulness or fantasy disposition, and creativity or narrative skill, are directly related. First, much of the evidence on children's playfulness is based on teachers' ratings, and teachers might tend to think that playfulness and creativity go together and let this influence their ratings, irrespective of whether it was actually so; direct observations of the children would be better. Also, a correlation may be due to some third factor which is the important causal influence; for example, some or all of the link between playfulness and creativity may be due to general intelligence influencing both (Lieberman, 1977; Fein, 1981).

This raises an important point about the significance of fantasy play. Children with HF disposition or who do a lot of fantasy play may tend to be those who are creative, intelligent, as well as co-operative, popular and less egocentric (Fein, 1981), and with higher levels of reading readiness (Becher and Wolfgang, 1977). Does this mean that encouraging fantasy play would encourage these other attributes? We cannot infer this from correlational studies; the intelligence might cause the fantasy, not the other way round. Experimental studies can potentially answer this question, though as we shall see, they have their own problems of methodology and interpretation.

Direct Training of Fantasy and Sociodramatic Play

The work of Smilansky (1968), and others since, has shown the possibility of enhancing the fantasy and sociodramatic play of children in nursery schools, playgroups and kindergartens, by means of adult tutoring in which an adult (usually a teacher) actively interacts with the children. This can involve either *outside intervention* or *inside intervention*. With outside intervention the teacher remains outside the play episode but provides comments or encouragement; for example, saying 'What are you going to cook for supper?' to two children in the Wendy House. With inside intervention the teacher actually takes a role and joins in the play; for example, saying 'Let's pretend that we are washing dishes', miming the actions, and perhaps assigning roles to the children.

Christie (1982a) provides a readable account of how to carry out and assess intervention in sociodramatic play. He suggests that the six essential elements for a teacher to work on are (1) imitative role play; (2) make-believe in regard to objects; (3) make-believe in regard to actions and situations; (4) interaction with play partners; (5) verbal communication related to the play episode and (6) persistence in the play episode. When the child has been observed participating in play that contains all these essential elements, Christie suggests that play intervention should be phased out. As he also points out, this sort of direct intervention is not appropriate for children who are already engaged in high-quality sociodramatic play, where indirect stimulation via vocabulary, props and theme ideas, is more relevant.

Since Smilansky's work, numerous researchers have confirmed that play tutoring does work; sociodramatic play can indeed be encouraged and developed in this way. This may be valuable in its own right, but will boosting sociodramatic play help a child in other ways? Some lines of evidence would suggest so. We have seen that the structure of such play episodes and the interpersonal co-operation and role-taking involved may make considerable demands on a child's social and perspective-taking skills. Correlational evidence links fantasy-play disposition with creativity and symbolic skills such as language, which may develop in step with it. If in fact there is a real causal influence here — if the experience of pretend play directly helps language and perspective-taking skills, for example — then boosting pretend play should develop these other areas of competence too.

In the 1970s a large number of studies were carried out, using what became virtually a research paradigm, employing play-tutoring and comparing its effects with a control condition. The basic research plan is outlined in Figure 1.1. These studies were mostly done in the USA, on kindergarten children from lower socioeconomic groups. The findings of some dozen research projects were generally positive: play-tutored children increased in social, cognitive and language skills, and creativity, more than control children (see Smith and Syddall, 1978, and Fein, 1981, for a review).

Figure 1.1: Typical Design of Research Projects on the Effects of Play Tutoring

Subjects	Usually children aged 3 to 5 years from lower socioeconomic backgrounds, attending nursery or kindergarten
Pre-test Assessments	Levels of spontaneous pretend play, and measures of social, linguistic, or cognitive development, creativity, etc.

Children then divided into

Experimental Group	*Control Group(s)*
Receive period of extra play tutoring; outside or inside intervention by adult to encourage fantasy or sociodramatic play, or role-playing activities	Receive period of (1) no treatment control — no extra tutoring; or (2) extra tutoring in some non-fantasy activities, e.g. arts and crafts, dimensionality training

Post-test Assessments	Usually same as at pre-test assessment

One example of research in this paradigm is that of Lovinger (1974). Eighteen 4-year-olds in a preschool nursery were assigned to an experimental group, and 20 to a control group. All the children were first observed, to record verbalisations in play, and were tested on the Verbal Expression scale of the Illinois Test of Psycholinguistic Abilities. There were no significant differences between the two groups at this stage. The experimental group then received extra play-tutoring intervention during the free play period of one hour a day, over 25 weeks; the control group experienced the regular nursery programme. The children's language abilities were then re-assessed. It was found that the play-tutored children, but not the control children, had improved on both spoken language and tested Verbal Expression.

Another example is the work of Saltz and Johnson (1974; see also Saltz and Brodie, 1982). Saltz and Johnson used thematic-fantasy-play training, and compared it to dimensionality training and no-treatment controls. The play-trained children were found, amongst other things, to have a better memory for stories, and when asked to tell stories from pictures they provided longer and better organised narratives (only post-tests were performed on these items, though the children were equated on pre-tests of intelligence). Similarly, Yawkey (1979) used a *social relations curriculum* with 5-year-olds, which involved setting up role-play experiences. Children in the control group had art and craft activities. The role-play group improved more on the Gates MacGinitie Reading Readiness Skills Test, and also on the Singer Imaginativeness Inventory (an extension of Singer's play-interview schedule mentioned earlier).

However, despite these and other positive findings, there are difficulties in the methodology and interpretation of findings of most or all of the play-training studies to date. These issues are discussed by Smith and Syddall (1978), Christie (1982b), and Brainerd (1982).

There are two common methodological problems. First, the testers have often been aware of the training condition of the children, so that scoring bias cannot be ruled out. Secondly, the control conditions have usually either involved no extra stimulation (as in Lovinger, 1974), or an unspecified amount of interaction (as in Saltz and Johnson, 1974, or Yawkey, 1979). The point of the latter criticism is that play tutoring involves both boosting pretend play, and a good deal of individual or small-group adult-child interaction and verbal communication. It may be the latter, and not the pretend play *per se*, which has benefits for language and other skills. Unless the control group is equated with the play-training group for verbal stimulation and adult-child interaction, this possibility cannot be excluded. In one study in which such a control

group was carefully equated on these measures, the differential improve-
ment of the play-trained children was largely restricted to pretend play,
and peer social participation (Smith, Dalgleish and Herzmark, 1981).

There are also problems in interpreting the pattern of results from
different studies (Brainerd, 1982). In some areas, notably perspective-
taking skills, some studies have obtained positive results and others have
not. The size of positive effects is sometimes quite small, even when
statistically significant. The permanency of any improvements is also
open to question, as very few of the studies have used a delayed post-
test some time after the play intervention has ceased. Finally, it should
be borne in mind that play training may have some results that could
be negatively evaluated in the classroom; for example, increases in noisy
physical activity (Smith, Dalgleish and Herzmark, 1981), and, in the case
of severely emotionally disturbed children, increases in overt aggression
and poor concentration (Nahme-Huang, Singer, Singer and Wheaton,
1977).

Having made these qualifications, we see that play training is clearly
an enjoyable activity, and even if it should prove the case that some or
many of the gains made by the children are due to the adult contact in
training rather than the play *per se*, nevertheless the gains are made.
Play training is clearly one effective way of bringing about sensitive
adult-child involvement, and (unlike many forms of adult involvement
in children's activities) it seems to increase peer interaction as well.

Theoretical Perspectives on Fantasy Play

The review of experimental training studies shows that we are still un-
certain about the exact importance of fantasy and sociodramatic play
in development. This is paralleled by the range of viable theoretical perspectives on these forms of play.

One school of thought, although at present times a minority one, is
that in fantasy play a child loses touch with reality to an undesirable
extent, failing to get to grips with real difficulties in his or her environment. Pretending that a block is a cake does not help the child learn
anything real about wooden blocks, or cakes, according to this line of
thought. This was the argument of Montessori (see Standing, 1957); the
positive side of this view is the emphasis on even quite young children
helping with real-life tasks, washing real dishes and baking real cakes
rather than pretend ones. This different emphasis may help to explain
any lesser encouragement of pretend play in working-class families

(Newson and Newson, 1968) and its possibly lower incidence in UK families of Asian origin (Child, in press).

Piaget was influenced by the Montessori tradition, and he also puts emphasis on the child's adaptation to external reality (Piaget, 1951; Rubin and Pepler, 1982). Fantasy play (called symbolic play by Piaget) is seen as a necessary stage of development, but one which in general is a reflection of the child's existing skills; assimilation rather than accommodation. Such play does consolidate existing skills, and it can give a child confidence in this; but it does not especially cause the growth of new skills.

On the other hand many theorists have seen fantasy play as having a more direct and positive importance. Freud and other psychoanalytic thinkers saw play as a means of wish fulfilment, and of working through anxious or traumatic events. This latter aspect, of the child gaining mastery over anxieties and conflicts, was continued by Erikson, and has lain behind the development of play-therapy techniques. Empirical evidence for the cathartic or mastery theories of play is rather sparse (Rubin, Fein and Vandenberg, in press).

Psychological theorists have, however, more often emphasised the cognitive or creative aspects of fantasy play. Vygotsky (1967) emphasised the distinction between literal, and non-literal, thought and language in pretend play, arguing that it therefore fostered symbolic and creative thinking. Mead (1932) discussed how sociodramatic play called on children to act out other roles and co-ordinate with each other, and thus developed perspective and role-taking abilities.

These hypothesised benefits of fantasy and sociodramatic play for symbolic thought, creativity and social cognition have been echoed by later writers such as Berlyne, Bateson, Bruner, Singer and Sutton-Smith. They also encouraged the play-training studies discussed earlier, which, as we have seen, give some support, strongly qualified by methodological reservations, to these positions.

Another theoretical position is that fantasy play may have direct or indirect benefits, but that these can be realised by other means as well. For example, I have argued (Smith, 1982) that fantasy makes play more complex, and therefore more useful as a developmental experience for the child; but other experiences, such as non-fantasy training, might be as or more effective in various domains — hence the varied results of the play-training studies. Rubin (1980b) considers that the primary benefit of fantasy play may be via the increased peer interaction which it can bring about, resulting in social-cognitive growth; but peer interaction does not necessarily take the form of sociodramatic play.

Summary: the Relevance of Fantasy Play for the Study of Language, Imagination and Writing Skills

The ability to fantasise or pretend is, like early language and like the recognition of self, a basic component of the symbolic ability of the child on which everything which is distinctively human will develop. The parallels between the structural development of early pretend play, and the structural development of early spoken language, are close; it may be the case that the two are very directly linked, although whether this is so and quite what such a linkage would imply in terms of developmental processes, changes and effects, has yet to be firmly established.

From 2 years of age onwards, a child's fantasy play has a non-literal narrative action structure which has obvious parallels with the later production of spoken or written stories. Relevant aspects of this correspondence are: the creation of imaginary roles, actions and events; the co-ordination of a sequential plan or story structure, including the initiation and termination of episodes; the reflection of stereotyped knowledge, including sex-role stereotypes, and exposure to the mass media, on the content of the narratives; and the potential role of an adult in encouraging and scaffolding narrative development. Relevant differences are: the appreciably earlier appearance of acted to written narratives, and the fact that in sociodramatic play at least the narrative is jointly constructed with one or more other play partners.

Children who have a high-fantasy disposition or engage in much pretend play, have generally been found to be more creative, socially skilled, and better at perspective-taking tasks. There are several ways of interpreting such findings. It may or may not be the case that the parallels of pretend-play narratives to written stories also imply a causative developmental link between the two. Such a link, if it is found, could be due to indirect factors; for example, pretend play might encourage perspective-taking skills, which could later be reflected in more mature story construction (Cowie, 1982).

Whether pretend play has certain causes, or consequences, can only be ascertained with reasonable certainty by careful investigations. Similarly, it could be all too easy to jump to conclusions about the causes or consequences of later imaginative writing. The research on pretend play has been extensive, and has uncovered a number of methodological problems and difficulties in interpretation. Such considerations too may have implications for the future study of how children's imaginative writing develops.

References

Becher, R.M. and Wolfgang, C.H. (1977) 'An Exploration of the Relationship Between Symbolic Representation in Dramatic Play and Art and the Cognitive and Reading-readiness Levels of Kindergarten Children', *Psychology in the Schools, 14*, 377-81

Brainerd, C.J. (1982) 'Effects of Group and Individualized Dramatic-play Training on Cognitive Development' in D.J. Pepler and K.H. Rubin (eds), *The Play of Children: Current Theory and Research*, S. Karger, Basel

Brooks-Gunn, J. and Matthews, W.S. (1979) *He and She: How Children Develop Their Sex-role Identity*, Prentice-Hall Inc., New Jersey

Chandler, M.J. (1973) 'Egocentrism and Antisocial Behavior: the Assessment and Training of Social Perspective-taking Skills', *Developmental Psychology, 9*, 326-32

Child, E. (in press) 'Play and Culture: a Study of English and Asian Children', *Leisure Studies*

Christie, J.F. (1982a) 'Sociodramatic Play Training', *Young Children, 37*, 25-32
— (1982b) 'Play: To Train or Not to Train?' in J. Loy (ed.), *The Paradoxes of Play*, Leisure Press, New York

Corrigan, R. (1982) 'The Control of Animate and Inanimate Components in Pretend Play and Language', *Child Development, 53*, 1343-53

Cowie, H. (1982) 'Can We Justify the Use of Fantasy in Educational Contexts?', *Research Intelligence, 12*, 15-16

Fein, G.G. (1975) 'A Transformational Analysis of Pretending', *Developmental Psychology, 11*, 291-6
— (1981) 'Pretend Play in Childhood: an Integrative Review', *Child Development, 52*, 1095-118

Field, T., De Stefano, L. and Koewler, J.H. (1982) 'Fantasy Play of Toddlers and Preschoolers', *Developmental Psychology, 18*, 503-8

Fischer, K.W. (1980) 'A Theory of Cognitive Development: the Control and Construction of Hierarchies of Skills', *Psychological Review, 87*, 477-531

Garvey, C. (1977) *Play*, Fontana/Open Books, London

Hartshorn, E. and Brantley, J.C. (1973) 'Effects of Dramatic Play on Classroom Problem-solving Ability', *The Journal of Educational Research, 66*, 243-6

Iannotti, R.J. (1978) 'Effect of Role-taking Experiences on Role Taking, Empathy, Altruism and Aggression', *Developmental Psychology, 14*, 119-24

Lieberman, J.N. (1977) *Playfulness: its Relationship to Imagination and Creativity*, Academic Press, New York

Lovinger, S.L. (1974) 'Socio-dramatic Play and Language Development in Preschool Disadvantaged Children', *Psychology in the Schools, 11*, 313-20

McCune-Nicolich, L. (1981) 'Toward Symbolic Functioning: Structure of Early Pretend Games and Potential Parallels with Language', *Child Development, 52*, 785-97
— and Bruskin, C. (1982) 'Combinatorial Competency in Symbolic Play and Language' in D.J. Pepler and K.H. Rubin (eds), *The Play of Children: Current Theory and Research*, S. Karger, Basel

McLoyd, V.C. (1982) 'Social-class Differences in Sociodramatic Play: a Critical Review', *Developmental Review, 2*, 1-30

Matthews, W.S. (1977) 'Modes of Transformation in the Initiation of Fantasy Play', *Developmental Psychology, 13*, 212-16
— (1978) 'Interruptions of Fantasy Play: a Matter of "Breaking Frame"'. Paper presented to meeting of the Eastern Psychological Association, Washington, DC

Mead, G.H. (1932) *Mind, Self and Society*, University of Chicago Press, Chicago

Moreno, J.L. (1946) *Psychodrama*, Beacon House, New York

Nahme-Huang, L., Singer, D.G., Singer, J.L. and Wheaton, A.B. (1977) 'Imaginative Play Training and Perceptual-motor Interventions with Emotionally Disturbed Hospitalized Children', *American Journal of Orthopsychiatry*, *47*, 238-49

Newson, J. and Newson, E. (1968) *Four Years Old in an Urban Community*, Allen and Unwin, London

Overton, W.F. and Jackson, J.P. (1973) 'The Representation of Imagined Objects in Action Sequences: a Developmental Study', *Child Development*, *44*, 309-14

Pepler, D.J. and Rubin, K.H. (eds) (1982) *The Play of Children: Current Theory and Research*, S. Karger, Basel

Piaget, J. (1951) *Play, Dreams and Imitation in Childhood*, Routledge & Kegan Paul, London

Pulaski, M.A. (1973) 'Toys and Imaginative Play' in J.L. Singer (ed.), *The Child's World of Make-Believe*, Academic Press, New York

Rubin, K.H. (ed.) (1980a) *New Directions for Child Development: Children's Play*, Jossey-Bass, San Francisco

—— (1980b) 'Fantasy Play: its Role in the Development of Social Skills and Social Cognition' in K.H. Rubin (ed.), *New Directions for Child Development: Children's Play*, Jossey-Bass, San Francisco

——, Fein, G.G. and Vandenberg, B. (eds) (in press) 'Play' in P.H. Mussen and E.M. Hetherington (eds), *Carmichael's Manual of Child Psychology* (vol. 3), Wiley, New York, 4th edn

—— and Pepler, D.J. (1982) 'Children's Play: Piaget's Views Reconsidered', *Contemporary Educational Psychology*, *7*, 289-300

Russell, C.L. and Russnaik, R.N. (1981) 'Language and Symbolic Play in Infancy: Independent or Related Abilities?', *Canadian Journal of Behavioral Science*, *13*, 95-104

Sachs, J. (1980) 'The Role of Adult-Child Play in Language Development' in K.H. Rubin (ed.), *New Directions for Child Development: Children's Play*, Jossey-Bass, San Francisco

Saltz, E. and Brodie, J. (1982) 'Pretend-play Training in Childhood: a Review and Critique' in D.J. Pepler and K.H. Rubin (eds), *The Play of Children: Current Theory and Research*, S. Karger, Basel

—— and Johnson, J. (1974) 'Training for Thematic-fantasy Play in Culturally Disadvantaged Children: Preliminary Results', *Journal of Educational Psychology*, *66*, 623-30

Singer, D.G. and Singer, J.L. (1976) 'Family Television Viewing Habits and the Spontaneous Play of Preschool Children', *American Journal of Orthopsychiatry*, *46*, 496-502

Singer, J.L. (1973) *The Child's World of Make-believe*, Academic Press, New York

Smilansky, S. (1968) *The Effects of Sociodramatic Play on Disadvantaged Preschool Children*, Wiley, New York

Smith, P.K. (1982) 'Does Play Matter? Functional and Evolutionary Aspects of Animal and Human Play', *The Behavioral and Brain Sciences*, *4*, 139-84

—— and Connolly, K.J. (1980) *The Ecology of Preschool Behaviour*, Cambridge University Press, Cambridge

——, Dalgleish, M. and Herzmark, G. (1981) 'A Comparison of the Effects of Fantasy-play Tutoring and Skills Tutoring in Nursery Classes', *International Journal of Behavioral Development*, *4*, 421-41

—— and Syddall, S. (1978) 'Play and Non-play Tutoring in Pre-school Children: Is it Play or Tutoring Which Matters?', *British Journal of Educational Psychology*, *48*, 315-25

Standing, E.M. (1957) *Maria Montessori: Her Life and Work*, Hollis and Carter, London

Ungerer, J.A. and Sigman, M. (1981) 'Symbolic Play and Language Comprehension in Autistic Children', *Journal of the American Academy of Child Psychiatry*, *20*, 318-37

Vygotsky, L.S. (1967) 'Play and its Role in the Mental Development of the Child', *Soviet Psychology*, *12*, 62-76

Wolf, D. and Grollman, S.H. (1982) 'Ways of Playing: Individual Differences in Imaginative Style' in D.J. Pepler and K.H. Rubin (eds), *The Play of Children: Current Theory and Research*, S. Karger, Basel

Yawkey, T.D. (1979) 'The Effects of Social Relationships, Curricula and Sex Differences on Reading and Imaginativeness in Young Children', *Alberta Journal of Educational Research*, *25*, 159-68

2 THE DEVELOPMENT OF REPRESENTATIONAL IMAGINATION

Joan Tamburrini

Introduction

The philosopher C.E.M. Joad is remembered, by those old enough to have listened to the radio programme 'Brains Trust', as often prefacing his replies to questions with, 'It depends what you mean by X . . .'. The phrase did not reflect equivocation on his part, but rather served to indicate that there were several meanings of 'X'. Most philosophers, if asked a question about imagination, would be likely to respond in a similar fashion and would begin with a clarification of the word 'imagination', for it has not a singular meaning, but refers to several different processes.

In order to examine trends in the development of imagination in children we need to unravel these different meanings. This chapter, therefore, begins with an analysis of three uses of imagination that are particularly relevant to our purposes. The remainder of the chapter is concerned with the development of imagination in certain contexts of representation. Human beings represent their experiences and their interpretations and feelings about external and internal realities in many ways – in fantasy play, drama, oral and written story-making, poetry, and drawing and painting. The contexts examined here are fantasy play, children's oral story-making, children's understanding and interpretation of stories and children's writing. The chapter is restricted to these contexts because they are the only ones where investigations have been carried out that are directly or indirectly concerned with the processes of imagination and are also developmental.

The Uses of Imagination

The following are two examples of children of different ages engaging in activities and encountering problems that involved them in the use of imagination in different ways. The examples occur in different contexts and there is an age difference of eight years between the children.

Nevertheless, there were some similarities in the kinds of imagination that were used.

Example 1

Josh is 3½ years old. He attends a nursery school, but the following activities were observed in his own home. At Christmas a number of people had given Josh sweets, including chocolates in colourful wrappings. However, he did not eat any, and neither did he allow anyone else to do so, but instead used them to construct what he called his 'arrangements'. At first these did not seem to represent any particular object, but rather reflected categorisations based on colour, shape and size. After several groupings of this kind, however, he did represent a particular object: some wrapped chocolates shaped like minarets were placed on a base of cuboid ones and he called the result a 'church'.

Josh's 'arrangements' covered a large area of the dining room floor, and as guests were coming to dinner his mother asked him to dismantle them. At first he was reluctant to do so, but when his mother carefully explained her difficulties if she could not begin to prepare the room for the dinner party, he saw her point of view and complied.

After several days constructing similar 'arrangements' Josh built a complex and beautiful house-like structure. Some parts of the house were constructed with wooden bricks, but for others he used sweets, including columns made from liquorice allsort sweets and windows of transparent rectangular ones. On its completion Josh said it was a cockatoo's house, and for many days afterwards he made up stories about the imaginary cockatoo.

This example illustrates three different uses of imagination. First, there was make-believe when Josh used the chocolates to represent church spires, and sweets to represent columns and windows, and when he pretended a cockatoo lived in the house he had constructed. Make-believe is one use of imagination. Secondly, Josh frequently engaged in predicting: for example, he predicted that the outcome of certain placings in his 'arrangements' would result in a structure that was stable as well as aesthetically pleasing. Predicting is another use of imagination. Thirdly, Josh was eventually able to understand his mother's point of view when she required him to dismantle his 'arrangements'. This is yet another use of imagination.

Example 2

Emma, aged 11 years, went on a visit with her class to a local beauty spot which was also of historic interest for its iron age fort. Emma was very interested in history, and also enjoyed writing poetry. On her return to school she combined these interests by writing a poem in which the group of imposing trees on top of the hill they had visited was likened to a group of warriors. The metaphor was elaborated at some length, the barks of the trees being likened to shields and the main branches to weapons, and the poem ended with a reference to the warriors' 'stored memories of ancient battles'. Emma revised her poem several times before she was satisfied with it and, in particular, she revised the first two lines until she was convinced that the reader or listener would be immediately aware of the metaphor.

Although the context is different, there are parallel uses of imagination to those described in the account of Josh's activities. Emma engaged in make-believe thinking when she wrote of the trees as if they were warriors and had stored memories of ancient battles. She did not believe that trees literally have memories any more than Josh believed a cockatoo really lived in the house he had constructed. Emma elaborated the metaphor at considerable length: the original idea to write 'as if' trees were ancient warriors was pursued in terms of 'if then' thinking — if the trees were likened to warriors then their barks could be likened to shields, and so on. When Josh predicted that the liquorice allsorts could be arranged as columns to support a roof he also engaged in the 'as if' use of imagination. Finally, just as Josh needed to put himself at another person's point of view to understand why he should dismantle his 'arrangements', so did Emma when she composed and revised her poem. She needed to put herself at other people's points of view in two respects: in trying to capture the feelings and experiences of the ancient warriors and in trying to put herself in the position of the reader of her poem.

The above examples thus illustrate three uses of imagination:

(1) We use 'as if' thinking whenever we imagine something to be other than it is literally or in actuality, and when we suppose something to be the case even though we do not yet know it to be so with certainty. The 'as if' use of imagination thus includes make-believe, conjecture and entertaining propositions. 'As if' imagination may be used in different contexts: there is a developmental range for instance from fantasy play in early childhood to drama in middle childhood and on, from oral story-making to imaginative writing; and contexts differ in terms of disciplines — we may entertain propositions concerned with moral problems, politics, the construction of a literary work or a painting, and we may generate hypotheses (a particular kind of proposition)

in science or history, for example.

(2) We also use imagination when we predict and when a starting point, in which something is imagined to be other than it is, is followed by working out what other events could be related in a causal, logical or complementary way; in other words when we elaborate a theme or a plot, or think about the implications of a proposition or hypothesis. These are all examples of the 'if then' use of imagination and, clearly, 'as if' thinking is often followed by 'if then' thinking.

(3) The third use of imagination illustrated in the accounts of Josh's activities and Emma's writing is 'role-taking', the identification and understanding of another person's point of view.

All three uses of imagination are involved in imaginative writing. When the writer constructs an imaginative narrative or theme he engages in the 'as if' use of imagination. Even though the narrative or theme may have its roots in his personal experience, he goes beyond it and writes 'as if' things have occurred that, though plausible, in reality have not. When the narrative or theme is complex, when various events are linked causally or in a complementary way, the writer's initial 'as if' proposition is followed by thinking in terms of a series of 'if then' outcomes. The writer also needs to engage in the role-taking use of imagination: he needs to try to identify, understand and empathise with the experiences of any characters that people his narrative; and he needs to identify and put himself in the position of his audience. If we ponder on the intellectual complexity thus entailed, it clearly presents difficulties for young children who will also be struggling with the difficulties of the written code itself. If, then, we are to understand these three kinds of imagination, we need to examine their uses in other contexts that precede them developmentally.

The Development of Representational Imagination

Play

One of the earliest contexts of the 'as if' use of imagination in development is make-believe or fantasy play in which a child transforms objects to mean something other than their literal meaning, and/or pretends to be someone other than he is.

Theorists have disagreed about the continuity between this kind of 'as if' imagination and its use in other contexts. Piaget (1962) emphasises discontinuity which, he argues, refers to the fact that though a young child uses objects as symbols for other objects and events in his play, he is primarily interested not in the symbols, but in what they are symbolising. Thus, he claims, imagination is the instrument of the play and not its content, whereas in story making, for example, the symbols are the content and the focus of his interest. For this reason Piaget writes of make-believe play as involving symbolic rather than representational imagination.

Vygotsky (1967), by contrast, emphasises continuity. The importance of make-believe play, he suggests, is that it liberates the child from literal meanings, or, as he puts it, situational constraints. The baby is bound by situational constraints in the sense that things dictate their use: a table is a place on which one puts meals, and a chair is something on which one sits. But in make-believe play chairs and tables can take on any non-literal meaning the child cares to give them − he acts and thinks 'as if' a chair or table is a house, a boat, a car or anything else he wishes. As imagination matures, meanings are organised and reorganised in the absence of conrete reference. Play is a transitional stage in this direction. When the child creates an imaginary situation in his play, meanings are severed from situational constraints, but he cannot yet sever thought from objects: so in order to imagine a horse, he needs to define his actions by means of using the horse in the stick as a pivot.

Both Piaget and Vygotsky theorised about play at a time when there was sparse experimental evidence to support their assertions, but over the last two decades or so there have been a number of studies concerned with an association between fantasy play and imagination or 'creativity', which Smith reviews in his chapter on fantasy play. As Smith says, there are too many methodological problems and difficulties in interpretation to say with certainty how fantasy play is related to imagination in other contexts, including imaginative writing, but there are, none the less, interesting parallels.

Smith examines aspects of development in children's fantasy play. One developmental trend he discusses is the lessening dependence on realistic objects for fantasy. For the youngest children the things that 'act as pivots' bear a close resemblance to the things they symbolise, but as development proceeds children make increasing use of less structured and unstructured materials. Another aspect of development is reflected in sociodramatic play in which children take different roles.

Both these 'as if' and 'role-taking' aspects of development in fantasy play can be described in terms of increasing distancing. Sigel (1981) has discussed the development of representational abilities in terms of increased 'distancing'. There is little distancing when the child reiterates his own fairly immediate and first-hand experiences in his representational activity. There is increased distancing when, though immediate experiences are the starting point, the child goes beyond them in imagining further events, when he draws on secondary experiences, and when he increasingly represents his conception of other people's perspectives.

Smith also describes structural aspects of the development of fantasy play. There is increasing complexity of structure as increasing numbers of objects are combined in play, and as play episodes are increasingly elaborated thematically and more sequences develop.

Oral Story-making

Oral story-making also emerges in early childhood, and is characterised by parallel developments in distancing and in complexity of structure. Pitcher and Prellinger (1963) studied stories told by 137 children between the ages of 2 and 5. Initially they used series of pictures about which they asked the children to tell a story because they assumed this would act as a helpful prop to the younger ones. They found, however, that the youngest children responded by simply pointing to and naming the objects in the pictures. They therefore abandoned this procedure and, instead, asked children, 'Tell me a story.' The main focus of Pitcher's and Prellinger's interpretation of the stories collected is a Freudian point of view. However, Applebee (1978) has re-examined their data and found evidence of both increasing distancing and a development of complexity of structural organisation.

A clear development in distancing was shown in terms of the settings of the stories, the characters and actions depicted. Two-year-olds tended to place the happenings within the home property, while by 5 years of age happenings took place in less familiar institutions, in foreign countries, in less definite places such as just 'forests' and 'mountains', and in fantasy worlds. Similarly, the characters and their actions depicted by most 2-year-olds were realistic, while by 5 both the characters and their actions were more distanced from self and immediate personal experience.

Pitcher and Prellinger do not directly discuss an increase in structural complexity, but they do report that at 4 and 5 children showed an increasing tendency to people their stories with more characters, to intensify their scrutiny of relationships among characters, and to be concerned with cause and effect. These tendencies suggest a development of structural complexity, for the more characters there are in a story and the more it includes related events, the more complex the structural organisation required. Applebee re-examined the stories in terms of structural organisation, and found six basic structures. The least structured organisation characterises what are hardly stories at all, but rather a string of events, a kind of free association showing few links from one sentence to the next. However, even at 2 years of age only one-sixth of the children's 'stories' were of this kind.

In the next stage of organisation, which Applebee calls a 'sequence', incident follows incident without any apparent causal links, though they are linked to a common core of the story. Frequently, these stories report a repeated action or events of the day. Most teachers of young children are familiar with the latter, the kind of story in which the character depicted gets up, has breakfast, goes shopping with mother, has dinner . . . and so on.

Applebee calls the third stage of structural organisation 'primitive narrative'. The core of the story is an object or event that is important to the child, around which are organised a collection of complementary events. The following story told by a 4-year-old is an example of 'primitive narrative': 'A little girl had a hamster. She left the door of the cage open. It got out. She cried. Mummy said it might come back but it didn't. She got a kitten for Christmas.'

At the fourth level of organisation a chain of events is narrated but there is a lack of focus – the incidents lead quite directly from one to another, but the attributes which link them continue to shift – characters pass in and out of the story, the type of action changes, the setting blurs. Applebee therefore calls this stage the 'unfocused chain narrative'.

By contrast the 'focused chain' of the next stage is a narrative which has at its centre a main character who goes through a series of linked events. It is essentially the 'continuing adventures of . . .' kind of story. The focused chain narrative accounted for about half the stories of the 5-year-old children. The last kind of organisation found in the stories allows the situation around which the story is constructed to develop over the course of the narrative as in the 'primitive narrative' stage, but now each event not only develops from the previous one, but also elaborates a new aspect of the situation.

Applebee examines these structural characteristics in the light of Vygotsky's (1962) account of concept development, and shows that they are similar to those described by Vygotsky. However, Applebee argues that both the complexity of the stories and their structural organisation are not simply separate manifestations of development related to age, but are related to each other. He carried out a statistical analysis on differences in complexity among major plot structures after controlling for age, an analysis which was concerned with the question of whether plot structure as well as age was related to the complexity of the stories. The results of the analysis suggest that there are differences in the complexity of the stories corresponding to differences in the structural organisation of the plots, and that these differences remain even after allowing for the fact that certain organisational structures are used mostly by the older children. This important finding that the level at which children perform may be related to task demands as well as age is of considerable importance, and will be discussed more fully later.

Children's Responses to Stories

Applebee also carried out a study of children's responses to stories. His subjects were 6, 9, 13 and 17 years of age. The 6 and 9-year-old children were asked, 'What is your favourite story? Tell me about it.' They were also asked why they liked or disliked particular stories. The older children were required to respond to a questionnaire, part of which asked, 'Pick any story or poem you know well and write about it.' The results indicate, Applebee claims, that there are stages in children's responses to stories which are characterised by Piaget's descriptions of preoperational, concrete operational and formal operational thought.

The most common response of the 6-year-old children (50 per cent) to the request, 'Tell me about it', was simply to retell the story. This kind of response requires the least reorganisation of the material. This, claims Applebee, is a manifestation of preoperational thought which Piaget describes as proceeding in a step-by-step fashion which parallels the concrete actions and events with which it is concerned, rather than being organised in terms of some overall category.

By the age of 9 only 9 per cent of the children retold the story, whereas 41 per cent presented a synopsis and 32 per cent a summary. The latter is an attempt to encapsulate the plot within a general category, and is characteristic, Applebee argues, of Piaget's stage of concrete operational thinking which involves the ability to organise material in terms of overall categories. The synopses seemed to be transitional between retelling and summarising – they were not classificatory summaries but rather reports of ongoing events, even though there was often more reorganisation and condensation than in simple retelling.

Formal operational thought is the term given by Piaget to propositional thinking. In terms of both distancing and structural organisation formal operational thought is an important advance in the development of imagination. It is not confined to the realm of concrete actualities as is concrete operational thought, but goes beyond what is given to a consideration of possibilities. In formal operational thinking a proposition or hypothesis is entertained, and the various things that it might entail or imply are considered, thus involving a more complex and coherent structure than concrete operational thought. Applebee shows that the responses of his adolescent subjects were manifestations of formal operational thought. They showed a concern with analysing the story and generalising about its meaning in contrast with the preadolescent children, whose concern was with retelling or recreating it. In particular their ability to distance themselves from the information given and to deal with the realm of possibilities was manifested in two ways. One was the children's concern with motivational principles, with teasing out cause and effect in the structure of the story, in the actions of the characters and even in the relationships between objective perceptions of the story and personal, subjective reactions to it. The other was the awareness of the implications of the theme or message of the story, as distinct from the actual people described and events narrated.

Children's Writing

The Crediton Project was a study carried out by Wilkinson, Barnsley, Hanna and Swan (1980) into the development of children's writing. Groups of children aged 7 plus, 10 plus and 13 plus were given four writing tasks designed to reflect development in terms of sense of audience, function and closeness to the child's first-hand experience. The four tasks were: an autobiographical narrative; an explanation task — an account of how to play a game; a fictional story whose content was to be related to a picture chosen by the child from a selection of three; and an argument presentation task — a piece of writing on 'would it work if children came to school when they liked, and could do what they liked there'. The developmental differences identified by Wilkinson and his colleagues were of various kinds, ranging from characteristics related to sense of audience to use of language, including register and syntax. However, the discussion here is confined to the three uses of imagination with which we are concerned.

The 'as if' use of imagination was, as was to be expected, particularly evident in the fictional story task. As Wilkinson and his colleagues point out, the invitation to write a story for which the picture selected is an illustration is an invitation to move beyond reality — to 'make up' a story. In one sense, a superficial one, there was a development towards realism, the older children producing more realistic themes than the younger ones. However, even when themes were realistic they were dealt with more imaginatively. The investigators used the terms 'fantasy' and 'imaginative' in special senses. 'Fantasy' in their terms tended to describe rather than interpret, whereas a piece which was interpretative as well as descriptive was called 'imaginative'. In these senses the children's writing showed a move from 'fantasy' to 'imaginative' pieces. The narrative of 10-year-olds mostly remained at the level of 'fantasy', and they tended to respond to the task with descriptions of violence even though the pictures were not particularly suggestive of violence. The older children, by contrast, were more interpretative in relating the feelings and emotions of the characters involved in the events they described.

It was stated above that writing requires the role-taking use of imagination in two respects: the writer needs to distance himself psychologically, to 'decentre', in order to put himself at the point of view of his readers and of the characters about whom he writes. The children's writing in the Crediton Project study showed developmental trends in both these respects.

All four tasks reveal the extent to which audience has been taken into account. In the explanation and argument tasks the youngest group found it difficult to decentre to the point of view of the reader. They seemed to be unsure of what information to give and partial information characterised the writing. In the story task they did not give sufficient clues to reconstruct the situation for the audience. At 10 plus the children gave more information and elaboration in both the explanation and argument tasks, though they were still sometimes unclear about what was relevant information. In the argument tasks chains of reasons for their opinions were given more often. In the story task they were able to give the reader more clues to help him understand the theme. By 13 plus partial acccounts were very rare — logical connections were made explicit, and the reader was given frequent information and explanation.

Development in the children's ability to use role-taking imagination in identifying and reporting the experiences and feelings of the characters about whom they wrote was evident in the fictional narrative task. The 7-year-olds did not on the whole express feelings, and their writing was 'a matter-of-fact world . . . peopled by cut-out figures'. The 10-year-olds showed an advance in this respect: some of their characters were given thoughts and words and seemed more three-dimensional. The 13-year-old children more often ascribed emotions to others. This was sometimes done explicitly, but also implicitly in what the characters

said and how they behaved. There was also a development in expressing
the emotional and social relationships between characters:

> For example, a characteristic of seven-year-olds was their inclusion
> in many of their stories of a 'Mummy' from whom their characters
> got lost or who acts as security for them. About one-third of the ten-
> year-olds referred to Mummy in an only slightly more distanced way.
> But in the scripts of the thirteen-year-olds 'Mummy' becomes a signi-
> ficant 'other' who has her own emotions the same as any character,
> and plays a social role in the family. (p. 148)

It was suggested earlier that the 'if then' use of imagination is reflected in the structural organisation of an episode of play, an oral story
or a piece of writing. Applebee's reinterpretation of the data of Pitcher
and Prellinger and his own study show that the development of structural organisation in the contexts studied reflects the development of
cognition generally. Wilkinson and his associates examined cognition in
children's writing with respect to the explanation and argument tasks.
One of the main strands of development reflected in the organisation of
the writing was the development of the capacity to generalise information which enabled the children to relate description and explanation
to relevant classifications. The 7-year-old children tended to describe
rather than explain and, as has already been stated, their descriptions
were usually partial. Thus, the organisation of their writing frequently
lacked coherence. The writing of the 10-year-olds had more coherence
because there were fewer partial accounts, and because they began to
explain as well as describe. But in the explanation tasks their accounts
tended to be sequentially organised. Thus, in explaining a game three-
quarters of them gave chronologically/spatially organised accounts,
whereas the 13-year-olds, because of their classificatory approach, were
less tied to sequential organisation. The argument task required sustained reasoning, and proved difficult even for the 10-year-old children,
leading many of them into self-contradiction. In addition the task involved two issues — freedom to go to school and freedom in school —
and at 10 children were unable to present an overall evaluation taking in
both issues. Inevitably, these difficulties affected coherence adversely.
By 13 plus the children were elaborating more fully: there were hardly
any partial accounts, and there were clear logical connections between
ideas. The result was a considerably greater degree of coherence. Finally,
at 13 plus some children were able 'to "go beyond the information
given", projecting a series of thematically related hypotheses which

none of the younger children in the sample manage to do'.

Wilkinson and his colleagues examined these shifts in the light of developmental differences postulated by Moffett (1968). However, several characteristics – the ability increasingly to 'decentre', the development from organising a narrative or report in a sequential way to achieving coherence in a structure that is less sequential, the development of classificatory thinking, and the emergence in the older children of the ability to 'go beyond the information given' – seem to parallel the stages noted by Applebee with respect to children's responses to stories and which, it will be remembered, he related to Piaget's account of the stages of cognitive development.

Cognitive Development and the Development of Imagination

In sum, these accounts of studies of children's oral story-making, their responses to stories and their writing all show developmental trends which reflect characteristics of cognitive development in general. There are, of course, individual differences within any one age range, but the sequence of development in these representational contexts and the characteristics at different stages show a marked resemblance to what has been found in studies of cognition in other domains.

Over the last two decades or so numerous studies have led developmental psychologists to question stage theories of cognitive development, particularly Piaget's account (see, in particular, Donaldson, 1978). While Piaget's account describes development in a general sort of way, the level of children's thinking, it is claimed, is more context bound than the results of his tests would lead us to suppose: several situational factors may affect children's performance, with the result that a child who gives evidence of preoperational thinking in one context may think in a concrete operational manner in another where those situational factors facilitate it; and, similarly, an adolescent who solves one of Piaget's problems in the domain of physical science at a formal operational level may well fail to perform at the same level in some other domain.

The examination of the development of representational imagination shows that it is context bound in two ways: there seem to be time lags in development among the four contexts examined here; and there are indications that situational features within the contexts affect children's performances. It is hardly surprising that the extent of distancing and level of structural organisation of which children are capable should vary, according to whether they are engaged in fantasy play, oral story-making or writing. In fantasy play there is not an entire absence of constraints. The materials available have some part in determining what is symbolised (see Pulaski, 1973), and when play becomes sociodramatic other participants exert their influence on a child. Nevertheless, the constraints on the content and structure of play are not as great as they are in other contexts. In general, in fantasy play children make the materials they use subserve their own purposes and pursue their own themes. Free association is given its head. But in oral story-making, free association, as we saw in Applebee's study of the data of Pitcher and Prellinger, leads to incoherence, to a failure to communicate. The need to communicate successfully is one of the constraints in oral story-making. Communicating in words requires that the content is more preorganised in thought than it is in play where one item may suggest the next and thus require fewer logical or causal links. In addition, the meanings of words are not arbitrary. To communicate successfully words must be used to convey their accepted meanings, in contrast with play, where the objects used as symbolisers are arbitrary — they may symbolise whatever the child chooses them to. In writing there are even more constraints. In oral story-making the response of the listener indicates to a child when he has communicated successfully and when he has not, and since he and his audience are in a face-to-face situation, he may substitute and supplement words with gestures and other expressions of feeling. In writing, by contrast, the message has to be conveyed entirely with words. Add to these the fact that the child has to contend with the problems of spelling and punctuation, and the greater difficulty of the written account than the oral one is obvious.

Perhaps less obvious are the situational constraints within the contexts which are likely to influence the level of a child's performance. Studies of cognitive development in other domains have isolated various situational factors affecting performance. Donaldson (1978) has distinguished between contexts involving 'embedded' thinking and those requiring 'disembedded' thinking. Embedded thinking is firmly based in personal experience and everyday transactions, whereas disembedded thinking is more distanced from personal experience and deals increasingly in abstractions and generalisations. Donaldson claims that young children's thinking is at its most capable in embedded contexts. She points out that a context favours embedded thinking when the objects involved are familiar to the child, and/or when the intentions are clear and match his experience of people's intentions.

A number of studies (e.g. Borke, 1975) have replaced the materials used in a standard Piagetian task with materials and situations more familiar to children, and found that under such conditions children were capable of 'concrete operational' thinking at a much younger age than in the standard task. For example Borke (1975) studied the ability of young children to identify another person's point of view when an array of miniature people in familiar domestic settings replaced the model of three mountains used in the standard task of Piaget and Inhelder (1956). Borke found that a good proportion of even 4-year-old children were able to do so, compared with the average age of 7 at which children are successful in the standard task. Similarly, other investigators have found that formal-operational thinking in certain domains occurs much later than in the tasks of Piaget and Inhelder (1958) which used problems in physical science, and this seems in part to relate again to familiarity. Wason and Johnson-Laird (1972), using logical problems unfamiliar to most people and requiring formal-operational thinking, found that many highly intelligent adults were unable to solve them correctly.

It will be remembered that Pitcher and Prellinger first intended to obtain their data by asking the children to tell a story about a series of pictures, having assumed that the pictures would act as a prop for the younger children. They abandoned this in favour of the instruction, 'Tell me a story', because the youngest age group responded by simply enumerating the objects in the pictures. We do not know why the youngest children responded in this way. It may be that they did not understand the intentions and interpreted them as an invitation to enumerate, or it may be that the invitation simply to tell a story allowed the child to draw on what was most personally significant to him and was thus a more embedded thinking task. In relation to this it is significant that when Wilkinson and his associates asked children to write a story which a picture chosen by them could illustrate, the youngest group tended to write about violence (a subject which doubtless dominates a great deal of their television viewing) even though none of the pictures was particularly suggestive of violence.

The cognitive complexity of a task is also the result of the sheer number of elements that have to be kept in mind. Light (1979) examined the role-taking abilities of a sample of 60 4-year-old children using a battery of six tasks. Although the children's performance on these tasks showed sufficient intercorrelation for Light to give them a composite score, there were also differences in children's performance which reflected the complexity of the task. For example, one task used a three-sided pyramid, on each face of which was a picture of a toy, and the child was required to identify the toy that the experimenter, sitting opposite the child, could see. Another task used the same three-sided pyramid, but the child was required to identify what a doll could 'see' at each of five positions. At two of these positions the doll could 'see' one toy and at the other three positions two toys. There were more successful responses to the former task than to the latter, the positions where the doll 'saw' two toys proving more difficult. Similarly, as Wilkinson and his colleagues point out, the argument-writing task was more demanding than the explanation one. Both required discursive writing, but there were two ways in which the argument task was the more difficult. To set out a coherent argument for freedom of choice in going to school and what is done there requires that the child keeps in mind both these elements and relates them. In addition, whereas for the explanation of a game temporal sequencing is adequate, the argument task requires logical connections to be made explicit.

In order to facilitate children's imaginative writing teachers need to be aware of the cognitive demands of the tasks they give children. It has been argued that cognitive difficulty is determined in part by the extent of the distancing required, and in part by the structural organisation necessitated by the content. The younger the child the less distancing can be expected. A teacher of the writer's acquaintance took her class of 6-year-old children to a country fair. It was a well-planned and well-organised visit, and a great deal of good-quality work in discussion, painting and model-making resulted from it. The teacher also gave the children a writing task — to imagine that they were the cow which had been taken to the fair and won first prize, and to write how that cow had felt. She noted with chagrin that this task produced work of poor quality, comparing unfavourably with other pieces of writing that the children had done. The work of Wilkinson and his associates showed that even when writing about themselves young children did not, on the whole, write about their feelings, that even 10-year-olds dealt with them in a cursory way, (e.g. 'I felt sad'), and that it was not until adolescence that feelings and emotions were expressed at any length and depth. If we consider that the teacher expected the children to identify not their own feelings but those of an animal, it is clear that this is too difficult for 6-year-old children. In middle childhood children can increasingly distance themselves from their own immediate experiences to write about other people in terms of what they do and what they look like, but it is not until adolescence that they can write in any sustained way about their personalities and emotions.

Psychological distancing is also required in keeping in mind the reader for whom one writes. This is related to structural organisation which, as has been shown, is itself related to content. Where a happening can adequately be narrated in terms of a simple temporal sequence, a child is faced with a much simpler task of organising his material and communicating it to the reader than he is when the content involves cause-effect relationships, and/or logical ones and/or interrelating issues. If the cognitive complexity of a task exceeds what a child is developmentally capable of, the result will of necessity fail to communicate adequately to the reader.

Summary

(1)   There are three uses of imagination particularly relevant to imaginative writing:

(a)   the 'as if' use of imagination when the writer distances himself from actuality to invent characters and imaginary events;

(b)   the 'role-taking' use of imagination in which the writer puts himself in the position of the characters about whom he writes and of the audience for whom he writes; and

(c)   the 'if then' use of imagination when the writer elaborates his initial 'as if' invention with writing of outcomes that are related in terms of temporal connections, cause-effect relations and logical connections. The more complex the 'if then' connections, the more complex are the structural organisation requirements of the task.

(2)   Developmental trends in distancing and in structural organisation are found in representational contexts that precede writing, i.e. in young children's fantasy play and in oral story-making.

(3)   Distancing in terms of identifying aspects of personality and emotions of characters in a written narrative emerges at adolescence as does the ability to modulate the writing according to audience.

(4)   Distancing in terms of 'as if' thinking reaches maturity in children's writing when they deal entirely with the realm of possibilities, when it is distanced 'from the information given'. This is one aspect of formal-operational thinking.

(5)   The other aspect concerns the structural organisation of an episode of thought, when the thinker teases out the various implications and outcomes of his hypothesis or proposition. These distancing and structural aspects which are combined in formal-operational thought would seem to emerge in writing at 13 plus, on the average.

(6)   The developmental trends that have been identified in studies

reported here reflect developmental trends that have been identified in studies of cognitive development in other domains. However, there are also variations according to contextual factors. The difficulty of a task is in part a matter of the extent to which it requires embedded or disembedded thinking. Embedded thinking requires less psychological distancing than disembedded thinking. Task difficulty is also determined by the kind of structural organisation demanded by the content.

References

Applebee, A.N. (1978) *The Child's Concept of Story*, University of Chicago Press, Chicago and London

Borke, H. (1975) 'Piaget's Mountains Revisted: Changes in the Egocentric Landscape', *Developmental Psychology*, *11*, 240-3

Donaldson, M. (1978) *Children's Minds*, Fontana/Collins, Glasgow

Light, P. (1979) *The Development of Social Sensitivity*, Cambridge University Press, Cambridge

Moffett, J. (1968) *Teaching the Universe of Discourse*, Houghton, Mifflin Co., Boston

Piaget, J. (1962) *Play, Dreams and Imitation in Childhood*, Routledge & Kegan Paul, London

— and Inhelder, B. (1956) *The Child's Conception of Space*, Routledge & Kegan Paul, London

— (1958) *The Growth of Logical Thinking from Childhood to Adolescence*, Basic Books, USA

Pitcher, E.G. and Prellinger, E. (1963) *Children Tell Stories*, International Universities Press, New York

Pulaski, M.A. (1973) 'Toys and Imaginative Play' in J.L. Singer (ed.), *The Child's World of Make-believe*, Academic Press, New York

Sigel, I.E. (1981) 'Social Experience in the Development of Representational Thought: Distancing Theory' in I.E. Sigel, D.M. Brodzinsky and R.M. Golinkoff (eds), *New Directions in Piagetian Theory and Practice*, Lawrence Erlbaum Associates, Hillsdale, NJ

Vygotsky, L.S. (1962) *Thought and Language*, M.I.T. Press, Cambridge, Mass.

— (1967) 'Play and its Role in the Mental Development of the Child', *Soviet Psychology*, *12*, 62-7

Wason, P.C. and Johnson-Laird, P.N. (1972) *Psychology of Reasoning: Structure and Content*, Batsford, London

Wilkinson, A., Barnsley, G., Hanna, P. and Swan, M. (1980) *Assessing Language Development*, Oxford University Press, Oxford

3 THE VALUE OF IMAGINATIVE WRITING

Helen Cowie

Introduction

> Fantasy is a natural human activity. It certainly does not destroy or even insult Reason; and it does not either blunt the appetite for, nor obscure the perception of, scientific verity. On the contrary. The keener and clearer is the reason, the better fantasy will it make. (Tolkien, 1964, p. 50)

To Tolkien, the enjoyment of fairy tales does not depend on whether they could happen in real life. Rather he argues that the pleasure which we feel when we experience a convincing product of the imagination can be explained as a perception of its *underlying* reality or truth. So he justifies the use of fantasy as a means of deepening understanding of ourselves, our relationships with others and the world which we inhabit. Children themselves often place a high value on their own imaginative writing, and although younger children may simply respond intuitively to their own stories, older children are capable of explaining quite rationally the issues which the characters and situations represent to them.

With this in mind, can we justify the use of imaginative writing in educational contexts? Is the reading and writing of stories simply an enjoyable way of passing time, or can it be viewed as a learning experience? Is Tolkien right to look below the surface of a piece of writing to a deeper layer of meaning, and does the creation of a narrative have any bearing on real life?

One way of approaching children's writing is to examine the developmental trends which emerge, since not only do linguistic skills improve, but also children demonstrate with age an increasing grasp of the psychological and social processes which are portrayed in their stories. In this chapter I shall discuss whether these developmental changes reflect increasing social and cognitive awareness on the part of the children, or whether the very act of writing about the self, other people and events helps children to come to terms with social, emotional and spiritual issues in their own lives. I will look first at extracts from stories written by children at different ages.

Typically, the narratives of 7-year-olds are straightforward chains of events which contain very little expression of emotion. At this age children focus on simple, physical traits in their characters; *what* happens is more important than *why* it happens, and they usually omit useful descriptive information which would help the reader understand the context within which the story takes place. For example, Lisa at seven writes: 'One day there was a witch and a little girl and one day a witch came at her house and took her away but in the nit she wook up and put her witch in the fier.'

Despite the horrific nature of the events in this story, the characters express no emotion, and the author gives little direct insight into the motives for their actions. There is no indication that Lisa has been able to identify with the witch, and it seems that, egocentrically, she assumes that the reader shares her perspective of the happenings in the story. Lisa's narrative appears egocentric, yet even at this age the use of dialogue can enable the child to enter more fully into the experiences of all the characters and, at the same time, develop a greater sense of reader-awareness. Here Catherine discovers that a conversation can enhance the effectiveness of a story as she shows how a sapling, newly planted in the farmer's field, gets to know an established tree:

> Leo turned round and said to the other tree whats your name my name is mini whats your name said mini my name is leo I licke your name Leo I licke yours mini Thank you Leo How old are you Leo three years old do you licke thise farm Mini yes I licke this farm very much I licke this farm as well said Leo.

When children read aloud this kind of story they will often role-play the characters by giving each a distinctive voice, with the result that the piece 'comes alive' for both author and audience. The links with earlier sociodramatic play (as described in Chapter 1) are clear, and a growing sensitivity to the feelings of the various characters can be seen. Ashley, aged 7, shows his understanding of the increased vividness for both reader and writer when he says to his teacher,

> I like dramatic stories. If you put people *saying* things it's much better. I find it's changed my stories. I started last year. It's more dramatic and exciting. Most people don't care and just do the story, just put things in, but if people say things it sounds dramatic.

By 9 or 10, children are beginning to show more empathy for others in their writing. Here Julian describes the feelings and intentions of a young Viking:

> The boat was rocked from side to side and most of the men were thrown into the sea but the strongest of them all was Asbjorn. He was a ten-year-old boy. He stood still as a statue on the deck. And when the last person was knocked overboard he blushed. After five weeks later Asbjorn saw land in sight, The next week he landed. There was a little humming noise in the distance — voices he thought. And the sound of ebony drums only one of me and thousands of that village. I do not know how to fight a whole village. Aha! I will creep in at night when they are all asleep and steal all their jewels and money and food.

Julian gives enough information about Asbjorn's state of mind for us to enter to some extent into the experience; in addition, he describes the setting in such a way that it is possible to visualise the scenes on board ship and in the strange country. The reader can see how he interweaves a growing understanding of people with a wider knowledge of the world. In a similar way, 10-year-old Daniel shows distinct awareness of the self-image of his hero, Ronald Biggs, and gives some impressions of the fluctuating emotions which an individual can experience:

> I was thirty-seven and I was deforced. I can't stand it any longer I said to myself one day and I disided to be a birglar. I was a birglar for three years and I became very wealthy but I steel wasn't satisfied. I disided to get into the bigger bussness and became a train robber.

It is interesting to note that in both of these extracts the hero is involved in an internal dialogue with himself as he plans what to do next. Although the story still consists of a chain of events recounted in strict chronological order, the time span is extended and the characters have their adventures in more elaborate and detailed contexts. In addition, there is far more psychological information about the reasons which underly the action than is normally found in the writing of younger children.

By the time of early adolescence, writers have a more heightened self-awareness and responsiveness to the feelings of others. They may even go beyond the literal to the metaphorical use of language, as Sian's account of a midnight encounter in a garden shows. Skilfully, she creates a mysterious atmosphere in the story through her description of moonlight and the ghostly shape of the statue. She uses a mature literary device — the rhetorical 'Where was John?' — in the third paragraph to indicate the heroine's thoughts at the moment. Her dialogue suggests the passage of time in a sophisticated manner, and the relationship between fantasy and reality is subtly handled. She acknowledges the surface source of the story — a television serial which 'worked into her mind' — but realises *after* writing it its deeper implications for herself as an adolescent girl. She says of writing that 'you can switch off from the world and pretend you are one of the characters' and identifies themes of loneliness and longing which preoccupy her at the moment:

> That night after my mother had left me I set my alarm for twelve o'clock. I didn't have any problem in going to sleep that night, I thought it would be lovely to see my friend John in our own secret moonlit garden just before I dozed off I put my alarm clock under my pillow and went to sleep.
> At twelve o'clock my alarm woke me. I had to creep very quietly past my mother's room and down the stairs. I opened the bathroom window, jumped out of it and down the path which led up to mine and John's moonlit garden.
> The next moment I was walking through a dream garden. Where was John? When I was walking through the moonlight the moon shone on a figure that looked like a boy's figure a figure rather like John's. I started to walk very slowly across the grass to where the person sat on the moonlit grass as I walked I whispered.
> 'John is that you?' no answer followed so I whispered 'John please answer if you don't I will go back to bed'. I knew that if I said that John really would answer if I said that. I still kept walking at last I reached the figure then John said
> 'Sarah you really are an ass of course its your old pal John'. 'Let's go for our walk in the garden while we can'. So we went for a walk around our garden at the end John said.
> 'Right meet you here this time tomorrow night'. 'Okay' I said and went up the stairs to bed. I was woken by my mother saying 'its time to get up'. I thought about last night the same question came into my mind was it a dream or not? I cannot explain as John was a statue which came alive with the moon. So I decided to think of it as a dream, then I remembered that I put a flower under my pillow which I picked last night. It was still there!

The mystery remains unresolved, but a group of girls from her class find

no difficulty in identifying with the heroine and her relationship with
the dream-like statue.

At 14 Velma, a pupil at a school for visually impaired children, moves
beyond a concern with herself to a deeper consideration of the effects
of time's passing on the human condition.

> *Time*
> Time changing, rearranging:
> Time like the syndrome of my mind
> Fled fast through the valley
> of a sombre past.
> Time that I could not see was there
> Walked my path, entwined my hair —
> Shadowed surveillance.
>
> Time mcadered my every breath,
> Showed no shame,
> Would not rest.
> Time stood in my shoes,
> And I was seen,
> The little girl I once had been.
> Time told revealing lies:
> Crippled beauty, blurred my eyes.
> He has no limits to his greed,
> Fufils his task, willingly leads.
> Changes bud to its flower:
> With alluring fingers
> Promised me power.
>
> Time marches through the ages of man,
> And all creation bows to his will.
> Time imperious, instrumental —
> Man stops.
> Kings try to escape him,
> They cannot, and I cannot.

This poem, by an unusually accomplished writer, shows how effectively the use of images can capture Velma's thoughts about life and
death. She seems to be standing back like a spectator, not only looking
at the changes which have happened to *her* as Time 'crippled beauty,
blurred my eyes', but also mourning the fact that life for us all has to
end.

What all the pieces seem to indicate is a growth with age in percept-iveness, empathy and self-awareness. It could, of course, be argued that these changes result solely from the development of the writers' own social cognition and from the adjustments which in any case they must make to their widening range of social experiences in real life, but the issue remains controversial. Some educators would argue that the writ-ings represent not only reflections of existing developmental trends, but are a part of an active construction of reality by the young writers themselves. It has even been argued that spiritual, religious and other deeply personal experiences can only be expressed in an imaginative form. Langer (1951), for example, says that thinking in images helps us to see patterns and structures in events, and that symbolic forms reveal 'the rationales of feelings, the rhythm and pattern of their rise and decline and intertwining in our minds'. Velma herself understands this point of view intuitively when she says that for her the only way of formulating her thoughts and feelings about abstract issues like the pur-pose of existence is through her imaginative writing. Similarly, Denise describes how, at the age of 10, she wrote a piece when her mouse died because it 'helped her to understand'.

Talking to children of different ages about the sources of their ideas for stories gives one interesting insights into their thinking processes, so before examining the various approaches to the interpretation and evaluation of imaginative writing by psychologists and educators, I would like to give some examples of ways in which children themselves perceive it.

Children's Views on Imaginative Writing

> I like making things up. At home I dream about this fantastic world. It doesn't have to be real. I can make it up, like when you have a magic pencil and whatever you want you take from the air.

Joanna, aged 11, discusses her story about the flight of a family of squirrels from a forest fire. The squirrels lose all their possessions in the fire and find refuge in a new wood where they are welcomed by a community of moles. It ends: 'Their misfortune and their bravery had been rewarded by wonderful people. Who could want more?'

The story is a fantasy about animals, yet the situation and the char-acterisations are based on real-life observation. The story is not as re-mote from Joanna's experience as a first reading might suggest, and, in fact, when asked about the sources of her ideas she says:

> I thought about it and I had been reading a book about animals going away from a forest fire and when I was writing the story my Mum and Dad were looking at new homes. At one time we were getting ready to go and we looked one more time and then Mummy changed her mind.

She admits that she was extremely anxious about the thought of leaving her familiar home environment, so it was reassuring to experience the move through an animal adventure.

Mark, aged 11, makes a similar point when he describes writing about an imaginary pilot, Joe Smith, who designs his own plane, test-flies it and crashes to his death.

> Mark: Say you're writing about yourself, you're playing the part of someone in it; you end it as most factual stories would end. Not many people fly aeroplanes on their first go. Mostly something breaks and they get killed. You're not in favour with yourself, more with the story. You don't care what happens to yourself. You pretend it's someone else. Really you *are* them.
> H.C.: You are Joe Smith?
> Mark: Yes, you are the Joe Smith and writing a diary of how you built an aeroplane and won a medal for it. In some stories, say there was a man called Joe Smith and it crashed, you run a commentary of your life in someone else's life.

Mark bases most of his stories on real events in his own life or on information which he has read in books. He admires authors who research the subject before they write and who create authentic characters and contexts. Of his favourite novelist, Willard Price, he says,

> In *Volcano Adventure* he's actually been into a volcano climbed down into it. It's like a diary. He's done many of the things he's written about. He's been to New Guinea and he finds out what it's like. It's realistic. You feel as if you're one of the people in the book. It makes you feel that you're walking through the jungle and capturing all these animals.

Through his reading and writing of stories, it seems that Mark is able to enter into the experience of another person and even take on the role of the other. As he himself says of imagination,

> It's like scanners in my head, a memory bank. I sort out the photo-
> graphs in my head, take out the right one and take negatives off it
> of ideas. You select the right thing you want and feed it through the
> computer.

Michelle, who is rather small for an 11-year-old, explains why she
wrote her story about a girl who shrinks when she drinks a magic liquid:

> I like writing about myself because usually when I want to talk
> about myself when small no-one wants to listen so I put it in my
> stories . . . I like people to feel that happened the way I remembered
> things, to let people know and share my memories and feelings. It
> depends on what I'm feeling. If I'm feeling I want to explain some-
> thing that's happened, I try to put it into my stories. I try to put as
> much memories as I can . . . When I write stories I try to *be* like I
> was and try to remember it. I go back and do it all over again.

She seems not only to be trying to come to terms with her own feelings
about being small, but also hoping that some of her readers may take
her perspective, and experience in imagination what smallness means.
Michelle understands intuitively that stories offer opportunities for
writers and readers to develop self-awareness and social sensitivity.

By contrast, Jon uses fantasy to explore what he calls possibilities,
and to try out experiences which in real life are unlikely to happen. His
stories are always about space, yet the interpersonal exchanges which
occur and the expressions of feeling and intention have their origins in
real life. For example, Jargon Plage, 'a slimy green tetrapod', experiences
fluctuating emotions as he carries out his doomed escape from the cell
on Planet Tetran and interacts with his robot guards. The main point
for Jon, however, seems to be to enable him to take on the role of
another person and so extend his range of experiences. He says:

> In adventures you could get a super muscle builder who could crash
> a car, or Asterix's magic potion. On other planets it's even better. You
> could be adapted to methane. You have even more possibilities. This
> earth has limited possibilities. We don't know what it's like on other
> planets. Adventure stories have possibilities, space stories have even
> more. You don't need to be limited by human life. This is the best
> mode I'm in. I may be able to incorporate social life into space stories.

Very young children are less articulate in describing the function which imaginative writing has for them. Their stories, I have suggested, usually contain plenty of action but little reference to inner feelings or motives. The accompanying picture is usually an integral and expressive part of the narrative and, although events can *seem* disconnected to the reader, they are probably clear in the mind of the writer. Five-year-old Francis, for example, is happy with his story *The Pirate's Magic Cave* and sees no need to elaborate for other people's benefit:

The pirates had a big boat
In the cave there were hundreds of gold guards
They're pretending they're his friends
When he's not looking they'll bash up his boat.

He says, 'It's my best one because I think it's more exciting than the Wizard one', and goes on, 'I like it ending nasty . . . and frightening things.' His friend Isabelle agrees, 'Sometimes I like happy endings and sometimes I like nasty ones, especially if they're nasty to princesses. I like them beaten up to have exciting bits!'

By 7 or 8 children can describe more about their own writing processes. Johanna's evaluation of one story shows her awareness of how she can in fantasy take on a new role:

I put imaginary things in and I thought about it a lot. It was a fantasy because I would like to have a tree house and rescue someone. I especially dream about rescuing people. They say, 'Thank you. You saved my life!'

Straightforward wish-fulfilment is a common theme amongst younger children when they talk about stories, yet a longing for magic things can often go alongside delight in the observation of everyday experiences. So Simon talks about the value which the reading and writing of stories has for him: 'Ideas come from my imagination. I imagine I'm in a secret garden. There's a magic vine that gives you everything you wish for . . .' Yet the content is rooted in reality: 'When I'm eighteen I'll look back to when I was eight and see what I wrote. I would think I was doing interesting things — finding birds, watching kestrels and kites, and finding acorns.'

The magic lands which have such a fascination for young writers often contain extremely realistic people and situations, as Joanne explains:

I need to put children in it. It makes it good if it's a fairy tale but not an actual fairy tale — not something that is true but it sounds true. They live in a cottage with mother and father and play with toys, like Moonface and Saucepan, and of course that is true. Some of the lands are true but some aren't. Those that sound true are ones where you buy things and they're a lot of money, so that's true in the shops. Some of it is impossible and some isn't.

She does seem to perceive links between the worlds of reality and imagination, and children of this age will often express dissatisfaction with a story simply because it goes beyond the bounds of credibility.

Young adolescents, who are more likely to deal with complexities of emotion and intention in their stories, will quite consciously describe aspects of the environment to achieve the right effect, and use the events of a narrative symbolically to illustrate an issue. Tracy, at 13, explains how she has deliberately created a sombre atmosphere as a backdrop to her story, *Doom for the Lion*, which is about the cruel killing of a lion by a tiger: 'The November sky was sinking and was heavy on the mountain. And the last of the yellow leaves were falling to the ground. The lion was getting ready for winter . . .' While she indicates the emotions of both killer and victim, at a deeper level she is concerned with the issue of violence and its long-term implications for other people. The story ends: 'His wife was taken to a zoo with his cubs to live behind bars. No more zebras or hunting no more freedom their lives were wrecked completely wrecked.' Other children in her class question the author's motives for writing such a gloomy piece, but they show that they share Tracy's concern about cruelty. She justifies the sad theme although she would rather have a happy ending:

Tracy: I liked writing about animals because I like animals. I like the words. I don't like the way the lion is killed.
Katy: Why did you write it then? You could have a fight and then have them slink off into the jungle.
Tracy: That's not good enough. That's not realistic. It's better to end the story completely.
Katy: I think the story shows that if it hadn't been for *man* the lion wouldn't have been killed. Is that the idea, that man shouldn't interfere?
Tracy: Yes. All this trying to interfere with the peaceful life that animals are trying to lead. They're going to chop down all these jungles to make more land, and they don't need more land. They're greedy.

Sian: The thing is, they say if a man goes and shoots someone in the street, he didn't do it on purpose . . . he's insane. They give him five years in prison. If a *lion* kills someone they *shoot* the poor thing. It's not fair. Animals don't understand . . .

Like Tolkien, these young people have perceived the deeper layer of meaning which can underlie the surface content of a story.

The Imaginary and the Real

These interpretations by young writers of their own work seem to indicate that this kind of activity is of value to them, but the implications for education continue to be controversial. Do children's symbolic transformations of real-life experiences into imaginative ones deepen their understanding or simply distort it? Should children be trained to differentiate clearly between reality and the world of the imagination?

In the nineteenth century it was actually considered by some to be harmful to read imaginative stories to young children. Tucker (1982, p. 67) for example, describes how one Victorian educator, Mrs Trimmer, criticised the use of fairy stories because they 'fill the heads of children with confused notions of wonderful and supernatural events'. Similarly, Montessori argued that it was wrong to encourage fantasy in preschool children since they were not intellectually capable of distinguishing between the imaginary and the real. (She quotes an example of one child who jumped out of the window in imitation of Goldilocks!) Unlike Froebel, who gave a central place in his educational philosophy to the development of the imagination in young children, she stressed that children should be trained to learn about real-life situations. To her, make-believe had no positive influence on the growth of the intellect.

A similar viewpoint appears in the Board of Education (1927) *Handbook of Suggestions for Teachers* in which the authors, while recognising that composition can be used to improve fluency and technical accuracy in written English, are still very cautious about the value of 'exercises in invention, such as fairy tales or imaginary autobiographies which illustrate merely the unrestrained play of the fancy and the love of make-believe'. They argue that 'fluency and fertility of invention are unfortunately not incompatible with serious inability to write a statement or description demanding accuracy, clearness of arrangement, sense of proportion and right choice of words'. In the present day there are still educators who deliberately exclude imaginative activities from their curriculum on the grounds that the school's domain is the real and not the imaginary. (The language programmes of Bereiter and Engelmann would be one example of this.) Others might admit that imaginative activities are enjoyable as pastimes, but they would argue that the teacher's role does not include the fostering of a world of make-believe. Fantasy play would be discouraged because its focus is not on real-life tasks; fiction would be used in the classroom as a means of developing children's reading skills, story-writing as a way of extending writing abilities. Even political arguments have been used to devalue the use of the imagination in the education of children. For example, in Russia, after the Revolution, social realism was deemed to be more suitable for children than fairy tales and myth.

The Inner World of Imagination

At the other extreme, influenced by the literature on psychoanalysis, some educators have argued that the symbolic images of fantasy — wicked stepmothers, cruel giants and fierce monsters — can help young children to distance themselves from the fears and anxieties which form part of their lives. By their involvement in imaginative stories and fantasy play children, it is claimed, are enabled to work through some of their emotional conflicts. The world of make-believe is viewed as playing a key role in the emotional development of the child. From this perspective, the themes of fantasy and imagination *are* real since they are about issues like life and death, loss of the parent, fear of separation and other anxieties of vital concern to the child. On the same theme, Gordon (1972, p. 78) suggests that through the forms of art 'man has found a way of breaking the seal that locks him fast into his inner world' and goes on:

> thus has man found, after all, a way of transmitting to others at least something of his intimate and personal experience, of gaining for it some social validation and of mediating to himself, to his own conscious self, a part of this elusive inner world.

She is saying that perhaps only by creating witches and giants, arduous journeys and incredible adventures are children enabled to find words to describe moving experiences and intangible ideas. Supporters of this viewpoint claim that through imaginative play, and the reading and writing of stories, children not only explore themes which are meaningful to them, but also achieve some kind of resolution of emotional conflicts. Holbrook (1966), for example, using creative writing as a means of helping difficult or backward children through their own personal crises, makes Freudian interpretations of their work. Thus, in one piece, a cloud symbolises hate and aggression, and its name, Black Skeleton, reveals the writer's 'fear of death'. Holbrook sees this boy as regressing to an infant stage, through writing, in order to understand conflicts within himself. There is an obvious danger here that, by adopting such an approach, teachers may wrongly project intense emotions on to the child and miss the real ideas which are being expressed.

Taking the Spectator Role in Imagination

These two broad approaches to the imaginative development of the child are strikingly different. The first views imagination as a flight from reality, an escapist activity which has no place in the school curriculum. The second argues that the internal world of the imagination *is* a real one. The first presents a rather narrow concept of reality; the second, with its therapeutic orientation, can run the risk of mistakenly seeing emotional problems in everything which the child produces. I would suggest that, though it has been constructive for educators to focus on the reality of the inner experience of the child, the resolution of emotional conflicts can only be one aspect of the imaginative process.

Recent studies have shown, however, that it is also possible to demonstrate links between the imagination and children's social and intellectual development. Hardy (1977) expresses a point of view which is commonly found in the literature on the philosophy of English teaching when she writes in her analysis of the function of narrative:

> We often tend to see the novel as competing with the world of happenings. I should prefer to see it as the continuation, in disguising and isolating art, of the remembering, dreaming, and planning that is in life imposed on the uncertain, attenuated, interrupted and unpredictable or meaningless flow of happenings. (p. 14)

Hardy is arguing that narrative is not only an aesthetic phenomenon invented by artists, but is a fundamental way of organising experience which underlies dreaming, day-dreaming, predicting events in the future, analysing happenings in the past, coming to terms with relationships and learning about ourselves. In order to live, she is saying, we make up stories about ourselves and others. In her view, two adults gossiping over the garden fence or a child fantasising about Bionic Man are, like the novelist, engaged in 'the narrative motions of human consciousness' (p. 12).

Britton (1970, 1977), in his influential work on children's imaginative writing, takes a similar perspective. Story-telling is not simply a form of escapism which will, with maturity, be replaced by more realistic concepts of the world, but is also one important means through which individuals build systematic representations of experiences which provide both an interpretation of the past and a system for anticipating, or even making, the future. Fantasy, he argues, mediates between the individual's psychological needs and the constraints of reality, and he argues that, as users of language, we orient ourselves in either of two ways, participant or spectator. When we take the participant role we are recording, reporting or classifying the world as it is, just as a scientist writes a report or a journalist records an event; by contrast, when we take the spectator role we attempt to shape our picture of the world in order to evaluate experience. Britton, Burgess, Martin, McLeod and Rosen (1975) write:

> As participants, our feelings will tend to be sparked off in action; as spectators, we are able to savour their quality as feelings. As participants, we are caught up in a kaleidoscope of emotions; as spectators, we have these emotions in perspective. (p. 81)

From this standpoint the writing of imaginative stories has the function of helping children to meet the demands of the real world more effectively.

Taking a similar perspective, Applebee (1978) demonstrates how very young children use stories as a means of distancing themselves from events in their own lives. By creating characters, actions and settings they gain insights into real-life happenings. He too notices developmental trends in social sensitivity, self-awareness and ability to identify underlying themes in narratives. Applebee's research is concerned with the stories which children tell and read. Other researchers (Wilkinson, Barnsley, Hanna and Swan, 1980; Cowie, 1982) show how young writers can use the world of imagination as a means of understanding their own lives.

This type of approach to narrative certainly confirms the self-reports of children, yet avoids the extremes of focusing too heavily on deep-seated emotional conflicts in the child. Furthermore, links exist between this approach and recent findings in the field of social cognition, in particular the work by psychologists on the purposes and effects of social role-taking.

The Relevance of Research in Social Role-taking

The literature on social cognition gives useful insights into the function which make-believe might have for children's social and intellectual development. Research into social role-taking — by which is meant the ability to relate the perspective of another person to one's own — was pioneered by Flavell (1968) with his identification of *levels* of role-taking ability. The earliest stage, he claims, involves a lack of recognition that the other person's viewpoint differs from one's own; the next shows awareness of the other's perspective but little understanding of it; in later stages, the child indicates a growth of empathic awareness about the intentions, thoughts and feelings of other people. Piaget (1932) had already pointed the way when he argued that early childhood involves a process of decentring in which both social and cognitive factors interact. The Piagetian view is that children come to take the perspective of others as egocentric thinking declines, and that with maturity comes the ability to understand what other people are thinking and feeling. Piaget (1932, p. 393) claims that through reciprocity and mutually shared meanings, the individual develops in understanding of self and others. In other words, the individual is actively constructing thought in co-operation with other people. Although Piaget has been criticised about his views on the actual age at which children are capable of this kind of social communication (Donaldson, 1978; Borke, 1971; Light, 1980), there is a growing body of research which confirms that self-understanding is reached through social activity, and that the individual comes to see himself or herself by taking on the role of the other. This process of social decentration seems to be aided by activities like sociodramatic play (Garvey and Berndt, 1975) and role-playing or acting (Hoffmann, 1976; Chandler, 1972, 1973; Hartup, 1970). (See also Smith's discussion in Chapter 1.) Light (1980), influenced by Mead's (1934) ideas on the effect of internal dialogues between self and other, stresses that the role-playing need not actually happen, but may be acted out in solitary play:

> The child may not only practise adult roles but also role-taking activities like those involved in competitive or co-operative situations. He

may rehearse past or future interactions with others, imagining the responses of another occupying a complementary role. In these respects solitary play may provide an important context for role-taking development. (p. 30)

This view of the social and cognitive benefits which may be the outcome of make-believe play suggests that imaginative activities do indeed have an important learning function both as a preparation for future social situations and as a deepening of understanding of self and others. Singer and Singer (1979) view the activity of fantasy as 'a form of information-processing or cognitive behaviour' and see 'the ability to stand situations on their heads and get perspective on them as originating in early childhood experiences with imaginative, make-believe play' (p. 211). Clearly this is an important area for investigation, and much research remains to be done to resolve the controversies arising from it. The essence of the argument is that symbolic activities – for example, those expressed in make-believe play, role-taking, story-telling or the writing of imaginative narratives – have an important function in the development of reflective thinking and social competence. The implications of this for child-rearing and education are enormous. Light, writing specifically about the value of fantasy play, concludes that symbolic play should be regarded as 'an indicator of the process whereby ego-centrism is transcended' (p. 75). Again, Smith (1982), pointing to the educational value of sociodramatic play and its function in developing innovative skills, writes, 'Fantasy provides play – which would otherwise be sensori-motor "practice" play (Piaget, 1951) – with internal goals which can structure it and bring it to a more useful level of complexity.'

The view that imaginative role-taking is much more than an assimilative activity which reflects a distorted view of reality and that it can play a constructive part in a child's social and intellectual development, is one which may be echoed in the research into children's writing. The writing of stories, if viewed along the same perspective, may be seen as an important learning activity in which not only are technical skills acquired, but children also discover psychological and social truths about themselves and others.

Conclusion

There seems to be growing evidence from a number of sources that imaginative activities are not only enjoyable in themselves, but also have clear intellectual, social and emotional benefits to the children who participate in them. As Furth (1978) writes:

> The playful attitude is a healthy and psychologically sensible strategy to cope with a world that is beyond the reach of adequate comprehension. It selectively focuses on what can be understood and avoids having to deal with other points of view that could disturb the present intellectual balance. (p. 102)

Moreover, the work on mutuality and reciprocity has important implications for the teaching of imaginative writing. If a writing community is created in the classroom, there are many benefits to the child. The conference, as described by Graves (Chapter 12) and by Cowie and Hanrott (Chapter 11) has the function of creating an unthreatening context within which ideas can be formulated, and roles experienced in a tentative and exploratory way. The growing sense of audience can be developed with important outcomes for social relationships in real life. Characters can be created which provide an opportunity for enacting situations which have already happened or speculating about events which might happen. Adventures may be experienced through the writing of stories without the problem of coping with everyday constraints. Further, children may use the stories as a means of re-enacting painful or disturbing events in their own lives and, through this symbolic enactment, keeping control of the situation and possibly resolving it. Again, mysterious or deeply personal thoughts and feelings can be expressed in a symbolic way which captures their meaning.

As we shall see in later chapters, some of the children's writing mainly *reflects* their world as they see it. This is particularly evident in the analysis of the sex-role stereotyping which appears in their stories from an early age. Davies, in Chapter 4, indicates the powerful influence of 'socialising agents' — parents, teachers and the mass media. Historically, too, children's writing is interesting since we see through their eyes how the contemporary scene appears to them. (The response to public hanging described by Linda Pollock in Chapter 5 is one example of this.) Yet at the same time this writing also shows that children may at times use it as a way of coming to terms with new or disturbing experiences. Their writing on issues like death, loss, separation, violence is in some ways a reflection of things as they *are* perceived by the child, but in other ways shows how they try to understand them (see Judy Ollington in Chapter 6). As one 12-year-old girl said, entering in imagination into the inner world of other people is like 'finding doorways into their land'.

In the field of writing in particular, research that investigates the social and cognitive learning which results from the use of the imagination has an important role to play in the justification of the arts curriculum in schools. The encouragement to write can encompass subjective and objective ways of knowing both about the inner world of experience and about external reality. More research needs to be done to test hypotheses that imaginative writing helps the child to shape ideas, to explore lines of thought in a playful or tentative way, and to develop in the capacity to take the perspective of other people; but investigations which focus only on the end-product run the risk of greatly underestimating the intentions of the child. More study needs to be done on the processes which underlie children's use of fantasy and the meaning which it has for them. Children themselves can illuminate the sources of their thinking, and sensitive observations of composing processes are feasible, as Emig (1971) and Graves (1983) have shown. The fact that there are wide individual differences in the capacity of children to use their imaginations in a constructive way is also a matter of importance since it raises the question of the extent to which these processes can be nurtured or inhibited by the responses of other people. We still know very little about the conditions within which the imagination of children can best be fostered, but again research into writing process by Britton, by Graves and by Wason suggests the need for trust in an audience and reciprocity between teacher and child; moreover, if a 'writing community' is created in the classroom the child is much more likely to find an authentic voice.

Finally, any study of the value of the imagination for cognitive development needs to set limits. There is a danger of going too far in either of two directions. Too great a reliance on fantasy can result in unstable, egocentric patterns of thought which have little meaning for other people and which lack form and coherence. On the other hand, if the individual denies the free flow of imaginative processes he is likely to be dominated by forms which come from outside and which lack life and feeling; in these conditions, the child's authentic voice may never be found. Smith (1982) makes this point in the context of play when he argues that 'creative outcomes are likely to be increased if there is a balance between fantasy play (assimilative) and more accommodative thoughts and behaviours' (p. 152).

It seems appropriate to end with John Fowles's aside to the reader in *The French Lieutenant's Woman*, where he writes that we are all novelists in the sense that we are in the habit of writing fictional futures for ourselves:

We screen in our minds hypotheses about how we might behave about what might happen to us; and these novelistic or cinematic hypotheses often have very much more effect on how we actually do behave, when the real future becomes the present, than we generally allow. (p. 294)

References

Applebee, A.N. (1978) *The Child's Concept of Story*, University of Chicago Press, Chicago

Board of Education (1927) *Handbook of Suggestions for Teachers*, HMSO, London

Borke, H. (1971) 'Interpersonal Perception of Young Children: Egocentrism or Empathy?', *Developmental Psychology*, 5, 263-9

Britton, J. (1970) *Language and Learning*, Allen Lane, London

— (1977) 'The Role of Fantasy' in M. Meek, G. Barton and A. Warlow (eds), *The Cool Web*, Bodley Head, London, pp. 40-7

—, Burgess, T., Martin, N., McLeod, A. and Rosen, H. (1975) *The Development of Writing Abilities 11-18*, Macmillan Education, London

Chandler, M. (1972) 'Egocentrism in Normal and Pathological Child Development' in F. Monks, W. Hartup and J. De Wit (eds), *Determinants of Behavioural Development*, Academic Press, London

— (1973) 'Egocentrism and Anti-social Behaviour: the Assessment and Training of Social Perspective-taking Skills', *Developmental Psychology*, 9, 326-32

Cowie, H. (1982) 'An Approach to the Evaluation of Children's Imaginative Writing, *Human Learning*, vol. 1, 213-21

Donaldson, M. (1978) *Children's Minds*, Fontana, London

Emig, J. (1971) *The Composing Process of Twelfth Graders* (NCTE Research Report 13), Champaign, Illinois

Flavell, J.H. (1968) *The Development of Role-taking and Communication Skills in Childhood*, Wiley, New York

Fowles, J. (1975) *The French Lieutenant's Woman*, Granada, London

Furth, H. (1978) 'Children's Societal Understanding and the Process of Equilibration' in W. Damon (ed.), *Social Cognition*, Jossey Bass, San Francisco

Garvey, C. and Berndt, R. (1975) 'The Organisation of Pretend Play'. Unpublished manuscript, Johns Hopkins University, reported in W. Damon (ed.), *Social Cognition*, Jossey Bass, San Francisco

Gordon, R. (1972) 'A Very Private World' in P.W. Sheehan (ed.), *The Function and Nature of Imagery*, Academic Press, New York

Graves, D. (1983) *Writing: Teachers and Children at Work*, Heinemann Educational, Exeter, New Hampshire

Hardy, B. (1977) 'Narrative as a Primary Act of Mind' in M. Meek, G. Barton and A. Warlow (eds), *The Cool Web*, Bodley Head, London

Hartup, W. (1970) 'Peer Interaction and Social Organisation' in P. Mussen (ed.), *Carmichael's Manual of Child Psychology*, vol. 2, Wiley, New York

Hoffman, M.L. (1976) 'Empathy, Role-taking, Guilt and the Development of Altruistic Motives' in T. Lickona (ed.), *Moral Development and Behaviour*, Holt, Rinehart & Winston, New York

Holbrook, D. (1966) 'Poetry and the Inward Life' in T. Blackburn (ed.), *Presenting Poetry*, Methuen, London

Langer, S. (1951) *Philosophy in a New Key: a Study in the Symbolism of Reason, Rite and Art*, Harvard University Press, New York

Light, P. (1980) *The Development of Social Sensitivity*, Cambridge University Press, Cambridge

Mead, G.H. (1934) *Mind, Self and Society*, University of Chicago Press, Chicago

Piaget, J. (1932) *The Moral Judgement of the Child*, Harcourt Press, New York
— (1951) *Play, Dreams and Imitation in Childhood*, Routledge & Kegan Paul, London

Singer, J.L. and Singer, D.G. (1979) 'The Values of the Imagination' in B. Sutton-Smith (ed.), *Play and Learning*, Gardner Press, New York

Smith, P.K. (1982) 'Does Play Matter? Functional and Evolutionary Aspects of Animal and Human Play', *The Behavioural and Brain Sciences*, 5, 139-84

Tolkien, J.R.R. (1964) *Tree and Leaf*, George Allen & Unwin, London

Tucker, N. (1982) *The Child and the Book*, Cambridge University Press, Cambridge

Wilkinson, A., Barnsley, G., Hanna, P. and Swan, M. (1980) *Assessing Language Development*, Oxford University Press, Oxford

Part Two: CHILDREN'S WRITING AND
THE DEVELOPMENT OF AWARENESS

INTRODUCTION

Helen Cowie

Danny, aged 11, writes about prisoners of war planning an escape from Colditz; Jon explains how a tetrapod outwits his robot guards; Julian describes the exploits of a heroic Viking; Matthew, aged 8, creates the character of a scientist who discovers strange properties in eagle's blood. The stories occur in a variety of places ranging from home to outer space, and the themes are about action and adventure. By contrast, Mary Anne writes about fear in the night at her father's house; Joanne, aged 11, describes a domestic scene in the house of a family of squirrels who, although they have an exciting escape from a forest fire, still end up safely in another home in a new part of the forest; Angela, at 14, discusses the predicament facing a pregnant teenage girl as she confronts her hostile parents. There are striking differences in setting and theme between boys' and girls' stories. In addition, male characters tend to be the ones who take the initiative in dangerous and demanding situations; they have a wide choice of occupational roles and are more likely to play a dominant part in the story. Female characters are more passive, and typically take on traditional roles; they tend to show dependent or helpless characteristics and are often rescued by males. In fact, from an early age children have expectations about the kinds of stories which it is appropriate for boys and girls to write. As one boy of 7 put it, 'You know, boys do sort of stories about Jumbo jets and outer space and all that, and exciting stories. Girls do poemish stories!'

In Chapter 4 Dilys Davies argues that writing is influenced by factors which are part of a wider socialisation process through which children learn sex-appropriate behaviour, and her extracts suggest that the values expressed in the stories are imposed on the authors by parents, teachers and the mass media. But is it enough to say that the narratives simply *reflect* the social world which these young people inhabit? Linda Pollock's study of twelve historical child and adolescent diaries suggests that such an interpretation is only part of the truth. In Chapter 5 she provides illuminating evidence which shows how certain young people in the past perceived themselves and others, and how their increasing maturity was accompanied by a growth in social sensitivity. She argues, in fact, that writing is one way through which these diarists seem to have learned to cope with problems in their lives, and have become familiar with the thoughts and feelings of other people. In addition, she indicates how the young writers seem to use their private diaries (even when the entries were read by relatives or tutors) as a way of coming to terms with their own emotions, some of which were extreme ones, like despair over ill-health or approaching death, and of understanding the complexities of their social environment. Her analysis suggests that the diarists are playing an *active* part in the process of growing towards maturity. Referring back to Joan Tamburrini's discussion in Chapter 2, one could argue that the authors are using their writing as a means of 'distancing' themselves from events and emotions in their own lives.

Of course the twelve diarists may be a self-selecting sample who have deliberately chosen this method of considering personal issues; it could be said that children who keep diaries are highly likely to use their writing for the purpose of taking the spectator role on experiences. However, in Chapter 6 Judy Ollington, from the perspective of the teacher of religious studies, goes further by arguing that some experiences and thoughts can *only* be expressed in images, poems, stories, dance and other symbolic forms. She admits that in some senses we are passively moulded by socialising agents from the culture, but she also claims that all children can be helped to make active use of images in order to communicate aesthetic and spiritual emotions. Thus, when one 11-year-old girl, Anna, explains that she liked her poem about love because she 'didn't say love was all kissing but also other things – the trees in winter with sparkling branches, talking to people, pictures, beautiful things like the sea', she seems to be trying to find her own images for expressing a deeply personal feeling. The images may not be new, but she is recreating them in her own words as a way of capturing an emotion and her thoughts about love at one point in her life. Judy Ollington also suggests that the images of story and myth help *all* children to come to terms with real issues in their lives; the fostering of an inner world of imagination by responsive parents and teachers will, she argues, give children an enriched perspective on themselves and other people, and on the religious, spiritual and aesthetic emotions which they are bound to experience.

The three contributors to this section give their own interpretations of the issues which children seem to explore in imaginative writing at different stages in their development.

4 SEX ROLE STEREOTYPING IN CHILDREN'S IMAGINATIVE WRITING

Dilys Davies

Introduction

Sex-role stereotypes, the norms which a society assigns as appropriate for males and females, are learned by children at an early age. One of the ways in which children express their experience and expectations is through the medium of imaginative story writing, where we can observe children's beliefs about the differing characteristics and behaviour of males and females in our society.

To explore how society's norms are reflected in children's writing, boys and girls of 15 years of age were shown a picture depicting a boat in a wood and were asked to write a story about it. The picture did not contain any people so the children were not responding to cues from stimulus figures in the picture, yet characters in the stories tended to be portrayed along sex-stereotypical lines.

Both boys and girls introduced far more male than female characters. Generally, male characters grasped the active, central roles in the stories, whilst female characters were shown in supportive and passive roles. The themes of the stories written by boys and girls illustrated marked differences. The stories of boys more often showed adventure, danger and physical aggression in themes of war, espionage, crime and activity in foreign countries. A typical example is a story written by Barry about a British pilot who is eventually rescued by the French Resistance. Barry begins his story with an atmosphere of danger and adventure: 'Flop down came the parachute. The explosion could be heard about a mile away while the airman hung from the tree with his parachute caught up.'

The stories of boys are often centred on action in foreign countries. Allan begins his story, *The Criminals*:

> Two men have got out of the Boeing 747 and got into a power boat with three hostages. They are in Africa, and have gone into the jungle where they will keep the hostages until they get the money for them.

In contrast, the stories of girls are often about domestic and family roles; the settings tend to be local. Barbara, for example, in *A Fun Day Out* describes a group of children playing with a boat. She introduces a domestic theme which portrays the traditional female role of providing and clearing away the food: 'Mary and Jane open the picnic hamper and they all tuck in hungrily . . . When everything has been eaten the girls clear away giggling and laughing together!'

Similarly, the boys and girls tend to assign attributes to the characters along sex-typed dimensions. Girls are generally more fearful and passive than the adventurous active boys. Carol writes: 'The two boys are all for taking the boat out but Jane who is not as bold as the boys is trying to stop them!' Emphasising physical strength, Allan describes how: 'the boat had been pulled up by two burly men'.

Girls typically play a supportive role to the dominant male characters, and are frequently depicted as in need of protection. In *Running Away*, where a boy and girl escape from an orphanage, Jane writes: 'Lisa, afraid, whispers to the twelve-year-old boy, "I'm scared, please let's go back . . ."' The boy then takes an assertive role, refusing to return, stating: 'We have to teach them a lesson. We have to show them we are not robot servants who they can order around.' The stories seem to indicate how deeply the sex-role stereotypes have been internalised by these young people since the characters act out in imaginary scenes the expectations which the authors themselves appear to have in real life. In this chapter I will discuss some of the factors which might lead children to reveal differing perceptions of male and female roles in their imaginative writing; in particular how sex-role stereotypes are communicated to children by the main socialising agents in our society, parents, teachers and the mass media.

Sex-role Socialisation of Children by Parents

Although it has been established that parents have sex-typed expectations regarding infants' behaviour, the evidence regarding parents' actual treatment of children in a sex-stereotyped fashion is more equivocal. There are a multitude of studies reported by researchers investigating sex differences along such dimensions as dependence–independence, aggression, interpersonal skills, cognitive abilities, toy and play preferences, sociability, dominance, achievement. Many researchers have reported that parents treat young boys and girls differently. Parents stimulate gross motor activity more with infant sons than daughters (Fagot, 1978), and give more verbal stimulation to infant daughters

(Maccoby and Jacklin, 1974). Studies carried out by Moss (1967) and Sears, Maccoby and Levin (1957) report sex differences in mother–child interaction. Sears *et al.* observed that mothers tended to pick up infant girls more often when they cried, while boys were frequently allowed to remain crying. Moss (1967) reported comparable findings; a high positive correlation existed between infant irritability and maternal contact for females from 3 to 12 weeks old. However, no correlation was found for 3-week-old males, and by 3 months a negative tendency was apparent. Moss hypothesised that the infant's cry instigated maternal intervention for female infants, but not for male infants, which is consistent with the data of Sears *et al.* Further, Moss observed that from 3 to 12 weeks, male infants were more often held, stimulated and aroused by their mothers. In the same study, it was observed that mothers imitated the vocalisations of female infants more often.

Reviewing the evidence, Maccoby and Jacklin conclude that although their 'survey of the research on socialisation of the two sexes has revealed surprisingly little differentiation in parent behaviour according to the sex of the child, there are some areas where different shaping does appear to occur' (pp. 338-9). These areas include dressing boys and girls differently, encouraging sex-typed interests, providing sex-appropriate toys and assigning sex-differentiated chores. Further, and even more strongly, parents 'discourage their children — particularly their sons — from engaging in activities they consider appropriate only for the opposite sex' (p. 339). They conclude:

> Boys seem to have more intense socialisation experiences than girls. They receive more pressure against engaging in sex-inappropriate behaviour, whereas the activities that girls are not supposed to engage in are much less clearly defined and less firmly enforced. Boys receive more punishment, but probably also more praise and encouragement . . . Whatever the explanation, the different amounts of socialisation pressure that boys and girls receive surely have consequences for the development of their personalities. (p. 348)

Similarly, Rudy (1968) and Hartley (1959) observe that for boys, sex-appropriate behaviour is emphasised earlier, and conformity to sex-role demands more rigidly enforced than for girls. As Hartley states, 'demands that boys conform to societal notions of what is manly come much earlier and are enforced with much more vigour than similar attitudes with respect to girls' (p. 458).

Further, parental sex-typing behaviour is assigning sex-differentiated chores and providing sex-appropriate toys may have implications for the ways in which children express perceptions of sex roles in their writing. For example, Whiting (1975), citing data from six cultures, describes how sex-assigned chores may contribute to later behavioural differences, and notes that girls are more frequently assigned domestic and child-care chores, whereas boys are assigned chores that take them away from the immediate vicinity of the home. For boys and girls, these sex differences in assigned work are associated with different frequencies of interaction with various categories of people. Girls interact more with adults and infants, whereas boys interact significantly more often with peers. Whiting observed that young girls in all cultures were significantly more nurturant than boys, and remained so in later childhood, while boys showed a significant increase in initiative after they began to take care of the pasturing and herding of animals. Hence Whiting's data draw attention to the possibility that a seemingly peripheral aspect of sex-typed socialisation, chore assignment, may have broader implications for other areas of development.

The provision of sex-typed toys by parents to boys and girls encourages children's awareness of sex-appropriate and sex-inappropriate activities. There is some evidence that parents buy different toys for their children (Rheingold and Cook, 1978); Goodenough (1957) indicated that parents bought similar toys for the children under 2 years of age but for the children over 2 years of age, they bought sex-typed toys. In this study no scientific toys were bought for girls by adults. Rheingold and Cook examined the contents of the rooms of 6-year-old children. Girls' rooms contained dolls, passive games and art material whilst boys' rooms contained trucks, bricks and equipment for active sports. Further, Fagot (1978) observed that although 2-year-old children showed marked differences in their toy and play preferences, parents did reinforce these behaviours. Girls preferred dolls and soft toys and boys preferred to play with blocks and manipulate objects. Parents gave boys significantly more positive responses when they played with blocks, and gave girls significantly more negative responses when they manipulated objects. Parents gave more positive responses to girls than boys, and more negative responses to boys for playing with dolls. The results of this study further emphasised that boys received more parental pressure against sex-typed inappropriate toy choice than did girls.

Parental sex-typing of children's toys and games has important implications for development. Research on children's games in a wide variety of cultures emphasises the importance of play in the socialisation process (Bruner, Jolly and Sylva, 1976); and Grief (1974) notes that the playing of sex-appropriate roles is an important factor in sex-role acquisition and development.

Block (1978) too points out that the evidence on differential sex-typing of children's interests and activities has important implications for the sex-role development of the child, such as the labelling of behaviour as sex-appropriate and sex-inappropriate, and criticises Maccoby and Jacklin's review on both theoretical and methodological grounds. Using data based on the Block Child Rearing Practices Report (1965) (CRPR) she examined child-rearing practices from two perspectives — parental self-reports and the perceptions by young adults of their own sex-role socialisation. Altogether, Block's data consisted of 17 independent samples, comprising 696 mothers, 548 fathers of children ranging between 3 and 20 years of age and 1227 young adults.

Regarding the differential socialisation of sons the CRPR data demonstrated:

(1)   Both mothers and fathers appear to emphasise achievement and competition more for sons than for daughters;
(2)   both parents encourage sons more than daughters to control the expression of emotion;
(3)   punishment is a more salient concern of parents of males than females;
(4)   there is greater emphasis on independence and the assumption of personal responsibility by parents of sons than of daughters, and this emphasis is more apparent in the responses of fathers than of mothers;
(5)   fathers are more authoritarian in the rearing of sons than of daughters: they are more strict, administer more physical punishment, and are less tolerant of aggression directed towards themselves by their sons;
(6)   mothers encourage their sons more than their daughters to conform to external standards.

Block suggests that these standards are manifestations of the greater concern for sex-appropriate behaviour in males than in females.

Hence Block's (1978) data support Maccoby and Jacklin's conclusion in that punishment, negative sanctions and conformity with regard to sex-appropriate behaviour is emphasised more in the child-rearing practices of the parents of sons than of the parents of daughters. Unlike Maccoby and Jacklin, Block also found more consistent emphasis in the socialisation of sons in the areas of achievement, competition, independence in the sense of personal responsibility, and in the control of emotion.

With regard to the differential socialisation of daughters, Block concludes:

1)   There is greater warmth and physical closeness in the parent–daughter relationship;
2)   both mothers and fathers of daughters have a greater expectation of 'lady-like' behaviours. They discourage rough-and-tumble play; mothers particularly expect daughters to stay clean whilst playing; fathers discourage fighting more in daughters than in sons;
3)   both parents exhibit a greater reluctance to punish daughters compared with sons;
4)   mothers exercise a closer supervision of daughters' activities compared with sons;
5)   daughters more than sons are encouraged by both parents to wonder and think about life, i.e. introspection is encouraged. Girls are also encouraged more to talk about their problems, are included more than sons in the discussion of family plans and are trusted more. (p. 38)

She also concludes that there is evidence for the differential socialisation of males and females; sex differentiation in socialisation emphases appears to increase with the age of the child, reaching a maximum during the high school years; there is evidence of specific sex-of-parent and sex-of-child effects.

Sex-role Stereotyping of Children by Teachers

Similarly, many studies in schools suggest that teachers differentially encourage sex-appropriate behaviour, and evaluate children's performances according to sex-stereotypical dimensions.

In a study of preschool classrooms, Fagot (1978) observed that boys received more positive teacher reaction when playing with blocks and art activities and more teacher criticism when they engaged in female-appropriate activities such as playing with dolls and dress-up; girls received more criticism when they played in the outside sandbox. Fagot notes that both playing with blocks and art activities are considered by teachers to be task-orientated academic behaviours. This supports the findings of Serbin, O'Leary, Kent and Tonick (1973) that boys, when engaged in activities considered by teachers to be appropriate task-related behaviour, receive higher levels of teacher reinforcement than do girls engaging in the same behaviour.

Serbin (1978) in a study of preschool classrooms observed that teachers encouraged boys more than girls for engaging in such activities as playing with bricks, trucks and the climbing apparatus; girls were encouraged to play with dolls and with games, such as a sewing game associated with the 'domestic' role. Serbin suggests that the encouragement of boys at such activities as manipulating objects and playing with climbing apparatus is associated with the development of skills at problem-solving tasks involving spatial reasoning. Similarly, in Britain, the work of King (1978) and Byrne (1978) suggests that teachers encourage boys to engage in tasks and activities involving mechanical and spatial skills, whilst girls are encouraged to engage in tasks involved in domestic skills.

Belotti (1974) in a study of the development of the feminine role in girls in Italian nursery schools observed that teachers actively encouraged girls to look after boys, to tidy up after them and help maintain peace and order. On the other hand, teachers were more tolerant of boys' disorder and rowdy games. Similarly, studying primary schools in Britain, Byrne (1978) states:

> Girls are praised for being quiet, clean, tidy, helpful; and criticised for being muddy, rough, noisy, lazy, untidy . . . On the other hand, boys are praised for toughness, for strength, for leadership, for organisation, for adult behaviour, for initiative and originality. (pp. 83-4)

Byrne suggests that the attitudes of teachers regarding sex-role behaviours are communicated to children so that well before the secondary school years children are aware of definite sex-role-appropriate behaviour. Girls have learned

> to like sedentary occupations, to be biddable and helpful and domesticated . . . and (that) boys have learned to be assertive, to fight . . . to show initiative, and to hide their emotions and stifle even the healthier of their fears. (pp. 83-4)

Bernard (1979) investigated the question of whether sex-role stereotypes and sex bias are present when a teacher evaluates a student. In this study 240 male and female teachers read and rated a description of either a male or female high school pupil who demonstrated either masculine or feminine sex-role behaviour, and whose major course of study was either English or physics. The description of sex-role behaviour contained adjectives described by Bem (1976) and Broverman, Vogel, Broverman, Clarkson and Rosenkrantz (1972) as stereotypically masculine or feminine. For example, the male sex-role-behaviour description contained such adjectives as 'independent', 'competitive' and 'assertive', whilst adjectives in the female sex-role-behaviour description included 'understanding', 'sympathetic', 'gentle' and 'warm'. The teachers were required to read and rate a written essay purported to have been written by the student, labelled as either John or Jane. Results demonstrated that the sex of the student influenced teachers' ratings of the written English essay. 'John' was rated higher than 'Jane' in having understood the question, and the answers attributed to 'John' were judged to be more logical and grammatical than 'Jane's'. An important finding of the study was the effect of student sex-role behaviour and course of study. For example, physics was judged to be an inappropriate choice of study for a student with feminine sex-role behaviour. Further, feminine sex-role behaviour was viewed by teachers as academically dysfunctional for a student studying physics. In both subjects, English and physics, a student who had been identified with masculine sex-role behaviour was assessed as superior across a number of dimensions of writing ability to a student associated with feminine sex-role behaviour. Bernard concludes that 'a teacher's impression of a student as defined by sex-role behaviours of that student may influence the manner in which a teacher examines the student's written work' (p. 562). Such evaluations are based on sex-role behavioural expectations rather than based on observed behaviour and performance-relevant criteria, and are the direct outcomes of the process of sex-role stereotyping.

In addition to any explicit instructions about sex roles, teachers may also socialise boys and girls differently through differences in interaction. Although teachers' interactions with pupils have not always been found to be related to the sex of the student, generally results indicate that boys receive a higher level of negative or a higher level of both positive and negative feedback. Boys have also been found to initiate more contacts with teachers (Serbin, 1978). Further, such studies indicate that even when girls do volunteer, teachers are less likely to respond to them.

Generally it seems that teachers' attitudes and sex-role expectancies influence the behaviour and attainment of children.

Sex-role Stereotyping of Children by the Mass Media

Children's Literature

There is wide agreement as to the sterotypic characteristics and behaviour ascribed to males and females, and despite changes in many societal values over the last few decades these stereotypes have maintained an unchanging quality. Further, sex-role stereotypes have for most people been incorporated into the individual's self-concept.

Children's literature and television programmes reflect cultural values, they contain sex-role prescriptions and standards providing an important vehicle for teaching children acceptable standards of behaviour and values perpetuated by the culture (Weitzman, Eifler, Holcada and Ross, 1972).

As Rowan (1979) points out, it is in our reinforcing effect on existing attitudes and behaviour that the mass media are most effective.

Research indicates that the sex roles presented to children in children's books generally, including school reading schemes, follow traditional stereotypical patterns.

In a study of the sex-role standards attributed to characters in children's books in the USA, Hillman (1978) compared the contents of children's books during two periods – the 1930s, and from the mid 1960s to the mid 1970s. The results of the investigations demonstrated that in both periods male figures were more numerous than females. Further, the range of occupations for males was much broader than for females, since approximately 160 occupations were listed for males while only 35 were listed for females. In addition to fulfilling a greater variety of work roles, males were depicted in jobs associated with power and prestige, while females were mainly depicted in domestic roles. While males were portrayed as being physically aggressive and competent, females were portrayed as exhibiting the characteristics of affiliation, dependence and sadness in both the periods investigated. Similar results were found in an investigation by Weitzman *et al.* (1972) of prize-winning books for children. Not only were women under-represented in the title, central roles and illustrations, but when they did appear their characterisations depicted traditional sex-role stereotypes. While men engage in a wide variety of roles and occupations, women are limited to the roles of wives and mothers. Typically, the stories portrayed boys as being active. Boys are presented in more exciting and adventurous roles, engage in more varied pursuits and demand more independence. In marked contrast, most of the girls in the stories are pictured as passive and immobile. Girls are more often portrayed indoors, hence placing limitations on their activities and potential for adventure. Further, Weitzman *et al.* note that even the youngest girls play traditional roles, with their actions directed towards helping and pleasing their brothers and fathers, thus confirming sex-role stereotypes.

Belotti (1974) considers a study carried out at New Jersey University which examined 15 collections of children's books and 144 reading schemes. The results indicated that the themes of the books stressed the dominance of boys and the passivity of girls. Lobban (1974) reviewed six reading schemes in common use in infant and primary schools in Britain. In a content analysis of stories from these series, Lobban coded the adult roles presented, the new skills learned, the leadership roles assumed in mixed activities, the activities shown and the toys and pets owned by children. The results indicated that the stories contained twice as many heroes as heroines. Most of the heroines were depicted in traditional female roles, such as learning to care for a new baby. When a story contained both a hero and heroine, Lobban states that the hero was nearly always dominant. Further, male characters had a greater range of activities. More adult male roles were shown, and male characters taught boys many new skills compared to the restricted range of new skills taught by female characters to girls. Whereas boys were shown watching adult men performing their occupational roles and tasks, girls were not shown observing adult female occupational roles. Hence, the results demonstrated a similar pattern to the results of studies conducted in the USA. Women and girls were portrayed as weak, submissive, passive and home based. Common themes entailed the adventurous, initiatory image of males and the dependent image of females. Their findings are confirmed by Sharpe (1976), reviewing British children's reading primers. Examining the roles played by girls and women, Sharpe notes that 'they are cast as the passive supporting characters for their vigorous male counterparts' (p. 93). Further, the different characteristics for boys and girls are implicitly endorsed: 'Little girls are good, sweet, quiet, and thoroughly angelic, and they like helping mother in the home.' Not only are boys not expected to behave like this, but furthermore Sharpe states 'it is their prerogative to be naughty'. When the two sexes are portrayed together, 'the boy is clearly the active, commanding and dominating figure, while the girl is a pliant and passive observer'.

It is not only the written word but pictures that reinforce and uphold traditional sex-role stereotypes in children's readers. Sharpe notes that

boys and girls are portrayed in costumes of traditional feminine and masculine characters, or in possible future roles. Boys put on costumes of cowboys, policemen, firemen, while the girls are dressing as princesses, nurses and brides. Toys that are pictured also follow the traditional roles. Girls have the inevitable doll, while boys play with cars, boats, planes and trains. (p. 94)

Sex-role stereotypes are also reflected in school text books, with possible implications for the sex appropriateness of the area of study. For example, Byrne (1978) reports an investigation she conducted in 1975 of science books being used in primary and middle schools in a selected area of Britain. She states: 'In all but one, every illustration showed boys in the active, experimental situation and girls standing admiringly, handing over a test tube or being shown what to do' (p. 89). Further, Nilsen (1975) concludes from an analysis of elementary text books in the USA, 'Boys are the dominant figures in the non-fiction section of the library because they are thought to be more able than girls in such fields as maths, science and statesmanship' (p. 208).

Children's comics follow a similar pattern of sex-role stereotyping. Braman (1977) categorises the comics widely read by children into two groups, the educational and the humorous. Braman states that the educational comics neglect women's roles, concentrating on such items as military information. Although the humorous comics are read by both sexes, male characters predominate by ten to one. Sharpe points out that for the age group between 7 and 13 years, comics can be divided according to whether they are appropriate for boys or girls. Their very titles reflect the orientation of the contents. The majority of boys' stories reflect action and adventure, whilst girls' stories are characterised by an absence of these features, focusing more on the personal and emotional elements. The sex-stereotypical themes are similarly reflected in adolescent and adult magazines (Silver, 1976). These researchers emphasise the point that women are mainly portrayed in the housekeeping role. Moreover, the traits emphasised in adolescent and adult magazines as being typically of women are those of passivity and dependence (Owen, 1972).

Newspapers, television, radio and films all transmit information about the nature and role of the sexes. Throughout the media, the sexes are presented in ways which are consistent with aspects of their stereotyped images. Further, the media reflect and reinforce sex-role stereotypes. Maccoby and Jacklin (1974, p. 139) state: 'The greater power of the male to control his own destiny is part of the cultural stereotype of maleness, and is inherent in the images of the two sexes portrayed on television and in print.'

Television

Gerbner (1978) describes television as the 'cosmic force' or unquestioned environment into which one is born. Television in the USA and in Great Britain reaches most homes, and is viewed for long and regular periods by children from an early age. In the USA 95 per cent of all homes have television (McArthur and Resko, 1975). Similarly, in Britain, Plowden (1980) reports that 99.6 per cent of all families have a television, and most are turned on at least once a day. Lalor (1980) states that television is regularly viewed from the age of 2 years upwards. Dunn (1980) comments that 'during the first years of life children are developing at a rate they never again approach'. Further, she indicates that 3 to 5-year-olds watch a great deal of television. Considering adolescents, Plowden (1980) states: 'If adolescence is taken to begin at twelve, then it is worth noting that the twelve to fourteens view, on average, more television a day . . . than any other age group' (p. 41).

Television not only entertains, but also persuades and informs. Researchers such as Plowden (1980) and Lalor (1980) emphasise the role of television in the socialisation process. Lalor states: 'Communication media are potential agencies of socialisation because they, like the family, the school and the child's peers, direct information and examples of behaviour toward the child' (p. 78). Further, Lalor points out that both in formal school lessons and in television viewing, children not only learn the factual information presented, but learn incidentally about themselves and society. Lalor terms this 'the hidden curriculum'. Thus, television presentations 'will have a bearing on children's attitudes to such things as sex roles, race, class, occupations . . . the status of individuals within our society and even the nature of reality' (p. 78).

Children not only watch television programmes specifically produced for children's viewing, but they also watch adult programmes. Traditional sex-role stereotypes are evident in both television programmes and in televised advertising commercials.

Jennings, Geis and Brown (1980) state that the main interests of women as illustrated in television commercials are 'in attracting and feeding men and cleaning their homes' (p. 203). Restricting women's interests to their concerns, Jennings *et al.* suggest, 'implies a corresponding lack of competence and confidence in the public domains of career and achievement skills' (p. 203). As McArthur and Resko (1975) indicate, children observe women depicted in television commercials as being preoccupied with the shininess of their floors and the whiteness of their wash. Television commercials carry implicit sex-role messages as well as explicit messages aimed at selling the product. As suggested by Singer and Kaplan (1976), the impact of such implicit messages may be all the more powerful precisely because the messages are indirect and unobtrusive.

Regarding television programmes, generally it seems that females are portrayed as passive and conforming compared with the more active and dominating roles played by men. Women are portrayed in a more restricted range of roles than men and are typically presented in a peripheral role to the male role.

Research on programmes specifically produced for children indicates that the sexes are presented in ways which are consistent with aspects of their stereotyped image. Investigating children's television programmes in the USA, Sternglanz and Serbin (1974) analysed male and female roles in ten popular programmes. Marked sex differences were observed in both the number of male and female roles portrayed, there being twice as many male roles, and in the behaviour displayed by male and female characters; males were more often portrayed as aggressive and constructive than females who were more often portrayed as being deferential. Moreover, males and females received different consequences for their behaviour. Males were more likely to be rewarded than females, whilst frequently there was neither reward nor punishment for females, the exception being that females were more often punished for high levels of activity than were males. British children's television programmes follow a similar pattern. Sharpe (1976) points out, 'On children's programmes and those for schools, the attitudes towards women show little variation from tradition.'

Lalor (1980) analysed programmes transmitted for children on both BBC and ITV networks over a six-week period. The results indicated the preponderance of male over female presenters generally. Moreover, Lalor states: 'Even when female characters are featured they tend to be used less frequently and to be more stereotyped.' Further, the occupations of males and females were found to follow sex-stereotyped lines. Lalor concludes from the investigations that 'the female role is characterised as that of mother and homemaker. The male role is to be strong, active, adventurous, resourceful, mechanical, happy in the great outdoors' (p. 80). In the programmes analysed, children were shown engaging in sex-typed activities and playing with sex-typed toys. For example, boys were shown possessing 'Action Men', whilst girls were shown possessing 'Cindy' dolls.

It is difficult to assess the impact of television viewing. However, we can assume that the smaller number of female than male characters on children's television, the behaviour they display, and the roles they play in cartoons, films and commercials do affect some children's developing view of the world and the sex roles within it.

Thus, throughout the media and in particular children's literature and television programmes, males and females are presented in ways consistent with their sex-stereotyped image. Different messages are conveyed as to the appropriate behaviour for males and females, thus providing an important source in both the learning and reinforcement of existing stereotyped sex roles.

Children's writing seems to reflect the cultural values which have been transmitted to them via the main socialising agents. Children are taught by parents, teachers and the mass media the appropriate norms of male and female behaviour. These norms are reflected in the themes and characters of their stories.

References

Belotti, E.G. (1974). Cited by E.M. Byrne, *Women and Education*, Tavistock, London

Bern, S.L. (1976) 'Probing the Promise of Androgyny' in A. Kaplan and J.P. Bean (eds), *Beyond Sex-Role Stereotypes*, Little, Brown & Company (Inc.), Boston

Bernard, M.E. (1979) 'Does Sex-role Behaviour Influence the Way Teachers Evaluate Students?', *Journal of Educational Psychology*, *71*, 553-62

Block, J.H. (1978) 'Another Look at Sex Differentiation in the Socialisation Behaviour of Mothers and Fathers' in J.A. Sherman and F.L. Denmark, (eds), *The Psychology of Women: Future Directions in Research*, Psychological Dimensions, Inc., New York

Braman, O. (1977) 'Comics' in J. King and M. Stott (eds), *Is This Your Life?*, Virago, London

Broverman, I.K., Vogel, 'S.R., Broverman, D.M., Clarkson, F.E. and Rosenkrantz, P.S. (1972) 'Sex-role Stereotypes: a Current Appraisal', *Journal of Social Issues*, *28*, 59-78

Bruner, J.S., Jolly, A. and Sylva, K. (eds) (1976) *Play: Its Role in Development and Evolution*, Penguin, Harmondsworth

Byrne, E.M. (1978) *Women and Education*, Tavistock, London

Dunn, G. (1980) 'Using and Understanding' in R. Rogers (ed.), *Television and the Family*, UK Association for the International Year of the Child, London

Fagot, B.I. (1978), 'The Influence of Sex of Child on Parental Reactions to Toddler Children', *Child Development*, *49*, 459-65

Gerbner, G. (1978) 'The Dynamics of Cultural Resistance' in G. Tuckman, A.K. Daniels and J. Bennet (eds), *Hearth and Home: Images of Women in the Mass Media*, Oxford University Press, Oxford

Goodenough, E.W. (1957) 'Interest in Persons as an Aspect of Sex Differences in Their Early Years', *Genetic Psychology Monographs*, *55*, 287-323

Grief, E.B. (1974) 'Sex-role Playing in Pre-school Children' in J.S. Bruner, A. Jolly and K. Sylva (eds) (1976) *Play*, Penguin, Harmondsworth, pp. 385-91

Hartley, R. (1959) 'Sex-role Pressures in the Socialisation of the Male Child', *Psychological Reports*, 5, 457-68

Hillman, J.G. (1978) 'An Analysis of Male and Female Roles in the Periods of Children's Literature', *Journal of Educational Research*, 68, 84-8

Jennings, J., Geis, F.L. and Brown, V. (1980) 'Influence of Television Commercials on Women's Self-confidence and Independent Judgement', *Journal of Personality and Social Psychology*, 38, 203-10

King, R.A. (1978) *All Things Bright and Beautiful*, Wiley, Chichester

Lalor, M. (1980) 'The Hidden Curriculum' in R. Rogers (ed.), *Television and the Family*, UK Association for the International Year of the Child and the University of London Department of Extra-mural Studies, London

Lobban, G. (1974) 'Presentation of Sex Roles in British Reading Schemes', *Forum*, 16, (2)

Maccoby, E.E. and Jacklin, C.N. (1974) *The Psychology of Sex Differences*, Stanford University Press, Stanford, Calif.

McArthur, L.Z. and Resko, B.G. (1975) 'The Portrayal of Men and Women in American T.V. Commercials', *Journal of Social Psychology*, 97, 209-20

Moss, J. (1967) 'Sex, Age and State as Determinants of Mother–Infant Interaction', *Merrill-Palmer Quarterly*, 13, 19-35

Nilsen, A.P. (1975) 'Women in Children's Literature' in E.S. Maccia *et al.* (eds), *Women and Education*, C.C.Thomas, New York

Owen, C. (1972) 'Feminine Roles and Social Mobility in Women's Weekly Magazines', *Sociological Review*, 10, 283-96

Plowden, L. (1980) 'Broadcasting Organisations' in R. Rogers (ed.), *Television and the Family*, UK Association for the International Year of the Child and the University of London Department of Extra-mural Studies, London

Rheingold, H.L. and Cook, K.V. (1978) 'The Content of Boys' and Girls' Rooms as an Index of Parents' Behaviour', *Child Development*, 46, 459-63

Rowan, J. (1979) 'Psychic Celibacy in Men' in O. Hartnett, G. Boden and M. Fuller (eds), *Sex Role Stereotyping*, Tavistock, London

Rudy, A.J. (1968) 'Sex-role Perceptions in Early Adolescence', *Adolescence*, 3, 453-70

Sears, R.R., Maccoby, E.E. and Levin, H. (1957) *Patterns of Child Rearing*, Row, Peterson, New York

Serbin, L.A. (1978) 'Teachers, Peers and Play Performances' in B. Sprung (ed.), *Perspectives on Non-Sexist Early Childhood Education*, Teachers College Press, New York

—, O'Leary, K.D., Kent, R.N. and Tonick, I.J. (1973) 'A Comparison of Teacher Response to the Pre-academic and Problem Behaviour of Boys and Girls', *Child Development*, 44, 796-804

Sharpe, S. (1976) *Just Like a Girl: How Girls Learn to be Women*, Penguin, Harmondsworth

Silver, S.J. (1976) *Then and Now. Women's Roles in McCall's, 1964 and 1974*. Paper presented at the meeting of the Popular Culture Association, Chicago, Illinois

Singer, R.D. and Kaplan, R.M. (1976) 'Introduction', *Journal of Social Issues*, 32, 1-7

Sternglanz, S.H. and Serbin, L.A. (1974) 'Sex-role Stereotyping in Children's Television Programs', *Developmental Psychology*, 10, 710-15

Weitzman, L., Eifler, D., Holcada, E. and Ross, C. (1972) 'Sex-role Socialisation in Picture Books for Pre-school Children', *American Journal of Sociology*, 77, 1125-50

Whiting, B.B. and Edwards, C.P. (1973) 'A Cross-cultural Analysis of Sex-differ-
    ences in the Behaviour of Children Aged Three Through Eleven', *Journal of
    Social Psychology*, *91*, 171-88

5 AN EXPLORATORY ANALYSIS OF CHILDREN'S DIARIES

Linda A. Pollock

Recent research into the writing skills of children and adolescents emphasises the importance of these for their social and psychological development. As Wilkinson, Bansley, Hanna and Swan (1980) state, 'The act of writing is itself a commitment . . . Writing is a means of discovering one's own uniqueness . . . Writing enables one to examine one's own feelings' (p. 60). Hardy (1977) points out that through writing we come to terms with relationships, analyse happenings in the past and learn about ourselves. Thus writing contributes to the lengthy process by which children and young people master the art of living in the real world, negotiating their way through what may seem to them to be insurmountable problems, and gradually appreciating the intentions and motives of others. Analysis of children's writing reveals that there are developmental trends in the decline of egocentricity and the expression of social sensitivity.

Although young children are not as self-centred and as unaware of the viewpoint and inner psychological state of other people as Piaget (1951, 1952, 1954) first led us to believe, they are still more egocentric than older children, and the latter more so than adolescents. Children disclose in their writing skills a growing ability to take into account the needs of the reader, for example by providing contextual information or by describing the characters in the story (Britton, Burgess, Martin, McLeod and Rosen, 1975; Cowie, 1982). Emotion, too, is rarely expressed in young children's written stories, and even though older children can depict the feelings they experienced, they ignore the internal state of other people. Adolescents, however, portray not only their own emotions, but are also concerned with the feelings of others (Wilkinson *et al.*, 1980). There is also an increasing differentiation in the concepts children and teenagers have of another person (Brooks-Gunn and Lewis, 1978; Light, 1979; Livesley and Bromley, 1973; Rogers, 1978).

The diaries of young people are a unique source for revealing the development, over time, of the above trends in individual children. This study has been concerned with a preliminary investigation into the content of twelve historical child and adolescent diaries. These texts date from the seventeenth century, and were written by both American and British children. Only a few child diaries are known to have survived – no preadolescent text has been discovered prior to the eighteenth century. Table 5.1 lists the children's ages at the commencement and finish of the diaries, their nationality, the years in which the texts were begun and the length of the texts. Table 5.2 gives the division of the sample into male and female, child and adolescent diaries.

Table 5.1: Age and Nationality of Diarists; Date and Length of Text

Name	Age began	Age ended	Nationality	Year of commencement	Length of text[a]
Marjory Fleming	7.2[b]	7.11	British	1810	131 pp
Rachael Hamilton-Gordon	9	9.3[c]	British	1882	22 ff
John Long	9.3	→[d]	American	1857	118 pp
Caroline Richards	10.0	→	American	1852	147 pp
Frederic Post	11.0	16.3	British	1830	285 pp
Elizabeth Wynne	11.4	→	British	1789	500 pp
Emily Shore	11.6	19.6	British	1830	351 pp
Anna Winslow	11.11	13.6	American	1790	73 pp
Stephen King-Hall	13.0	→	British	1906	20 pp
James Gallatin	16.2	→	American	1813	118 pp
Anna May	17.2	17.7	American	1840	96 pp
Roger Lowe	18[e]	→	British	1663	97 pp

Notes: a. Only the length of text written before the age of 20 is given.
b. The editor included in the published text a letter written by Marjory at the age of 6 years.
c. Rachael's date of birth is unknown, hence an estimate of her age is given.
d. → signifies that the diary was continued into adulthood.
e. Roger's exact date of birth is unknown, an estimate of his age is provided.

Table 5.2: Division of Sample by Age and Sex

	Child	Adolescent	Total
Male	2	5	7
Female	6	5	11
Total	8	10	18

It was decided to concentrate on a small sample so that the character and development of each child, together with the content of the entries would be fully conveyed. An additional bibliography of diaries not used here, but which contain sufficient detail for a similar analysis to be performed, has been supplied at the end of the chapter for those wishing to pursue this line of enquiry further. The material collected has been organised around three main areas: egocentrism, expression of affect and social perception. The results demonstrate that it is possible to use diaries as one way of tracing a child's growing social sensitivity.

Egocentrism

In discussing the topic of egocentrism in relation to diaries, the audience factor must be considered. Diaries do tend to be private documents, written for oneself, and therefore there is no need to take the reader's needs into account. However, in the case of several of the young child diarists, adults obviously read the texts and the children were aware of this. Marjory and Elizabeth were both instructed to keep a diary by their tutor, who then corrected the misspelt words. Caroline decided to keep a diary of her own volition, but later let her school teacher read it. The texts of Anna Winslow, John and Stephen were read by their parents, and this was also probably the case with Rachael's diary. On the other hand, the adolescent diaries were secretive and read only by the author. For example, James reflected 'I often wonder if anybody got hold of my diary after I am dead what an ass they would think of me. I will leave strict instructions to burn it' (pp. 114-15).

Marjory, at the age of 7 years 2 months, began her diary thus 'Many people are hanged for Highway robbery Housebreking Murder & c & c'. She followed this with the statement 'Isabella teaches me everything I know' (p. 3). She, characteristic of most 7-year-olds, clearly felt no need to set herself in any kind of context, nor to explain that Isabella was her adult cousin with whom Marjory spent most of her sixth to eighth years, but simply commenced writing. Compare this with the first entry of Caroline, which reveals a better ordering of information and provides more contextual details.

> I am ten years old to-day, and I think I will write a journal and tell who I am and what I am doing. I have lived with my Grandfather and Grandmother Beales ever since I was seven years old, and Anna, too, since she was four. Our brothers, James and John, came too, but they are at East Bloomfield at Mrs Stephen Clark's Academy. (p. 1)

Apart from not explaining that Anna was her younger sister, Caroline did inform us as to who she was herself. Emily, at the age of 11 years 6 months, was even more specific:

Our family consists of papa, mamma, and five children. Papa is cur-
ate, during part of the year, for Mr Cust Rector of Cockayne Hatley,
a little village two miles and a half from us. We live at Potton, a little
market town in the confines of Bedfordshire and Cambridgeshire.
Papa takes pupils; his greatest number is six. (p. 1)

Emily then went on to give much more information about her family.
Hence she not only explained herself, but also the rest of the family
members and their situation. The account no longer centres on herself.

Curiously enough, the adolescent diarists did not give contextual
detail, their first entries are very context-dependent. James, aged 16
years 2 months, started his diary with the following paragraph: 'The
Russian Minister Count Dashkoff offered mediation, on the part of the
Emperor Alexander, to the Secretary of State. Father thinks this very
important and of great weight' (p. 1). Anna May, at the age of 17 years
2 months, commenced her text in an introspective vein:

Treasure of my thoughts! Dear companion of solitary hours! When
sad I recall my thoughts in solemn measure, and when gay, in strain
as light as the happy air. Herein I inscribe the workings of my secret
soul. (p. 1)

Another way of tracing a child's ability to describe events and situations to other people, taking into account what the latter need to know
or even perhaps what they would like to know, is to examine the descriptive passages of the diaries. Despite the problem that diaries do not
contain many such passages, and still fewer examples of fantasy writing,
they can illustrate the growing expertise of handling language and im-
parting information with increasing age. Wilkinson *et al.* (1980) have
discovered that young children's sentences are narrative, descriptive,
affirmative, literal, factual and self-oriented. An example of this type
of writing can be found in a letter Marjory wrote to her mother at the
age of 6. Though this is remarkably coherent for her age, it reveals the
strange juxtaposition of sentences and ideas characteristic of young
children's writing.

My dear Mud,
My sleaves is tucked up, and it was very disagreeable, my collar, and
I abhored it amoniable. I saw the most prettyist two tame pidgeons
you ever saw and two very wee small kittens like our cat . . . The
hawk is in great spirits, it is a nice beast, the gentlest animal that ever

was Seen. Six canaries, two green linnets, and a Thrush. Isa has been away for a long time and I've been wearying for her Sadly. (p.161)

The first sentence is totally context-dependent, and there is no connection between the various topics. However, at the age of 7 years 6 months Marjory was capable of using metaphorical language, writing in a poem in which she related the tale of an imagined lover:

> We walked apon the distant hills
> And often goes into the mills
> Very soft and wite his cheeks
> His hair is fair and grey his breaks
> His teath is like the daisy fair
> The only fault is on his hair. (p. 26)

Marjory returned home later that year. She wrote to Isabella while recovering from a severe bout of measles, and depicted in this poem a chastened, saddened little girl, whose experience with pain has done much to quench her vitality. Putting her feelings into a poem helped her to cope with what she had undergone. The poem, composed at the age of 7 years 11 months, also provides the first instance of the use of a metaphor.

> O Isa pain did visit me
> I was at the last extremity
> How often did I think of you
> I wished your graceful form to view
> To clasp you in my weak embrace
> Indeed I thought Id run my race
> Good Care Im Sure was of me taken
> But indeed I was much shaken
> At last I daily strength did gain
> And O at last away went pain. (p. 174)

The recovery was short lived. She succumbed to meningitis and died only four days after composing the poem.

Marjory was certainly precocious in her writing ability. She displayed a capability for depicting feelings and using metaphorical language which was far in advance of her contemporaries as well as earlier or modern children. Wilkinson *et al.* (1980) state that children begin to use similes about the age of 10 years and metaphors from the age of 11.

Two nineteenth-century 9-year-olds included in their texts composi-
tions which are far more literal and factual than Marjory's efforts. For
instance, Rachael described the rice fields she saw while travelling from
New Zealand to London in 1882:

> We saw lots of rice growing. It grows in water and they let the water
> into the fields for the rice, and let it out again when it is not wanted.
> In some fields the rice was just beginning to grow; in others it was
> very big; in others it was ripe and in others it had been mown. In
> some fields the rice was being threshed — this is how they do it. The
> rice is spread out on the ground and then bullocks are driven round
> and round on it till all the grain is stamped out. (p. 217)

Although this passage is literal, Rachael none the less considered the
reader and explained what he or she needed to know. John, at the age
of 9 years 9 months, attempted to put forward the case for the evils of
alcohol.

> Intemperamence is a great evil. It is a great evil because if we are
> made drunk by folks, we shall be led on to *gambling*; and then, per-
> haps, be led on to stealing, to get money to gamble with, and then
> lose that by gambling: After we lose that, we may *murder* someone
> for money, and then be found out and put into State's prison, and
> then hung: all of this comes from intemperamence. I hope there is no
> one at our school who will be a rum drinker, or a rum seller. (p. 26)

It is not quite logical that people gamble only when drunk, or that all
drunk people gamble, but the rest of the essay is well structured and coherent. John could also find a use for alcohol, thus disclosing an ability
to see both sides of an argument. He concluded with the remark 'it is
necessary for people to put on wounds that are very bad'.

Anna Winslow's text also provides evidence on her language development. At the age of 12 years 10 months she wrote about a party she
attended and presented only her own point of view.

> There was a large company assembled in a handsome, large, upper
> room in the new end of the house. We had two fiddles, and I had the
> honor to open the diversion of the evening in a minuet with miss
> Soley . . . Our treat was nuts, raisins, Cakes, Wine, punch, hot and
> cold, all in great plenty . . . For variety we woo'd a widow, hunted
> the whistle, threaded the needle. (pp. 16-17)

Seven months after this event she became the proud owner of a head-dress of the latest fashion, a 'Heddus roll'. When this contraption was worn, the distance from the roots of her hair to the top of the roll was one inch longer than the distance from the roots to her chin! She described this acquisition to her mother:

> aunt Storer said it ought to be made less, Aunt Denning said it ought not to be made at all. It makes my head itch and ach, and burn like anything Mamma. This famous roll is not made wholly of a red *Cow Tail*, but is a mixture of that, and horsehair (very coarse) and a little human hair of yellow hue, that I suppose was taken out of the back part of an old wig. (p. 71)

She put the roll in the context of her feelings about it together with the opinions of her aunts with whom she was staying.

An older diarist, Emily, at the age of 18 years 5 months, commented on a nature scene. She was not only concerned with the beauty of the scene, but also the feelings which this beauty engendered in her and others.

> There was a sort of a fairy beauty in the scenery of the lovely Forest; the blue sky glowed through the delicate embroidered veil of the leafless sprays with extraordinary lustre. The lights and shades, the variety of tints and distances, the purity of the atmosphere, I have never seen surpassed . . . We ran about shouting to each other, sometimes plunging into a shady hollow; sometimes standing on a grassy ride or terrace, and looking down on commons gleaming with sunshine and embedded with wood. (p. 241)

It is notable that a few of the above quotations refer to emotional states. Perhaps more than any other subject, diaries depict the increasing ability to express feelings of affect, to articulate not only the feelings present in oneself, but also to recognise the emotions present in other persons.

Expression of Affect

Young writers do not display in words feelings of fear, panic, joy or sorrow. Marjory's statement at the beginning of her diary has already been quoted. She expressed no compassion for those due to be hanged and no sympathy for their plight. Similarly Rachael, aged 9, noted of a storm:

> It has been very rough indeed ever since we left Adelaide . . . and the deck has been so wet with waves coming over it that we have not been able to go up on deck. Last night 12 fowls 2 geese and 1 turkey were drowned and two of the sheep and a lamb. (p. 214)

The description is quite flat, there is no sense of panic or fear. Accounts of fire outbreaks appeared in several of the texts, and these clearly demonstrate an age progression in the expression of affect.

At the age of 10 years 1 month John wrote:

> Last night I came very near burning up the house. I went into a closit in Grandmother's room to get my shoes; and then father, mother, and I were sitting in the sitting room, and we smelt a strange smell, and father got up and went into the closet and it was all on fire. He got water and put it out. (p. 12)

John did not explain how he came to start a fire, but even more strangely no-one was afraid or panic-stricken in his story. It is almost as if the very act of writing ironed all emotion out. Caroline, at the age of 13 years 3 months, noted:

> We were awakened very early this morning by the cry of fire and the ringing of bells and could see the sky red with flames and knew it was the stores and we thought they were all burning up. Pretty soon we heard our big brass door knocker being pounded fast and Grandfather said, 'who's there?' 'Melville Arnold for the bank keys', we heard. Grandfather handed them out and dressed as fast as he could and went down, while Anna and I just lay there and watched the flames and shook. (pp. 52-3)

She did convey alarm by the use of the phrase 'pounded fast' and depicted the fear of herself and her sister. However, she did not elaborate on the internal state of any one else. On the other hand, John certainly revealed a sense of concern for others when he described another fire, at the age of 16.

> Bridgham's tavern, with the store, and barn, and outbuildings were entirely consumed. Luckily it was so calm the fire crossed neither

the water nor the street. No great injury to any persons. Part of the furniture saved. $4,000 lost. Men and women worked like good ones. (p. 69)

Nevertheless, older adolescents could still be preoccupied with their own emotions when placed in a stressful situation. For instance, Anna May was miserable when she left home to attend college, and seemed to be unaware that her peers could also be homesick. She wrote at the age of 17 years 2 months:

Oh dear! What a misery is mine! Would that I were only at home! I am feeling so lonely and miserable. I cannot get one of my lessons; they seem so new and hard to me. What must I do? Could I only see my parents today, what would I give! Or, could I only receive a letter from them how happy should I be! I am alone, so solitary. O dear me! I weep bitterly to think I came. If I could only go home. (pp. 1-2)

Similarly, when Stephen, aged 18 years 2 months, was participating in some naval gun tests, he was interested solely in his state of mind, and portrayed no compassion whatsoever for his fellow cadets in the same position.

to my horror I found myself standing on top of the turret whilst it slowly trained round to bear on the object. In vain I looked out for a chance of escaping, there was none. So bracing myself up against the stanchion on the roof, I awaited the fatal moment . . . My heart nearly stopped, and the agony of fear, deadly fear, took hold of me, which was succeeded by a sort of calm resignation. (p. 355)

Illness and Death

Death in earlier centuries was something which was ever-present and which affected all sections of the population, not just the elderly. The young were especially vulnerable. Of the sample of twelve young people studied here, four had died before the age of 20: Marjory at not quite 8 years, Frederic at the age of 16 years 3 months, Emily at 19 years 6 months and Anna Winslow shortly before her twentieth birthday. Thus, illness and death formed a major part of their lives. How they learnt to cope with this is depicted in their diaries, illustrating an age progression in empathy and the articulation of distress. The youngest diarist, Marjory, was more concerned with her own reaction to Isabella's sleepless night than concerned for the latter's well-being. She remarked, at the age of 7 years 3 months:

> Some days ago Isabella had a tereable fit of the toothake and she walkied with a long nightshift at dead of night like a ghost and [I] thought she was one . . . a ghostly figure she was indeed enought to ma[ke] a saint tremble it mad[e] me quever & shake from top to toe. (p. 11)

Six months later, though, Marjory related a tale of the drowning of puppies and disclosed her feelings of outrage and shock.

> it is shoking to think that the dog & cat should bear them & they are drownded after [all]. I would rather have a man dog than a women dog because they do not bear like women dogs, it is a hard case it is shoking. (p. 65)

Caroline, aged 10 years 1 month, described two sad little girls during the illness of both their grandparents.

> Grandfather and Grandmother have been very sick and we were afraid something dreadful was going to happen. We are so glad that they are well again . . . It was so lonesome for us to sit down to the table and just have Hannah wait on us. We did not have any blessing because there was no one to ask it . . . We had such lumps in our throats we could not eat much and we cried ourselves to sleep two or three nights. (pp. 8-9)

Two and a half years later she was, however, surprised at the calmness with which her grandmother received the news of her sister's death. The latter received a letter telling her of her sister's demise:

> she was knitting before she got it and she laid it down a few moments and looked quite sad and said, 'So sister Anna is dead'. Then after a little she went on with her work. Anna watched her and when we were alone she said to me, 'Caroline, some day when you are about ninety you may be eating an apple or reading or doing something and you will get a letter telling of my decease and after you have read it you will go on as usual and just say, 'so sister Anna is dead'. I told her that I knew if I lived to be a hundred and heard that she was dead I should cry my eyes out, if I had any. (p. 45)

At the age of 12 years 6 months Caroline had no insight into how upset her grandmother was, and no inkling that the latter was concealing her grief in order not to upset the two girls.

Two diarists had to come to terms with their own approaching deaths — Frederic and Emily, both dying from tuberculosis. There is only a brief mention of this in Frederic's diary. At the age of 14 years 10 months he noted 'I am very subject to a cough. Indeed, I am a very tender plant, difficult to rear; whether I shall ever attain maturity, Thou, Lord, alone knowest' (p. 83). In contrast, Emily's text contains much more information on her reaction to her illness. She began to feel ill at the age of 16 years 6 months, and from that date was required to spend her winters away from home in a milder part of the country. A letter from an old childhood friend during one of these sojourns in 1836 brought on a bout of nostalgia, revealing Emily's sense of loss and regret.

> Indeed, it is now a different existence; life seems changed to me, young as I am, since I parted with Eliz.; one of its chief features is blotted out of the landscape [i.e. health]. My heart aches when I think of those past pleasant days, as I now write this my eyes are almost blinded with tears. (p. 229)

A month after writing the above, she was more resigned to her ill-health, and accepted that she could no longer study as much as she would like to. 'Well, it is no use to go on always struggling with weakness and in-capability of exertion. I cannot hold out for ever and now I begin to feel thoroughly ill. I am afraid I must relax' (p. 231). By the age of 18 years 6 months she recognised that her frailty caused distress to others.

> It is painful, however, to be the object of such constant care and anxiety to my parents, especially my poor father, who has harass-ment enough in his wearing profession without my (innocently) adding to it. It is impossible to describe how he watches me, and how, without being fidgety, he catches at any glimps of my being better. (p. 265)

Despite the fact that Emily, for the most part, acknowledged that she was dying, she continued to endure moments of anguish for what might have been. A few months before her death she recalled her childhood:

> I live it all over again, and I cannot avoid weeping. There is no lan-guage to describe the sharp pain of past and regretted happiness. I

was much happier as a child than I am now, or ever shall be. (p. 320)

Inner World of Feeling

The adolescent diaries bring to light the turbulent emotions of these young people, their swings from joy to despair. They appear to be using their diaries as one method of keeping a grip on their inner world of feeling. As Elkind (1967) states of twentieth-century adolescents 'Only he can suffer with such agonised intensity, or experience such exquisite rapture' (p. 83). The adolescent diarists were aware of their frequent mood changes — Anna May, aged 17 years 4 months, commented 'My mood is very changeful. I am now sad, now gay. Why is it thus?' (p. 40). The young people suffered greatly if they felt that their trust had been abused, expressing in their comments a bitter sense of betrayal. John was let down by a room-mate when he was almost 16. He complained:

> He has deceived and disappointed and wronged me. I will never forget or forgive it in him . . . I think him mean and dishonorable in his treatment of me, and in the future walks of life I shall always fear and distrust [him], however bright a glare he may spread in the faces of others. (p. 73)

Roger, too, suffered a betrayal of friendship when he was about 19. The brother of the girl he was courting at the time threatened to reveal the romance to the girl's father, who disapproved of Roger.

> this stinkeing Raskell betrayed his one sister and me, who I went allways with and spent my monys for his sake and advised hime the best I could . . . He said as soone as his sister angerd hime he would tell his father all — and this is the activge of a seemeing pretended freind to me as can be, when in truth is no better than a deivelish, malicious, dissembleing, knavish rascall . . . this was a matter of much greife to me and I was very sad upon it. (p. 47)

At the other extreme, Emily, aged 18 years 7 months, portrayed her intense delight at the first evening walk she had managed to enjoy for several months.

> Oh, it was delicious . . . it seemed to me like paradise . . . the sky was cloudless, the birds singing joyously . . . And oh, the soft, soft, cool green turf! I ran about it as if I was still a child; I stooped down and pressed it with my hand, I quite loved it . . . I rushed about hither

and thither, unable to control my delight. (pp. 245-6)

Social Perception

'"Social perception" has been defined as the "process by which man comes to know and to think about the other persons, their characteristics, qualities and inner states"' (Brooks-Gunn and Lewis, 1978, p. 79). In this section the diarists' perception of themselves will be discussed as well as their perceptions of others. Young children, at least from the evidence contained in their diaries, were not concerned with their own characters or development. This is in marked contrast to the adolescents — a characteristic of their texts is entries on the exploration of their characters. They were aware that they are on the threshhold of life, and were preoccupied with trying to eradicate their childish faults, ready to take their place in the adult world. Many of them were surprised at the speed at which their childhood was passing, and felt that the preparation time was running out. Frederic wrote on his fifteenth birthday:

> What a many events are crowded into that small space! and yet I am scarcely launched on the world's wide ocean! My life has not, yet, been an eventful one. This, however, is an eventful time in my history — that epoch when the pursuits of boyhood are gradually relinquished, and verge towards the man. (p. 86)

Elizabeth remarked on her seventeenth birthday:

> This is a day that made me reflect very seriously as I accomplished my seventeenth year and I must own I think it prodigiously old as it is not far from twenty. This made me spend a very dull birthday as at the bottom of my heart I was very sad to think I was beginning the eighteenth year of my life and that till now I had wasted my time in a very foolish way but I took my resolution to begin to be more applied to things that will be of more use to me in future and to enjoy life as it is very short. I was quite Philosophical and mean to remain it. (vol. 2, p. 24)

These teenagers subjected their personalities and behaviours to a minute dissection. At the age of 17, John noted:

> When I am old, I shall not, like most people, look back upon my

collage days with feelings of great joy. My college life, unlike the generality, is not very pleasant. One reason is that in my disposition, being some like my father, I cannot be very happy in any foreign situation. I look continually at the dark and not the bright side of the picture. (p. 73)

Emily, also age 17, reflected:

There is completely a world within me, unknown, unexplored, by any but myself. I see well that my feelings, my qualities, my character, are understood by none else, I am not what I am supposed to be; I am liked and loved far more than I deserve. I hate — yes, I truly hate myself; for I see the depths of sin within me, which are hidden from all other eyes. (p. 175)

The diaries demonstrate a growing recognition, with increasing maturity, of the motives, emotions and intentions of others. The young people start to realise that other persons have an inner psychological state. At the age of 7 Marjory was aware of the effect her behaviour could have on others, thus disclosing an ability to understand their state of mind.

To Day I have been very ungrateful and bad and disobedient. Isabella gave me my writing I wrote so ill that she took it away and locted it up in her desk where I stood trying to open it till she made me come and read my bible but I was in a bad humour and red it so carlessly and ill that she took it from me and her blood ran cold but she never punished me. (p. 43)

She, in comparison with the rest of the sample, seems to have been far in advance of her years in the attainment of social maturity. The remaining children, right up to adolescence, had more difficulty comprehending another's point of view.

Caroline, aged 10, commented on some cakes which her elder brother had brought 'They were splendid. I offered John one and he said he would rather throw it over the fence than to eat it. I can't understand that' (p. 4). However, by the age of 13 she had some inkling of the intentions of others:

Anna told Grandmother that she saw Mrs George Wilson looking very steadily at us in prayer meeting the other night and she thought she might be planning to 'write us up'. Grandmother said she did not think Mrs Wilson was so short of material as that would imply, and she feared she had some other reason for looking at us. I think dear Grandmother has a little grain of sarcasm in her nature, but she only uses it on extra occasions. (p. 51)

She not only perceived, but judged the motive of her grandmother. By the age of 17 Caroline was reconciled to the more undesirable, from her point of view, aspects of her grandmother's character. 'Grandmother knows that we think she is a perfect angel even if she does seem rather strict sometimes. Whether we are 7 or 17 we are children to her just the same' (p. 124).

Anna Winslow, by the age of 12, was also capable of explaining and inferring the behaviour of another person. She remarked on a new acquaintance:

Last monday I went with my aunt to visit Mrs Beacon. I was exceedingly pleased with the visit, and so I *ought* to be, my aunt says, for there was much notice taken of me, particularly by Mr Beacon. I think I like him better every time I see him, I suppose he takes the kinder notice of me, because last thursday evening he was here, and when I was out of the room, aunt told him that I minded his preaching & could repeat what he said. (pp. 3-4)

Two months later she wrote of her father 'My Hon'd Papa has never signified to me his approbation of my journals, from whence I infer, that he either never reads them, or does not give himself the trouble to remember any of their contents' (p. 18).

The teenage texts illustrate the increasing differentiation of children's concepts of other people. John, aged almost 16, pondered:

We always, when we meet with new characters, form first impressions so-called of each one. So I find in my class . . . There is one whose name is M—, of whom my first impressions are unfavourable. He seems to have a small mind, to be one that would laugh at his schoolmate if a mistake is made, while if he were in the same condition he would not wish to be so treated. Another; Mr —, seems to be self-conceited. Has a peculiar smile when another is reading wrong, as if, were it in his own hands, he could himself perform the task more easily. (p. 60)

James, nearly 20, related:

> I am very sorry for mamma; I can see she is not happy. Father is so occupied that I do not think he notices it. It is hard for her: she speaks so little French, has really no friends whom she care for, and her position is a very difficult one. The Court is so hemmed in by etiquette to which she is not accustomed. She does not understand the ways of Frenchwoman and is continually shocked. (pp. 99-100)

The judgements the diarists made of another person progressed from the bare statement 'I like' or 'I dislike' to the reasons for such feelings. They began to characterise other people, their global concepts of them became differentiated (Livesley and Bromley, 1973) and, by adolescence, the children recognised the good and bad aspects of another's character (Rogers, 1978), as well as appreciating that people were not always what they appeared to be. John, at the age of 9 years 6 months, merely stated 'I liked him for a schoolmaster. I like Mr Atwood, too' (p. 7). Six years later he was more explicit, writing of a new teacher that he was

> a very pleasant man — one whom I like thus far, since he does not appear too sour and cross, but pleasant and willing to aid one, and not seeming to take delight in wounding the feelings of any of his pupils. (p. 56)

Elizabeth, at the age of 13, described one lady as 'one of the most disagreable creatures of the world' (vol. 1, p. 65). At 15 years 6 months she noted of her hostess 'She affects much sincerity and on that account is often very rude, but at the bottom of her heart is as faulse as a cat' (vol. 1, p. 220). Two years after this she wrote ruefully:

> I had cause today to find out that often the persons that are thought to be the most virtuous and clever, have at the bottom of it all great faults, and behave in some occasions very ungentleman like. (vol. 2, p. 43)

Moral Judgements

Moral judgements of their own behaviour reveal a similar trend to that depicted above. The young diarists did not take their intentions into account when considering whether or not they had done anything wrong. They judged in terms of punishment and reward as well as the physical consequences of their actions (Wilkinson *et al.*, 1980). In Marjory's world, despite her precociousness, everything was black and white. She did not concern herself with motives. For example, at the age of 7 years 9 months she stated 'every body just now hates me & I deserve it for I dont behave well' (p. 82). An older diarist, Caroline, aged 13 years 3 months, was very conscious of the fact that she had broken an injunction of her grandparents. Although she meant no harm in doing so, she judged her behaviour in terms of good relations and the immediate social context and did feel guilty. The two sisters had slipped out to attend a night sleigh party, against their grandparents' wishes.

> but we did not enjoy ourselves at all and did not join in the singing. I had no idea that sleigh-rides could make any one feel so bad. It was not very cold, but I just shivered all the time . . . I was so glad when we got near home so we could get out. (p. 55)

By the age of 14 years 4 months she had begun to rationalise matters: 'I went to school this afternoon and kept the rules, so to-night I had the satisfaction of saying "perfect" when called upon, and if I did not like to keep the rules, it is some pleasure to say that' (p. 56).

Older adolescents judged a particular action in terms of notions of intention and fairness. John, aged almost 15, was late for chapel one morning and was due for a reprimand from the college master.

> I don't [care] much, for my intentions were good, and it was from no desire to shirk from my duty — from which, if from everything else, I do not mean to depart. Yet it is some disgrace to me, and I should rather [have] been in season. (p. 58)

Stephen, at the age of 16 years 1 month, considered the justness or otherwise of a punishment he had received. 'Mr Hammond gave me a drill in Divinity for laughing, it was grossly unfair, as I only laughed at an Israelitish King's name ie. Rab-Shakeh' (p. 341).

Coming to Terms With Life Itself

Diaries are not only one way of improving the use of language, and not only a source for tracing the development of a child's social sensitivity. They are also an aid to a child's comprehension of the world and of life. Writing down their problems helped the children and teenagers to come to terms with them. Thus, diaries are one method by which children learn to cope with and meet the demands of the real world. These problems ranged from the simple, although not to them, troubles of childhood to the more complex worries of adolescence. For instance, Marjory at the age of 7 years 6 months wrote 'I am now going to tell you about the horible and wretc[hed] plaige that my multiplication gives me you cant conceive it – the most Devilish thing is 8 times 8 & 7 times 7 it is what nature itselfe cant endure' (p. 46). John, aged 10 years 7 months, confided his great homesickness when he was sent to a weekly boarding school for a while, to his diary. 'I shall be glad when next Saturday comes for I shall go home then and see the folks. I get real homesick here; it is such a lonesome place, the days seem weeks to me' (p. 33). Elizabeth was torn two ways trying to cope with a more difficult problem. At the age of 18 years 9 months she was about to marry the man she loved, but this meant emigrating to a new country and leaving her family behind.

> Though I must acknowledge that this event makes me perfectly happy, yet I dread it and the idea of leaving so suddenly my Father Mother and sisters, distresses me I can hardly make up my mind to it. I was quite miserable after the whole was determined upon. Mamma and my sisters burst into tears, I did not know what to say, what to do . . . How shall I accustom myself to live without them? Oh God, I wont think of it, it must to happen; it is for my good and happiness, I wished it myself and now that what I desired might happen, it frightens me and I think the undertaking almost too great. (vol. 2, p. 161)

The texts demonstrate that the path towards maturity is strewn with obstacles for the young people to negotiate, and that they do not always find this an easy task.

Conclusion

The diaries studied reveal that there is a growth of social sensitivity with increasing age. The diarists displayed, as they approached adulthood, a greater ability to pass on information, to recognise and articulate the emotions possessed by themselves and others, as well as a deeper understanding of what makes people act in the way that they do. It is also clear that, despite the developmental trends, there is a great deal of chronological variation in this field. Some children were far in advance of others.

References

Britton, J., Burgess, T., Martin, N., McLeod, A. and Rosen, H. (1975) *The Development of Writing Abilities (11-18)*, Macmillan Education, London

Brooks-Gunn, J. and Lewis, M. (1978) 'Early Social Knowledge – the Development of Knowledge About Others' in H. McGurk (ed.), *Issues in Childhood Social Development*, Methuen, London, pp. 79-106

Cowie, H. (1982) 'An Approach to the Evaluation of Children's Imaginative Writing', *Human Learning*, vol. 1, pp. 213-21

Elkind, D. (1967) 'Egocentrism in Adolescence' in D. Rogers (ed.), *Issues in Adolescent Psychology*, Meredith Corporation, New York, 2nd edn, pp. 79-85

Fleming, M. (1934) *The Complete Marjory Fleming*, edited by F. Sidgwick, Sidgwick & Jackson Ltd, London

Gallatin, J. (1914) *A Great Peace Maker*, William Heinemann, London

Hamilton-Gordon, R. 'A Child's Journal of a Voyage from Wellington, New Zealand to London', The British Library, Add Mss 49271, ff. 207-28

Hardy, B. (1977) 'Narrative as a Primary Act of Mind' in M. Meek (ed.), *The Cool Web*, Bodley Head, London, pp. 12-23

Hoffman, M. (1976) 'Empathy, Role-taking, Guilt, and Development of Altruistic Motives' in T. Lickona (ed.), *Moral Development and Behaviour*, Holt, Rinehart & Winston, New York, pp. 124-43

King-Hall, S. (1936) 'The Diaries of Stephen King-Hall' in L. King-Hall (ed.), *Sea-Saga*, Victor Gollancz Ltd, London, pp. 335-506

Light, P. (1979) *The Development of Social Sensitivity*, Cambridge University Press, Cambridge

Livesley, W.J. and Bromley, D.B. (1973) *Person Perception in Childhood and Adolescence*, John Wiley & Sons Ltd, London

Long, J. (1923) *America of Yesterday*, edited by L. Mayo, The Atlantic Monthly Press, Boston

Lowe, R. (1938) *The Diary of Roger Lowe*, edited by W. Sachse, Longmans, Green & Co. London

May, A. (1941) *Journal of Anna May*, edited by G. Robinson, privately printed, Cambridge, Mass.

Piaget, J. (1951) *The Child's Conception of the World*, Routledge & Kegan Paul, London

— (1952) *The Language and Thought of the Child*, Routledge & Kegan Paul, London

— (1954) *The Construction of Reality in the Child*, Basic Books, New York

Post, F. (1838) *Extracts from the Diary of the late Frederic James Post*

Richards, C. (1913) *Village Life in America*, Henry Holt & Co, New York

Rogers, C. (1978) 'The Child's Perception of Other People' in H. McGurk (ed.), *Issues in Childhood Social Development*, Methuen, London, pp. 107-29

Shore, E. (1898) *Journal of Emily Shore*, Kegan Paul, Trench, Trübner & Co. Ltd, London

Wilkinson, A., Barnsley, G., Hanna, P. and Swan, M. (1980) *Assessing Language Development*, Oxford University Press, Oxford

Winslow, A. (1894) *Diary of a Boston School Girl*, edited by A. Earle, Houghton, Mifflin & Co., Boston

Wynne, E. (1935) *The Wynne Diaries*, edited by A. Fremantle, Oxford University Press, London, passim

Additional Child Diaries Not Used in the Study

Alcott, L. (1889) *Life Letters and Journals*, edited by E. Cheney, Robert Brothers, Boston

Bowen, S. (1942) 'Diary of Four Bowen Children' in E. Bowen, *Bowen's Court*, Longmans, Green & Co., London, pp. 241-52

Brown, M. (1905) *The Diary of a Girl in France*, edited by H.N. Shore, John Murray, London

Colt, J. (1936) *Young Colt's Diary*, edited by C. Terrott, Grayson and Grayson, London

Cowles, J. (1931) *The Diaries of Julia Cowles*, edited by L. Moseley, Yale University Press, New Haven

Eves, S. (1881) 'Extracts from Journal', *The Pennsylvania Magazine of History and Biography*, *5*, 19-36, 191-205

Fairfax, S. (1904) 'Diary of a Little Colonial Girl', *The Virginia Magazine of History and Biography*, *11*, 212-14

Gaskell, M. (1883) *Records of an Eton Schoolboy*, edited by C. Gaskell, printed privately, London

May, A. (1941) *Journal of Anna May*, edited by G. Robinson, printed privately, Cambridge, Mass.

Newbolt, F. (1904) *The Diary of a Fag*, F.E. Robinson & Co, London

— (1927) *The Diary of a Praeposter*, Philip Allan & Co Ltd, London

Orr, L. (1871) *Journal of a Young Lady of Virginia*, edited by E. Mason, John Murphy & Co., Baltimore

Ramés, M. (1911) 'Marie Louise Ramés' Journal' in H. Huntington, *Memories, Personages, Peoples, Places*, Constable & Co. Ltd, London, pp. 228-96

de Rothschild, A. (1935) 'Diary' in L. Cohen (ed.), *Lady de Rothschild and her daughters 1821-1931*, John Murray, London, pp. 75-108

Russell, H. 'Diary', The National Library of Scotland, MS no. 3233

Selwyn, T. (1903) *Eton in 1829-30*, edited by E. Warre, John Murray, London

Shippen, N. (1935) *Her Journal Book*, edited by E. Armes, J.B. Lippincott & Co., Philadelphia

Wister, S. (1902) *Sally Wister's Journal*, edited by A. Myers, Ferris and Leach, Philadelphia

Wortley, V. (1852) *A Young Traveller's Journal*, T. Bosworth, London

6 IMAGES FOR LIFE?

Judy Ollington

Ring a ring a roses
A pocket full of posies
Tishoo tishoo
We all fall down!

This ancient Christian dance, danced on graves at the time of the Black Death and now a children's game, provides an image through which to reflect on the aesthetic dimension of religious education (RE). There are many elements which deserve attention. It is a circle dance, and the circle provides a clue to that deep necessity of the human mind to synthesise, to form a whole out of the disparate elements of life. It is a response to a terrible experience, a peculiarly human response which creates a form which transcends a particular event and still has power and life in the totally different context of a children's nursery class. It is a cultural form into which generations of children have been initiated. It lives, because within the simple movement patterns and rhythmic song, a range of contradictory emotions are contained. It ends with dislocation and laughter. An understanding of these activities, synthesising and dislocating, forming, transforming and transcending will help to reveal the significance of the aesthetic and the religious realm. This chapter attempts to explicate that claim.

'Make a circle.' Children do not, in fact, need to receive that instruction from the adult world; it is the form which first emerges from the apparently random scribbles of infants from whatever cultural background (Arnheim, 1954, ch. 4). It is the form which most adequately expresses the need to create a world from the totality of things. Form must emerge from chaos; 'a still point in a turning world' (Eliot, 1963, p. 191) has to be sought. The human mind must synthesise in order to experience anything, and the way this synthesis is made helps to determine the nature of the personality and the kind of relationships which are made.

With what shall I make the circle? With all that I am and all that there is; that is the ultimate demand which drives the human spirit. The young child responds by total absorption in creative activity and endless

109

exploration of the world around. The need to find 'still points' is the need to objectify. The goal is attained by movements in two very different directions. The route of disciplined detachment and careful observation which science ultimately took led to the discovery of unity in abstract principles and general laws. This achievement was made through the development of the language of logic and mathematics; the ultimate pattern of things was expressed in a form of stable signs. Such objectification made possible the great advances in technology. The price of such progress was high, for it could only be made by leaving behind the world of immediate experience, of sound, sight, touch, grief and hope, ecstasy and despair. Art and religion take another route which strives for an even greater unity in holding fast to the intensity and transient particularity of human experience and the complexity of 'all that is'. The struggle is still to objectify — to make objects which give form to the lasting truth of immediate experience. The forms are not those of mathematics and logic, but images taken from the sensed world and transformed into metaphor, symbol, poem, story, song, music and dance. Without such forms the world would be manipulable but unfit for human habitation. Human beings can only live in a world shaped by forms and symbols which give them a sense of significance. 'Poetically man dwells' claims Heidegger (1976, p. 131), and expresses the fact that men and women do not passively and unreflectively endure pain or revel in pleasure, but spontaneously respond to experience. They have the power to act upon and shape the world and thus transform it. It is through this power that freedom comes.

What has all this to do with RE? 'Ring a ring a roses', it was noted, was a given cultural form. The child once initiated into it will play the game again and again. Religions form circles. That is, they provide forms through which the whole of life can be viewed and lived. They are given cultural forms, and the way fully to understand them is to join the circle and play the game. Yet 'game' is a misleading metaphor, for the game is life itself. A characterisation of religion which is illuminating here is one provided by Geertz (1966). Religion is a system of sacred symbols which

> function to synthesise a people's ethos — the tone, character and quality of their life, its moral and aesthetic style and mood — and their world view — the picture they have of the way things in sheer actuality are, their most comprehensive ideas of order. (p. 215)

Religion defines for a people what is 'really real', not in some abstract metaphysical sense, but in the sense of that which is trusted and forms the springboard for action. It is this understanding of religion which will provide part of the foundation for this argument, though it will prove necessary to extend and modify it.

Within such a model it is not possible to make a sharp distinction between the religious and the aesthetic. In societies where one religion dominates, as in medieval Europe, art and religion are clearly seen to be one. Story, dance, drama, ritual, song, architecture and social order are all part of one circle. In such a world the images live; they reverberate, for individuals find in them echoes of their own life and experience and respond with the creation of fresh forms. When such a synthesis breaks down there is a tendency at first to identify religion with the traditional cultural form and to be oblivious to the new forms which religion is taking. From such blindness there emerges that terrible hybrid 'religious art' or 'religious poetry', which is usually bad art and bad religion. If Geertz's wider definition is taken, it is possible to perceive the new forms which religion is taking, and to recognise that art and religion move in the same direction, and that their goal is the creation of a world of human significance.

How does the task of RE appear within such a model? Its prime aim is to assist pupils in their synthesis of experience. Goethe (1850) describes the process as

> that of turning into an image, into a poem, everything that delighted or troubled or otherwise occupied my attention, of coming to some understanding with myself thereupon, as well as to rectify my conception of external things as to set my mind at rest about them.

That is the experience of a great poet, but the same struggle is echoed in this dialogue between teacher and a twelve-year-old pupil in an RE lesson.

> Miss, what is death . . .?
> What do you mean?
> Well, I was reading this comic and this girl she was dying and above her head there was this great purple bird with a black beak, red eyes and cruel claws. Is that death?

This is a paradigm of the kind of question which lives at the heart of RE. The content may range wide over everything that delights, troubles or otherwise occupies, but the answer can only be given in the form of images, poems, stories, rituals or festivals.

This synthesising is a primary and inevitable activity of the human mind. It is the concern of education because no-one creates a world alone. Alone, there would be no external world as we conceive it; our conception is mediated through language, and our understanding structured by the symbolic cultural forms into which we have been initiated. Significantly, the pupil's question is provoked by a comic. The powerful images and stories which are in fact playing the most influential part in the world formation of the majority of pupils come from advertisements, television games, the pop song and surrounding architecture, not from any religious tradition or major work of art.

It is within this context that the task of religious and aesthetic education should be understood. There are three main elements in this undertaking. First, the aim is to provide a richer store of images. In this, aesthetic and religious education play a similar role in giving pupils access to the cultural heritage of the human race. Content will vary, with RE embracing ritual, myth and sacred scripture, but approach and method need to be the same. Second, it is important to develop the skills necessary to turn images into poems, paintings or music, daydreams into stories, gesture into dance. This is one of the major tasks of aesthetic education, but it is one on which RE is dependent. Limitation in expression has as its counterpart an inevitable limitation in perception. The artist seeks objectivity, and the development of artistic skills leads to a more profound struggle to reflect what is really there. Lastly, there is a need to help pupils to reflect upon and be responsible for the images which they have. In one sense we are passive recipients of images — they emerge from the unconscious in dream and creative work, they are provided by the cultural milieu in which we are placed, and they have great power because they are always linked to an emotional response; but we do not need to be held captive by them. It is part of the task of RE to encourage this liberation. 'Is that death?' asks the child. This is a metaphysical question in the sense suggested by Emmett (1949, p. 215); metaphysics is the search for metaphors which form appropriate models for co-ordinating experience. Developing responsibility for images will involve countering one powerful image with another of equal power but with different implications, looking at lines made between images as for example in advertisements, and discussing the kinds of experiences and actions which emerge from certain symbolic frameworks.

Such reflection is inevitably disturbing because it threatens the original synthesis. This brings us to the other verb suggested by the dance, 'We all fall down.' The drive to synthesise, to form the circle, is countered by what would appear to be an equally strong impatience with it and delight in breaking free. The movement forward threatens the movement round. The professional dance first emerges from the Jewish faith with its fierce distrust of the image. This distrust of the image is also characteristic of Islam, and is a recurring theme in the history of Christianity. What can lead to the dislocation of the circle? Anything which forces recognition that it is not big enough. This can be the full recognition that others live within coherent symbol structures totally different from those with which one is familiar. It can be the ruthlessly honest determination to face the tension between the reality of a particular experience and the traditional forms of understanding of which Job is a classic example. It can be the power of a great work of art providing a new image with which to appraise reality. Both artist and religious visionary are driven to break the traditional structures and create new patterns by a passionate desire to grasp reality, which always leads to an awareness of the gap between the symbol and that which it attempts to reflect. Both share a sense of transcendence, and it is this sense which threatens the traditional forms which seek to contain experience, but also gives hope to move beyond their destruction.

It is the recognition of the inevitability of dislocation if the task of synthesis is to be undertaken within an educational setting that causes the major controversy about the kind of RE suggested here. To reflect upon the pervading symbol structures within which significance is to be found is a very dangerous undertaking, for on such synthesis depend the integrity of personality, the stability of family and community life and the acceptance of social and political structures. 'Mankind, can bear anything', says Geertz (1966) 'except the thought that God is mad.' To avoid such a threat, a number of different positions may be taken about which only brief comment can be made here: (a) RE should be abolished to be replaced by social studies and moral education. This is an inadequate solution, for if the full implications of moral and social education are explored, they will lead to consideration of issues which are the province of RE – the exploration of significant symbols and the concern for the 'really real'. (b) RE should be taught 'objectively'. This inevitably means that the aesthetic dimension must be excluded, for it is important that the subject should lead to understanding without ever posing the question of truth. To create a story, to dance, to paint, to act out a ritual, is to enter a world which restructures reality and therefore possibly endangers existing structures. This objective approach presents problems because a true understanding of religion can only be gained by that inside vision which the aesthetic perspective provides. Any other approach will fail to motivate most pupils. (c) RE should be confined to an attempt to initiate pupils into the Christian vision of the world and other faiths or views should be perceived only from that standpoint. This is probably the view of the subject which prevails in many schools, in spite of the strong educational objections reiterated in most of the literature in the last decade. The philosophical, social, psychological and theological problems inherent in such a position have been well expounded. This approach is not feasible within a pluralist society.

In contrast to these positions, a view of RE is here presented in which the aesthetic plays a crucial role and an adequate rationale can only be provided by a fuller explication of what was earlier referred to as 'a sense of transcendence'. It is only possible to do this in metaphoric terms. Both artist and religious visionary are aware of a space beyond the given circles. It is this awareness which enables them to break free from the traditional forms and create anew. Newness and freedom are both signs of imaginative power. The sense that there is 'more there' than we have yet found forms to enshrine, that reality for ever eludes our grasp, is an essential foundation for attitudes of worship, contemplation and imaginative creation. The characterisation of religion with which this paper began needs to be extended to include this sense of transcendence, this sense which drives human beings to press against the limits of their situation, to dream dreams and dare the impossible. It must form an essential part of any definition of religion on which RE is based.

A brief consideration of the practical implications of this model will suggest how it can illuminate some of the recent developments in the RE curriculum. In the early years the task of synthesising must take priority. The controversial Plowden injunction (DES, 1967), not to encourage doubt until faith is established, still holds good if by faith is meant the creation of a coherent world. On such a synthesis depends the establishment of trust and hope and the development of personality. It is perhaps because they serve this function that the life themes first created by Goldman (1964) have survived in primary school RE. Nevertheless, much haziness surrounds the rationale of this work. Many misconceptions are dispelled if it is recognised that the metaphoric process is central to all experience. Experience is never immediate, for links are always made between one experience and another. It is upon this foundation that frameworks are created and fundamental attitudes shaped. The life theme is an attempt to develop this potential for educational ends.

What exactly might that mean? The most coherent defence of the life theme in the early days was based on a Christian incarnational theology (Hull, 1972). Within a particular religious community, this rationale makes sense. The theme works when family life and community worship serve to reinforce the links suggested. It is in the secondary school that the problem becomes acute and justification at times vague. The rationale defended here places the life theme within the context of religious and aesthetic education with the aim of enriching the store of images and developing expressive skills. Themes suggested in the first post-Goldman syllabuses were chosen because of their links with the Bible but they were, significantly, images which transcended a particular religious tradition: bread, light, fire, wind, seasons. The work of many psychologists and phenomenologists bears witness to the fact that there are certain images which powerfully reflect the nature of the human situation (Bacheland, 1969; Jung, 1958; Eliade, 1976).

Examples of how this happens in practice may help to illustrate the point. A class of 7 to 11-year-olds in a small country school had been working for half a term on a theme of wind and fire. They had explained it in many ways, building bonfires, making kites, dancing and painting. By chance an old poster for the Booker novel prize was found. It depicted a bronze statue holding a bowl of fire, and because it seemed to fit the theme, it was put up on the wall. No attention was drawn to it. It was just there. Tim, aged 9, stood in front of the picture. Eventually he fetched his teacher and tried to tell him about what he saw. The teacher was a sympathetic and imaginative person but could not grasp what the boy was trying to tell him. Tim had never written any poetry before, but in a desperate attempt to communicate he wrote this:

From this great bronze bowl
The flames leap high
and lighten up
the darkened sky *
The figure though of stony bronze
Glints in the light of crackling flames.
It never seems to tire of standing there
Holding the great bowl
of living fire
Standing there
So real yet
Without life or love.

He had got to the heart of the theme, felt the contrast between life and death and something of the significance of the symbol of fire. A similar thought is reflected in this piece by a 13-year-old girl arising out of the nature work on Autumn:

> Leaves are a great source of my pleasure. It is Autumn I like best because you, in my mind, see the leaves at their best it is as though they do it to show off and be better than the companion trees around them which I think is great fun also to play a game of catching the leaves when they come down before they touch the ground it is the fascinating colours as they blend together in a mad dance before they glide down to rest on the long grass only to be chased by the cat as though it were a mouse, tear it to shreds. Perhaps it is the sound of the crunch when a dog takes a flying leap for a ball that was thrown, they still seem to hold life even though they are dead. They are seeming to be happy even though they are sombre.

In a similar way the fundamental themes of darkness and light recur in children's writing in this moving poem by a dyslexic child:

> *The Cave*
> Out of a cave came a
> crak from the dark
> Murmurs of help help cried
> the thing in the dark
> Please help me please please
> come on help me
> The voice came from the
> dark corner of the cave
> Creeping slowly in looking
> listening to hear where the
> voice came from
> Help Help the voice said
> once again Help Help it said.

In all the examples given there was a good and close relationship between teacher and pupil prompting the desire for communication. It was a relationship in which the teacher provided some imaginative stimulus in the form of picture or theme, yet was sensitive enough to leave space for the pupils' creative response. It is significant that the two poems quoted were created out of a sense of intense frustration resolved in the discovery of an image which communicates. Many of the themes suggested are related to a fundamental sense of space and time.

Parallel to the development of mathematical and scientific understanding of space and time is the equally important development of the sense of the symbolic significance of both. In time, the fundamental task is to find a creative response to change — change of mood, of age, of status, fortune or relationship. Here images from nature, tree, fire, seasons, flowers, enliven, while the unchanging plastic flower or concrete block deaden sensibility. Traditional religious forms of festival, rites of passage, story, dance and ritual serve the same function. In space, the sense of wonder and of possibility are developed through contemplation of the very small and infinitely great. Shells, nests, attics, cellars, tunnels, paths, caves, stars, mountains and deserts, all provide stimulus for imaginative exploration. The experience of contrast and contradiction is also fundamental to all people and reflected in images of light and darkness, life and death, male and female, good and evil. The possible range of relationships with the world and others, dependence and independence, trust and fear, contemplation and exploitation, can be seen through exploration of the images of mother, father, friend, judge, king, servant, master, child and artist. From such basic imagery themes begin, and the teacher's task is to provide the initial stimulus, the context of freedom in which imaginative work can develop, to introduce the work of great artists and the appropriate religious forms of festival, architecture, song or myth.

The mention of myth leads to consideration of an important element which is now entering into the newer syllabuses. The Goldman-inspired curriculum pursued image to the detriment of story. It is now widely recognised that without myth there can be no religion. By myth is meant here a story which is seen to have significance for human life. Narrative is one of the most important forms of synthesis. It is the form through which image and action are united, where the human being and the unpredictable happenings to which he is subject are shaped into a pattern which makes living possible. It is through the fairy story that the young child is best introduced to the mythic realm. Here again, the now vast literature on the subject reveals the recurring themes in the fairy stories of diverse peoples (Bettelheim, 1978). Themes of journey, of task, images of the varied forms of evil, dragon, giant, goblin, witch; the simpleton hero, the animal helper, the strange transformation and the vision of ultimate attainment — all provide the child with imaginative resources for coming to terms with life. The Bible story, banished by Goldman for fear that the child might confuse it with fairy story, has a place if the imaginative truth and psychological importance of the latter is recognised.

Between the ages of 6 and 7 the child begins to define more clearly the frontiers between the world of fairy tale and the world of common-sense reality. 'You don't come alive again when you're dead', comments a 7-year-old at the end of *Snow White*. It is vital for sanity and survival that pupils are encouraged in this grasp of everyday reality. The middle years are inevitably a period when the child needs to distance herself from the all-enveloping power of myth. The imaginative world is never-theless of vital importance if everyday life is to have depth and signifi-cance. The sense of the circumference of that world must be established without loss of a sense of its power. At the same time, the child is com-ing to understand the scientific world which contrasts in a different way with the everyday sense of things. The teacher's task is to help the child keep three balls in the air, the commonsense world, the imaginative world and the scientific world, and in later years their interdependence will be recognised.

The secondary years are a time when the task of gaining a sense of responsibility for images will predominate. It is also a time when pupils need help in facing dislocation and working towards a broader and more profound synthesis. Myths which were left behind in childhood can be rediscovered in a new way by the adult mind. Such a lifelong process will not be completed by 18. All that can be aimed at in the secondary years is a widening of perspectives revealing that there is territory to explore and a development of attitudes which prevent the narrow absolution of restricted vision. Now is the time when the arts play a crucial role. Pupils need to be encouraged to reflect on the images given in our present culture. Great art challenges given perception, for it forces us to look again when the conventional image has been shattered. There needs to be no difference in approach to the artistic work or the religious leader, the sacred scriptures or visions of life. Much recent scholarship in the New Testament field has drawn attention to the fact that the Gospels are best understood as artistic creation. Treated as such, they inspire creative response and give new vision. The movement towards a synthesis which most truly reflects reality will not be an easy one. It will involve risk, but risk and vision are inextricably connected. To reflect on images, to encounter new and challenging forms, to begin to see the world through the eyes of others and to recognise the multi-plicity of perspectives is to enter on a journey. 'Ring a ring a roses' ends in dislocation, but it is possible to laugh and get up again. Laughter is the creative response to the shattering of a small world. Laughter, not despair, is only possible when it is recognised that the world does not end when one shaping of it shatters. The spirit which can laugh is able to care about and yet ultimately hold loosely to all structures. It is on such an attitude of gaiety, courage and trust that RE rests.

References

Arnheim, R. (1954) *Art and Visual Perception*, Faber, London

Bacheland, G. (1969) *Poetics of Space*, Beacon, Boston

Bettelheim, B. (1976) *Uses of Enchantment*, Thames & Hudson, London

DES (1967) *Children and their Primary Schools, vol. 1* (Plowden Report), HMSO, London

Eliade, M. (1976) *Patterns in Comparative Religion*, Sheed & Ward, London

Eliot, T.S. (1963) 'Burnt Norton', *Collected Poems*, Faber & Faber, London

Emmett, D. (1949) *The Nature of Metaphysical Thinking*, Macmillan, London

Geertz, C. (1966) 'Religion as a Cultural System' in M. Banton (ed.), *Anthropological Approaches to the Study of Religion*, Tavistock, London

Goethe, J.W. (1850) 'Truth and Poetry' in E. Cassirer (1979) *Symbol Myth and Culture*, Yale University Press, New Haven and London

Goldman, R. (1964) *Religious Thinking from Childhood to Adolescence*, Routledge & Kegan Paul, London

Heidegger, M. *The Piety of Thinking*, translated by J.G. Hart and J.C. Maraldo (1976), Indiana

Hull, J. (1972) *The Theology of Themes*, CEM Press, London

Jung, C.G. (1958) *Psyche and Symbol*, Doubleday Anchor, New York

Part Three: THE WRITING PROCESS

INTRODUCTION

Helen Cowie

In Chapters 7 and 8 we see how accomplished writers face the problems of finding an authentic voice and avoiding the contorted language which obscures meaning. Peter Wason, in his discussion of ways of freeing oneself from writing blocks, recommends two alternating phases: (1) an uncritical 'exteriorisation of thought' in which ideas can be expressed in any form; and (2) a critical process of revision. The first can be used either to free the mind from unnecessary material which is blocking expression or to put the writer in touch with his own, as yet, unformulated ideas. The second requires a more objective appraisal of the form and content of the writing. He argues that through the interweaving of these two approaches a committed voice can be found. As Don Murray puts it, 'The writer has a split brain — creator and critic — or competing forces — freedom and discipline.' In fact, Don Murray, in Chapter 8, also explores the revision process in extracts from a journal which he kept while he was writing a novel and some non-fiction pieces. We read about the pain involved in the composing process and the sense of well-being when writing flows. At the same time, Don Graves draws parallels between the experience of this accomplished novelist and the writing of young children who, he claims, can learn to 'rehearse' their writing and to use effective revision strategies. They too, in the right kind of environment, can discover a 'voice' in their writing with which to express their thoughts. He echoes Vygotsky (1962, p. 149) who used a striking image to describe the process as a change from inner speech, 'that dynamic, shifting, unstable thing fluttering between word and thought' to the more precisely formulated mode of written speech through the deliberate structuring of the web of meaning.

In Chapter 9 Barry Kroll provides a different approach to the analysis of children's writing by using the method of the story-grammar — a representation of the structure of a narrative in the form of a tree diagram — in order to give insight into ways in which children develop a story. He shows that the child's concept of what makes an effective narrative is likely to have a strong influence on his or her writing, and it seems to me that there are interesting connections to be made with the telling and reading of stories.

In these three chapters we gain important insights into the processes which underlie even the simplest piece of writing. The fact that children seem to show a concern for the form as well as the content of their stories gives strong support for the view that there are parallels to be drawn between the child's writing processes and those of the mature writer. Again, the teacher's role seems to be crucial not only in the evaluation of the end-product, but also in his or her interest in the child's intentions (whether realised or not) and changing concepts of what makes good writing. It is appropriate to introduce this section with the answer which one 10-year-old gave me when I asked him if he planned stories in advance:

> I had all these ideas and I just fitted them together for the story. We had a day to think about it. I thought about it beforehand . . . You get a sudden inspiration. I think of it as all the ideas placed all over the place and I have to think of a way to connect all the ideas up. Once I have connected two ideas it's easier to connect up all the others . . . I may be stuck and then suddenly the ideas come a little further on . . . If it's very quiet you're able to think. You get so many ideas that if you talked about them they might get pushed out.

Reference

Vygotsky, L.S. (1962) *Thought and Language*, MIT Press, Cambridge, Mass.

7 CONFORMITY AND COMMITMENT IN WRITING

Peter C. Wason

It is argued that conformity to stereotyped styles of writing tends to conceal a sense of commitment to what is being said. The effect is both to alienate the individual from the practice of writing, and to encourage a kind of obscurantism which may be inimical to clear thinking. The conditions for recovering a committed voice and the benefits of so doing are described.

Conformity

'You a member of the estalishment then?' I was talking to a small group of trainee managers from a leading computer firm about a pet deductive problem of mine. 'It's those funny words you use in your writing. When you talk to us it all becomes clear.' Remote and forbidding, my prose had apparently been perceived as an example of what Claire Lerman (1981) calls the 'institutional voice', cultivated over about twenty-five years to fit the constraints of learned journals. I defended myself by saying that if I were to unpack my words for an untutored audience, then my articles would have to be very much longer, but this argument did not satisfy my managers at all. Still, they had a point. They felt, and I think a lot of us would agree, that a great deal of what lands on our desks is impenetrably obscure. Furthermore, they implied by the term 'establishment' that it was needlessly and perhaps deliberately obscure. Increasingly, it would seem, the voice of a person with something to say is lost.

In some cases one would be inclined to think this is a good thing. Consider technical reports which purport to provide no more than factual information, e.g. 'The Loads Exerted by Grass Silage on Bunker Silo Walls' — surely to write about that in a committed way would be inappropriate. And yet I am unsure. In the 1950s a flourishing group, The Presentation of Technical Information Group, led by the late Professor R.O. Kapp, was set up at University College London, precisely to study ways of rendering such information more interesting and palatable. I am

reluctant to draw a limit between different kinds of writing, although I
suppose that a philosophical paper allows more scope for commitment
than a technical report. What I try to do in this essay is to sketch the
forces which induce conformity on style, and speculate on how commitment may be recovered through writing.

At its very worst, a peculiarly offensive style does seem to infect
the literature of the social sciences and relatively new disciplines which
borrow concepts from a variety of older ones, e.g. semiotics and design.
This style is conspicuously absent in philosophy (especially the philosophy of mind) and in the natural sciences. One may ask why it is tol-
erated and published when it appears to be so unintelligible. Perhaps
the layman, anxious to increase his knowledge, is being held at arm's
length.

There is a counter-argument to this criticism. In an influential book,
Kuhn (1962) pointed out that even the observations of the scientist are
determined by the paradigm in which the research is done. They are
certainly not 'objective'. Hence, if something as basic as observation is
conceptually loaded, it is hardly surprising that the reporting of results
is similarly affected. But this counter-argument is a defence of specialised, or technical, literature and I exempt such writing from my attack.
The unfortunate tendency of the layman to dismiss anything he cannot
immediately understand will be corrected.

Three Types of Obscurity

I distinguish three types of obscurity in writing; (1) is venial, (2) is un-
avoidable, and (3) is pernicious.

(1) There is a fairly common, but relatively trivial kind of obscurity
which results from grammatical error. It is often manifested in ambiguity which seldom has really serious consequences. All of us in the
trade would, I am sure, be guilty at times of this kind of obscurity if
our writings were to be put under the microscope of the purist. We delight to pounce on it, especially when it occurs in our students' essays,
but I shall say no more about it here because I do not want (now) to
be a nag.

(2) There is the obscurity of technical, or specialised writing. A moment's reflection will persuade one that it is inevitable and legitimate. The
development of knowledge in nearly every domain entails an increasingly specialised vocabulary so that it is notoriously difficult for experts
in even related fields to understand each other. Some specialists affect
to despise the vulgarising works which seek to interpret such literature,

but that seems to be their own limitation. In any case, I am not alarmed by this problem.

(3) There is the obscurity of power which I shall call obscurantism. I believe it to be particularly important as an obstacle to effective writing. It is represented by the language of some social institutions, and it aims to be objective and impersonal. Its effect is to delimit an area of enquiry so that the uninitiated fail to understand it, but remain suitably impressed by what they take to be erudition. In the social sciences, at any rate, the abstruse has a compelling attraction, especially for some students who may imitate this style for two reasons. First, it appears to set the seal of scientific respectability on their own writing, and secondly, it need not betray original thought or commitment. This institutional style may also be inimical to the exercise of thinking – a plausible hypothesis anticipated in politics by Orwell (1948), and argued with zeal by Andreski (1972) in relation to social sciences.

It is with third type of obscurity that I am concerned. It flourishes best (if carefully nurtured) in academia and in government bureaucracy – institutions characterised by the attempt to be objective and to impose conformity.

The Language of Academia

It is as a university teacher that I am primarily concerned about the effects of the obscurantist style. The issue has been admirably summed up by one of my correspondents who had been a student counsellor:

> Somewhere along the line we take nice, co-operative children or adolescents, and we convince them that if you write incomprehensibly you are an expert, and if simply, puerile. In fact you personally, and perhaps a majority of the members of staff in most universities, would more or less reverse that. If you write simply, you are an expert. If you write simply about very difficult topics, you are an outstanding expert. It is incomprehensible writing which is puerile. But given the apparent fact that most staff prefer simplicity, or at least say they prefer it, how does it happen that those nice, co-operative students become so invincibly certain of the direct opposite? (Malcolm France, personal communication, 5.5.75)

Not only students. Quite a time ago I offered to republish the paper of a friend in a book I was editing if only he were to rewrite it in such a way that it would be comprehensible. My offer was declined. Perhaps he thought the paper was wrong, or intellectually worthless, even though I thought it highly original. After all, creative people do often denigrate their earlier work, or perhaps he thought the paper would be in some way less objective if it were to be expressed in plain English. Who can tell? Another correspondent illuminated for me the roots of conformity:

> My own theory is that these peculiarities of style result from an inferiority complex on the part of psychologists and sociologists: (they are comparatively rare with physicists, biologists, doctors etc. – except psychiatrists). We feel that we are not yet accepted as really scientific, so we try to impress ourselves and our public, by adopting what sounds like a scientific vocabulary. At the same time, to show how widely we read, we take both our ideas and our language from foreigners rather than compatriots – in my day it was German authorities who were usually quoted (Wundt rather than Sherrington or Ward); later French (Binet rather than Galton); now of course it is American . . . 'Girls of seven have another way of saying the same thing' sounds too humdrum: so it becomes 'The seven-year-old female school population are differentiated by an idiosyncracy (*sic*) in the strategy of their learning behaviour' (Cyril Burt, personal communication, 19.12.69)

In rather the same vein, other academics (e.g. Mahoney, 1976, p. 85; Van den Berghe, 1970, pp. 97-8) have, tongue in cheek, cautioned the student to use 'seasoned jargon' if he wants to get anywhere at all. J. Scott Armstrong of the Wharton School, University of Pennsylvania, forgoes irony in saying virtually the same thing:

> It soon becomes obvious that the purpose of writing is not to communicate but to impress. The ability to write in an incomprehensible way is useful for people who have nothing to say. And in the time you spend making it easier to read, you could be writing another incomprehensible paper. (*The Times*, 9.4.80)

Finally, I cannot resist quoting the start of a letter by Bob Short (*sic*) entitled 'Monosyllabic Writing' which appears in Faraday's (1816-46) unpublished commonplace book:

> Sir, I think it would be well for all if our mode of speech could be made more plain as well in what we write as what we say – so that

each might read as he runs. I know there are those who will laugh at this but why should they?

The criticism of verbosity and obscurantism is clearly not a contemporary phenomenon, but the forces which perpetuate it are too entrenched to yield to individual voices. I might add copious examples of pretentious writing from my own data base, but I have done this elsewhere (Wason, 1980). In any case, it seems a little unfair to slang the efforts of my own students and associates when anyone might dig up similar cases in my own papers. But it is not just our seats of learning which are responsible for the cultivation of obscurantism. In fact, it pales into insignificance when it is compared with the style of officials. In the spirit of fairness, and for the sake of the record, I shall describe my own attack on official language before returning to my target.

The Language of Bureaucracy

The language of official forms and instructions has long been accepted as a minor irritant and a feeble joke. I think Sheila Jones and I were the first academics to become seriously interested in this problem in the mid-1960s (e.g. Jones, 1968; Wason, 1962; Wason, 1968). We even received a grant from the Medical Research Council to investigate it, and we introduced the term 'logical tree' (which subsequently became algorithm) into the vocabulary of government circles. We demonstrated experimentally that in several cases the language of interrelated rules was almost impossible to understand in continuous prose because of the complexity of the syntax, and we forecast that the problem would be exacerbated in the future because the drafting of legislation proceeds by accretion. Moreover, we developed a technique which, in principle, eliminates consumer difficulty.

A nice example of such language occurred in a 1960s leaflet,

Late Paid and Unpaid contributions

Contributions paid late cannot normally count for death grant (other than towards the test of yearly average) unless they were paid before the death on which the grant is claimed and before the death of the insured person if that was earlier. But if the insured person died before the person on whose death the grant is claimed, contributions which, although paid late, have already been taken into account for the purpose of a claim for widow's benefit or retirement pension, will count towards death grant.

One begins to wonder *who* has died. A fascinating problem in identity and temporal relationships for the bereaved person to solve. Of course, it must be remembered that leaflets from which this extract was taken are not designed to state the law, but to *help* the ordinary man or woman to understand it (see also Wason and Johnson-Laird, 1972, Chapter 17).

After a few ripples of excitement and much shuffling around from one government department to another, guided by a more or less benevolent Treasury, the interest appeared to wane. But it gets aroused again periodically, as one group of assiduous proselytisers after another takes up the cause. The most active of these groups today, The Plain English Campaign, led by Chrissie Maher and Martin Cutts of the Salford Form Market, have developed a missionary zeal in their desire to root out all symptoms of officialese. This has involved the shredding of forms in front of the Houses of Parliament, a gesture which apparently achieved only an evanescent publicity.

The problem is a real one, and in an ideal society it would not exist, but it is more complex than most critics appreciate. After a fair amount of experience of dealing with enlightened officials spurred on by the interest of the media, my submission is that piecemeal onslaughts and articulate advocacy will change nothing. It might be an interesting psychological exercise to penetrate the mental processes of the writers of official leaflets (as we once contemplated doing), but the dominance of bureaucratic obscurantism would remain untouched because it is motivated (in a very broad sense) by political interest. Lucidity is not the prime consideration of those who wield power, as even a socialist minister of the Crown confessed to us in a casual remark. In such cases control is truly exerted through the written word: rules are made to bind people.

At this point I included a section, *The Obscurantism Test*, in the original article. I now think it is both too speculative and too technical to reproduce here. Basically, the idea is that if a passage of expository prose can be *reduced* in length without loss of informative meaning, then it is obscurantist; if it has to be *expanded* to be made comprehensible then it consists of specialised language. It was shown, for example, how an extract from a particular sociological text could be radically reduced without loss of meaning, and how an opening sentence from a particular mathematical paper would require expansion in order to be understood by the layman.

However, the idea is really a conjecture rather than a test. It would need much research on different kinds of discourse, as well as considerable psychological experimentation, before its feasibility can be established.

Commitment

Intentionally, or unintentionally, an obscurantist use of language conceals the commitment of the author. In contrast, memorable prose seems to be written with a highly distinctive and committed voice. It is something which is essentially human and individual; neither a machine nor a committee could write in this way. And contrary to popular belief, I think it cannot be imitated. It comes from having a particular attitude to what you want to say. But how do you find out what you have to say? Perhaps you knew it all along. This I seriously doubt.

An Affective Problem

'Why don't you write an article analysing exactly what is wrong with all those monstrous sentences you have in that file?' somebody once said to me. He thought it would be helpful to be aware of error in writing. But in spite of numerous manuals, and in spite of the rather bourgeois obsession with the niceties of style (typified by Philip Howard's column in *The Times*), we know deep down that the possession of prescriptive rules does not overcome the central problem of writing. It is generally acknowledged that writing is hard work, but it is not like giving a lecture, or playing chess, which are just as intellectually demanding, but which possess sufficient constraints to start and terminate performance. 'It's a skill, isn't it?' a former student has just said to me on the telephone. 'Yes, it's a skill', I replied. She meant that it is something which improves with practice. Partly right — practice is a necessary, but not a sufficient condition for what I call 'happy writing', a kind of writing, familiar to experienced writers, in which the output is associated with a sense of elation and commitment (or engagement). My answer on the telephone had ignored the affective problem (Wason, 1980).

Any kind of serious writing involves a confrontation with the self because it creates an object which is both a part of the self and a part of the world of ideas. In reading the text, or working over it, the writer is shown a reflection of himself. The object can be criticised, elaborated or destroyed. And doing any of these things, I have argued, modifies the consciousness of the writer (Wason, 1970).

Such processes are basically affective. They involve a perception of the self and especially self-esteem. Lionel Trilling told me that, when he was teaching rhetoric at Colombia University in the 1930s, some of his students expressed an admiration for his own writing, but said they could not possibly write like that because 'they were not gentlemen'. A similar elitist assumption, held by more than one of my friends, is that writing is a gift which they do not (regrettably) share. One has only to think about the fetishistic rituals that some authors have performed before starting to write, in order to appreciate that writing, or at any rate happy writing, does not seem to respond to a volitional act. One does not surround oneself with rotten apples before sitting down to do the income tax; there is no need to invoke a muse for such a menial task. Elsewhere I have disputed this 'natural function theory' (the wait-for-it effect) as stemming from our romantic notions of creativity, and I cited journalism as a counter-example. But I am now inclined to think I was wrong.

Happy writing demands a relaxed attitude. All too often, most individuals are convinced that writing is going to be difficult, and so of course it does become difficult and peculiarly unpleasant. Hence, I am impressed by some of the techniques advocated by Rohman (1965), such as analogical exercises, in his 'prewriting method'. Like meditation, or prayer, writing depends on an inner dialogue which is non-volitional. It is something which is not entirely under conscious control. The importance of this problem has been more widely acknowledged in the United States with the attention paid to writing workshops in university departments. More conservative academics, of course, will view this particular scene with scepticism and distaste because it touches on the emotional life.

The Myth of Conceptual Innocence

One might entertain the romantic fantasy that voice has been lost through experience. One might suppose that in some golden age we saw the world with fresh eyes, and could write about it in an unaffected way, and that we ought to be able to recover that vision. This idea which derives from Blake, Rousseau and Wordsworth (among others) is obviously attractive and does not seem to me entirely false. It is attested by the aesthetic quality of young children's drawings.

In *Zen and the Art of Motorcycle Maintenance* (Pirsig, 1974) the protagonist Phaedrus, a teacher of rhetoric, encounters one of his students who wants to write a 500-word essay about the United States. This is never even attempted. Success only comes when the topic is finally restricted: 'Narrow it down to the front of one building on the main street . . . the Opera House. Start with the upper left-hand brick.' The result is a 5000-word essay. This release from a block is attributed to a fresh-found ability to look and see rather than to repeat what she had already heard so many times before. As a result of trying out further exercises, Phaedrus concludes that the compulsion to imitate (absent in young children) has to be broken down before real rhetoric teaching could start. The recovery of voice is achieved through detailed descriptive writing. The analysis seems to me basically correct: conformity to a stereotyped objective standard has a stultifying effect on the writing of most students. The value of the exercise, however, remains unclear. The critical question is whether such writing would help the individual to write in other ways, especially in more abstract or general terms which do not depend on observation. At any rate, Nancy Kuriloff (1980), a writing therapist in California, who specialises in the treatment of writing block, seems to have developed a similar technique: 'Write about stone . . . Don't stop. Don't correct. If you get stuck, write about how it feels to get stuck.' She has a profound but simple point: the important thing in writing is to keep going. The superior wisdom of everyman's 'Critic' (as she calls it) must be denied.

Discovery

In 1970 the editor of *Physics Bulletin* invited me to write an article on writing scientific papers, perhaps expecting some useful hints and rules of composition put over in an encouraging manner. He received an hypothesis about the generative power of writing, and I received six requests for off-prints (Wason, 1970). My technique, described in that paper, consists in the serial alternation of two distinct modes of writing: (a) an uncritical exteriorisation of thought, and (b) a critical rewriting of the exteriorised mass. Hartley (1980) claims that this technique is idiosyncratic, and I am delighted to hear that I escape the charge of redundancy. My argument is that when these two modes are allowed to interact (successively between drafts, not concurrently within drafts) they facilitate, clarify, and enlarge thought. Happy writing becomes an important source of discovery. Let me repeat myself and say just a little about these two modes.

Exteriorisation may seem inimical to intellectuals because it implies the production of an object in a free-associative manner, akin to Freud's primary process. Particularly repugnant, one would think, is the toleration of the rubbish often produced by this mode. So much incoherent, hackneyed, and altogether bad material may tempt the writer to correct as he goes along, or start afresh. Such a bow towards Kuriloff's 'Critic' tends to induce inhibition because the mode of trying to say something cogently interferes with the mode of finding out what to say at all. This would be the point at which the pen is laid down on the desk.

The more considered mode which attacks and moulds the exteriorised object in a critical way would also appear alien to many individuals.

Personally, I find it congenial to see what I think and then analyse what I say. However, Murray (1978), in a perceptive essay, claims it possesses a vaguely clandestine quality. He argues that the discovery of meaning through rewriting from the 'zero draft' has not been studied because it has not been experienced (or admitted) by writers in the less imaginative forms of writing, and because it is not considered academically respectable. Two professors of his acquaintance implied that they were ashamed of writing in this way, and did not discuss it with their students. My own experience confirms that many individuals simply do not know what it means to rewrite anything in a different way. One of my friends even claims that her successive drafts get worse instead of better. There is, to a large number of people, something odd about the very idea of rewriting. Is it that unconsciously rewriting is like prevarication in speech? Or is it connected with the idea that self-expression implies a self which is somehow sacrosanct and inviolable?

The thesis that discovery (or invention) is a function of writing, and especially of rewriting, is more familiar to rhetoricians (e.g. Young, 1978) than to experimental psychologists. Techniques of writing need to be developed in the psychological laboratory which might enable the individual to be liberated from that tunnel vision which forces only a narrow point of view, and hence precludes discovery. Our experience suggests that some school children are highly receptive to novel techniques in composition (Wason and Williams, 1978). The Whorfian hypothesis (that language moulds thought) does seem to have stronger claims in writing than in speech. This, of course, is an optimistic declaration which befits publication in an American journal. Actually, I am sanguine that the undoubted fruits of writing can be captured in an experimental investigation. The counter-argument is that the control entailed by an experiment is incompatible with the conditions for happy writing.

Therapy

Committed writing may be (in computer terms) a unique way to empty the store so that more space is made available for new ideas. It follows that what is written is not necessarily of value to anyone else. The writing of angry memos, without sending them, is proverbially supposed to have a cathartic effect on the emotions of frustrated managers. Similarly, the headaches caused by intellectual confusion might be alleviated by putting them down on paper. I owe this interesting hypothesis to a conversation with Ivor Stilitz, and recently observed a concrete instance of the effect which was more compelling than any experimental result.

10 June 1980. Jan Smedslund from Oslo discusses with me some problems of rationality and the extent to which this is an empirical issue. I am not conscious that I can help much beyond listening sympathetically. He is blocked in his thinking about the problem, and tells me that this is stopping him from writing. I suggest (of course) that it might help to write.

The next day he telephones to say that immediately after leaving me he wrote for two hours without interruption and covered four pages. 'What came out was totally unexpected, and this really surprised me.' It was also wrong, but it apparently clarified the topic, and enabled the writer to locate the source of the block in his thinking. Thus a conceptual difficulty had been illuminated, not by thought or discussion, but by emptying the store of deficient material.

I was blocked before writing this essay, and indeed, I could not decide whether to write it at all. This indecision is unusual for me because I generally find writing can be relied upon to put myself into a good mood. Moreover, I set myself firm deadlines which I invariably meet ahead of time. On holiday I realised that I was not taking my own medicine, so I wrote down a kind of scenario which, like Smedslund's piece, was also unplanned (see appendix). On reflection, it represented a statement to myself of how I stood at the moment of writing, but the effect was to make me feel less alienated from my own thoughts and feelings. I experienced a disproportionate exaltation after having written something objectively trivial. And in a couple of days I was at last able to begin a first draft without too much trouble. It was as if this writing of a scenario had to be done before more serious work could start.

Let me cite one more example, a more serious one, of writing which may achieve a similar purpose. In 1979 Virginia Valian sent me some essays in exploratory self-analysis written in a particularly fluent and natural style. Many of the topics clustered round the problems of being a woman in a predominantly male academic world. For instance, the attitude towards difficulties in cooking and in academic work are compared. The overall impression to me was that such writing was an attempt to render an individual life more meaningful and coherent. What interested me, however, was that the author possessed an unusual need to write, for just these purposes, and I pointed this out to her. She confessed that, before reading my letter, this idea would have seemed incredible because of the pain she experienced in writing, but now its truth seemed obvious. Indeed, the essays are being cast in the form of a book, *A Life's Work*.

These three examples, Jan Smedslund's, my own and Virginia Valian's, illustrate the therapeutic power of committed (and yet perhaps involuntary) writing. It is evident that such writing may empty the store, or, at a higher level, impose a pattern on daily experience. And perhaps for some people this kind of writing is necessary (even though it may not be recognised as such) in order to get on with the main business of living. My constant attempts to cajole friends and colleagues into writing may have some rational justification.

Conclusion

Beneath the surface of this essay there is the continuous awareness of the sorrow and difficulty which so many people experience in writing. It has been written in the faith that this apparent difficulty is not resolved by exhortation or by precept, but that it can be overcome if only such people were to free themselves from the tutelage to stereotyped models to which they assume (consciously or unconsciously) that they should conform. Through the process of writing and rewriting a committed voice can be recovered in which such individuals are allowed to find out what they think, say what they think, and then stop. To them this essay is dedicated.

Appendix

A Scenario: the Setting of a Scene: 17 July 1980

Let me set the scene. I am writing this in our Suffolk cottage. It is a typical summer day — cold, damp and overcast. This morning I mowed an incredible amount of grass, and then had a nap in the afternoon. Ming returned from Sudbury market to announce that she is starting a campaign for the more humane treatment of pigs. I think this is a splendid cause, and we talk about it. After a bit I continue to stare out of the window. Two crammed note-books and four files lie on my desk giving the illusion of industry and scholarship. Away from it all, as they say: no students, no committees, no tedious bus journeys to college, the ideal situation for productive work. Perhaps. We have a nice vegetarian meal. I write down a couple of sentences, and then stomp about my study. I walk into the main room only to be confronted by Mr Reagan at the Republican Convention. Even this does not depress me; I cannot get on but I am totally preoccupied. I write down a few more sentences, stoke up the boiler, and then decide to go to bed. But a torrent of thoughts assails me as soon as I hit the pillow. A familiar situation, I can hear you saying: a case of writing block. Not familiar to me. Well, instead of making such a fuss about it, you should write that other paper – you know, the one about pragmatics – which will probably go much better. You haven't written anything for at least four months, you know . . . (At this point the scenario turned into a dialogue with myself.)

Shop Hill Cottage, Alpheton, Suffolk.

> The impulse of the pen.
>   Left alone, thought goes as it will.
>   As it follows the pen, it loses its freedom.
> It wants to go one way,
>   the pen another.
>   It is like a blind man
> led astray by his cane, and what I
>   come to write
> is no longer what I wished to write.
>   Jules Renard

References

Andreski, S. (1972) *Social Science as Sorcery*, Deutsch, London

Hartley, J. (1980) *The Psychology of Written Communication*, Kogan Page, London

Jones, S. (1968) *Design of Instruction*, HMSO, London

Kuhn, T.S. (1962) *The Structure of Scientific Revolutions*, University of Chicago Press, Chicago

Kuriloff, N. *Time*, 14.6.1980

Lerman, C. (1981) 'The Institutional Voice and Control of Topic' in H. Davies and P. Walton (eds). *Language, Image, Media*, Blackwells, Oxford (in press)

Mahoney, M.J. (1976) *Scientist as Subject: the Psychological Imperative*, Ballinger, Cambridge, Mass.

Murray, D. (1978) Internal Revision: a Process of Discovery' in C.R. Cooper and L. Odell (eds), *Research on Composing*, National Council of Teachers of English, Urbana

Orwell, G. (1948) 'Politics and the English Language' in S. Orwell and I. Angus (eds), *The Collected Essays, Journalism and Letters of George Orwell, IV, In Front of Your Nose 1945-1950*, Penguin, Harmondsworth (1970)

Pirsig, R.M. (1974) *Zen and the Art of Motorcycle Maintenance: an Enquiry Into Values*, Bodley Head, London

Rohman, D.G. (1965) 'Pre-writing: the Stage of Discovery in the Writing Process', *College Composition and Communication, 16*, 106-12

Valian, V.V. (1977) 'Learning to Work' in S. Ruddick and P. Daniels (eds), *Working It Out*, Pantheon, New York

Van den Berghe, P. (1970) *Academic Gamesmanship: How to Make a Ph.D Pay*, Abelard-Schuman, London

Wason, P.C. (1962) *Psychological Aspects of Negation*, Communication Research Centre, University College, London

— (1968) 'The Drafting of Rules', *New Law Journal, 118*, 548-9

— (1970) 'On Writing Scientific Papers' *Physics Bulletin, 21*, 407-8, reprinted in J. Hartley (ed.), *The Psychology of Written Communication* (1980), Kogan Page, London

— (1980) Specific Thoughts on the Writing Process' in L.W. Gregg and E. Steinberg (eds), *Cognitive Processes in Writing*, Erlbaum, Hillsdale, N.J.

— and Johnson-Laird, P.N. (1972) *The Psychology of Reasoning: Structure and Content*, Batsford, London

— and Williams, J.E. (1978) 'Collaborative Writing Games', *Resources in Education, 7*, 13

Young, R.E. (1978) 'Paradigms and Problems: Needed Research in Rhetoric Invention' in C.R. Cooper and L. Odell (eds), *Research on Composing*, National Council of Teachers of English, Urbana

REVISION IN THE WRITER'S WORKSHOP AND IN THE CLASSROOM

Donald M. Murray and Donald H. Graves

This chapter explores the revision process in writing in extracts from a journal which one of us (DMM) kept while writing a novel and some non-fiction pieces. Alongside these extracts, DHG draws parallels with the writing of young children.

MURRAY

Yesterday, Aviva called and, apologetically, asked me to cut my chapter on 'The Feel of Writing' from sixteen pages to twelve. She was surprised at my delight. Given no choice but to cut, I become the surgeon. It would go fast, and I knew the piece would be better for the surgery.

Steph pointed out in my draft of a chapter for the Donovan-McClelland book that I incorrectly used 'for' in the second paragraph. She suggested 'because'. My reaction was normal; I rejected her suggestion, as I would any editor's suggestion. I over-reacted and rewrote the whole paragraph. When I receive criticism, I normally put the draft aside and start a new one. It is probably the way I reestablish control over my territory. Childish. But the paragraph was better. 'For' became 'who'.

The principal changes in the chapter for Donovan and McClelland were inserts which developed important points towards the end of the piece, or which wove concepts from the early part of the piece through the rest of it. The early pages were rewritten many, many times. The

GRAVES

Rebellion is not the exclusive property of the professional writer. I find it a healthy sign when children rebel in order to maintain control of their information or language. The child may be 'wrong', but the greater issue in the long run will be the child's sense of control of the writing process. We are experts at stealing children's writing voices.

Our data show that children as young as 8 years of age are capable of writing to *find out* what they mean. For such children, six to ten unassigned drafts is not unusual.

changes were reinforcements of what was discovered through the early re-writing of the beginning.

Yesterday I drafted a tentative new beginning of the novel; revising be-coming rehearsing. I know what has to happen in the new beginning. In addition to all the usual things, such as introducing the story, the main characters, setting the scene, estab-lishing the voice, I have to allow Ian to discover the murder of Lucinda's children, which he didn't know in the last draft until the middle of the novel. Sometime this summer, I real-ised he had to know from the begin-ning and that knowledge would give a necessary energy to the beginning of the novel. I recalled William Gibson's advice in *Shakespeare's Game*, 'A play begins when a world in some state of equipoise, always uneasy, is broken by a happening.'

I don't think while writing; I see. I watched him find the old newspaper clippings, saw, felt his reaction to the news. I do not think what Ian should do; I watch him and record what he does. And yet the technical problem has been thought out before. Planted. Was the scene I watched what grew from that seed?

To cut sixteen pages to twelve for Aviva, I count the lines on a page – 27 – estimate where editorial changes have added lines, and come up with a total: 109 lines to cut.

I have observed surgeons. I cut fast, clean strokes, no hesitation, and subtract each line from the total. Thirty minutes, and I am at the end and have cut 117 lines, 8 over. I cut 827 words and added 67. I have 8 lines to use to clarify, restore, or de-velop if necessary. Now I go through and look at the notes in the margins of copies I have given colleagues, after

Murray has a different pace from that permitted in most school situations. He waits, listens, suspends judgment. He is surprised by his characters and information. The waiting is the best aid to redrafting. 'Oh, this is missing. I forgot to say why he was upset.' Papers due within the same class period, or even in the short space of a few days, do not aid listening or that important sense of ownership of the writing.

Starting with first grade, children have to become proficient in the time-space dimensions of writing on paper. 'This will be a two-page paper; oh, I'm stuck, where will I put this long word?'

I have cut on instinct.

As I walked home from school today I rehearsed yesterday's idea. I could start the novel without a new first chapter, weaving the new material through the old.

When children write regularly, they rehearse while watching TV, riding on buses, in all sorts of places. Just knowing they will write every day enables them to think about writing when they are not actually writing. Professional writers 'panic' at the thought of losing one day's writing, simply because it ruins thinking in between writing sessions. Picking up the cold trail for amateur or pro is a disheartening task. Children who compose as few as two to three times a week, lose out on the important thinking that goes on between writing episodes.

Revision of one article I am doing is not revision by my definition. There are no new visions or insights, just simple editing for clarification. It is a bad article. It needs no work, has no possibilities hidden between its words.

When I reread a draft and disgust cramps my bowels, I've learned to back off. It's taken me a long time to realise that I can't force a solution to a writing problem. What do I do when I'm stuck? I quit.

It has taken me years to realise that quitting doesn't make you a quitter. The football coach still yells in my ear. I keep coming back to the writing desk and keep quitting – without guilt (without too much guilt).

The 'can I have another piece of paper' syndrome is in many classrooms, especially where there are good readers who write infrequently. Their writing tools lag well behind their ability to read. They are painfully aware of the discrepancy between their written text and what they wish they could say.

I am surprised how calm I am at the slow start of the revision of the novel. I feel it is perking, somewhere. I have identified a technical problem in the first chapter – the dialogue on the telephone – and I have a rough sequence of action. I have to get to the typewriter and that's not easy with the teaching schedule I've established for myself. I resent this dependence on the typewriter to get this revision going. Usually I revise by pen, but this particular Olympia Electric is necessary on these pages in some way I can't understand. Perhaps I have to make the writing real by seeing it in type. That may make it an object that I can study.

Beginnings are terrifying. You have to capture the reader instantly, and there is so much exposition and description that has to be wound into the narrative, so it can rapidly uncoil in the reader's mind.

I have to make sure that the new beginning is in the voice of the novel. Each piece of work has its own voice. If that voice is strong and I can hear it then I can easily return and confidently revise after interruptions. If the voice isn't clear, then I don't have a piece of writing, and there's no point in revising.

I rarely refer to the notes I make about a work in process during the writing.

I have been working on the novel in my head, but I am being drawn into the drafting by a force like gravity.

Chapter one just took off, and I'm running after it as fast as I can.

I was outside the novel and then, by writing, I was inside it. I have no longer any conscious consideration of technical matters. The novel has begun to tell me what to do.

Children erase, make brushing movements as if to make the paper crisp and clean. Sometimes they need to recopy, just to see it lined up, or just to simulate what final copy might be like. Unfortunately, too many children are intolerant of cross-outs and manipulations needed to make the text 'messy in order to make it clear' (Calkins, 1980)

Six-year-olds are not terrified in the least. But with each passing year, as a sense of options, or fear of failure, or growing sense of audience appears, the terror of the blank page becomes more real. This fear occurs with the best of teaching. Imagine the terror of the blank page when the teacher is punitive!

I waited patiently, and now the story is working. I have three pages of draft without consciously selecting from the dozens of strategic choices in my journal and in my head.

Three pages in 35 minutes. I'm itching to start the next novel. The better one piece of writing is going, the more insistently the other pieces demand writing. There is an explosion of possibility. I want to do poems, stories, articles, plays – to prune, to paint.

When children receive more time for writing, and on a regular basis, they learn to wait more effectively. When children wait, they may conference with the teacher, or with other children, or just sit and read what they have already written. This gives distance to the text and greatly aids the act of revision.

And waiting is the prelude to the creative burst. It is rare, whether the writer be child or professional, that the *high quality burst* is not preceded by effective listening and waiting. Such activity has great carry-over to other curricular areas, simply because the child is in touch with himself or herself as a learner. Listening does that.

As educators, I think we have to ask ourselves if we provide such high-quality listening time for children with our over-inflated curricula and time slots that must be filled.

Regular writing helps children to put the spelling and mechanical aspects of writing behind them. Only then can children give greater attention to the information. Regular daily writing, with effective challenge and response to the writing, aids the writer to reflect on the craft itself.

I am aware, when I am writing as fast as I was this morning, that I am weaving threads, but I am not conscious of picking up the threads and using them any more than an experienced weaver is conscious of the learned act of weaving. I simply sense the need for action, referring back to a previous action, for setting up the beginning of a new pattern, of drawing together, knotting, loosening up, busy, busy, busy, at my clattering loom, but not thinking. Doing. That's the best thing about craft, you can get beyond thinking.

Is it the vocation of the artist to cele-
brate life by showing the moments of
order within disorder? The greater
the art, the more temporary these
orders? Or the more the artist makes
us aware of the forces threatening the
temporary order, the more moving
the work?

It is one of those rare mornings when
the desk is clear, my tools are at
hand, Mozart is on the radio, and
the autumn sun pours through the
yellow, baring trees. I feel happy —
and I have a slight headache, a bit of
cramp in the bowels, fear that the
work will not go — or go well. But
the timer is on. I must type up what
is written to get to the point where I
can weld the new beginning to the
previous draft.

The draft is rolling. It is developing,
increasing, growing full with additional information, revelations, connections. I follow it as it speaks, and
then when it is really going well, I am
compelled to step back, to go to the
john, heat another cup of coffee, put
a record on the phonograph, stand
back, get distance, see if it is really
going as well as I thought.

Murray mentions that he is *compelled*
to step back from his writing. During
the high point of an episode, I have
seen children get up to sharpen pen-
cils, wander around the room (where
permitted) or talk to another child.
This is particularly true if the child
is trying something new, a logical
transition not tried before, or a new
description. The intensity of engagement actually demands disengage-
ment.

I am happiest when making imaginary
worlds; I am still the only child whose
playmates live in the walls.

This writing must be like skiing
Tuckerman, hurtling down, almost
out of control, the skis not quite
touching the snow, faster, faster.

If I type my own draft a hundred
times, I would write a hundred different novels, for this imagined world
is so real and has so many dimensions
it can be seen a hundred different

ways.

Fitting, joining, cutting, shaping, smoothing – the busy cabinetmaker in his shop.

Is there enough? Too much? Again and again, line by line, paragraph by paragraph, page by page, I must ask these same questions. And answering them by writing, ask them again of the new lines.

'How long should it be? Are there pages enough?' The concept, 'It is good if it is long', begins at age 6 and continues on through advanced doctoral degrees. Small wonder that the idea of cutting rarely enters into the teaching of writing. Through effective questions, teachers can elicit information needed to heighten one section and thereby make other sections seem unnecessary. Such questions as, 'Tell me in one sentence what this is about', can be a help with cutting.

It is easy to move chunks of writing around, or to fit new chunks in. There is never one way, but many ways.

The use of carets, wide margins, scissors and paste, for reorganising an early draft is useful for young writers. With daily writing and good teacher conferences, there is a cluster of 8-year-olds who are ready for this kind of activity. Too many children see writing, particularly their own, as fixed, immovable. They need to see how it can be moved around and with profit. If teachers model these tools of reorganisation with their own writing, children can see how the space–time issues of writing are solved in revision. We can live a lifetime and never see craftspersons revising their work.

Reading your own prose is an act of faith. It takes courage to leave in, not to cut, not to change.

I am suspicious when it works the way I want it to work.

Writing without thought. Just writing. Not thinking about writing and then writing, but writing/thinking, writing that is thought.

There comes a time when you have to admit that the work can't be perfect. It will never match the vision.

Teachers who sense that an impossible road of perfection is defeating a writer, need to help the writer to end the selection. They can even model an ending to their own writing. 'It isn't perfect. I *feel* it isn't where I want it to be, but I am going to end the piece just the same.' Children *need to see their teachers write*, not to copy but to sense their involvement in the task of writing.

Put something in on one side of the draft and something pops out on the other.

(From a letter I wrote to another writer . . .) 'I've gotten the first draft of the first chapter of the novel revised and typed and moved ahead to those dreadful, awful, terrible chapters immediately after the first chapter (the first third of the novel). I knew that they would read like shit, but I knew that if I could grit my teeth I could face them and fight my way through. I sailed through them in a matter of hours, and I saw that the piece of writing had demanded the new beginning I thought so radical. To put it differently, I thought I would have to make a lot of changes to justify the new beginning. In fact, the "changes" were made before the new beginning.'

When the beginning is right the rest follows, and more quickly. As young writers develop, they learn to make decisions about the content of their writing at an earlier time. For example, some children do effective decision-making at the point of topic choice. One topic is chosen, two excluded. Indeed, this can be an effective movement of revision. Then there are those who will try three to five leads. The more advanced the writer, the more they realise the importance of early decisions.

It took me from spring to autumn to create the new beginning of the novel. To put it differently, it took me months to hear what the novel had to tell me about its story. If I had listened to the draft it would have told me how to begin the novel. It did tell me. When I found the right beginning there were no major changes to be made in the text. The novel was waiting to be begun that way.

I am completely within the text. I

start to add a sentence, and it is already there, written last January, just the way I would write it now. It must be the right sentence.

I wonder if extensive rewriting is not mostly a failure of prewriting, or allowing adequate time for rehearsal, a matter of plucking the fruit before it is ripe.

But you have to bite the fruit to know it is really ripe.

Much of the reordering in the text is making sure that the most important material is at the point of emphasis in the paragraph, in the sentence, in the scene. Where are the points of emphasis? At the end and at the beginning. The important information must be those points.

This is the same location of attention with the young writers — beginnings and endings. For the young writers this is the easiest location to help them with revision.

It's so hard to go back and face your copy. It is a mirror. It does not show the person you hoped to be but the person you are.

This page explodes with possibility. I must control it. I see a thousand stories at once, each superimposed on the other.

Children who find that their selection is about two or three subjects, not one, should not be dismayed. When they keep a list of future topics, or collections of discarded material cut out of other drafts, they already have a start on another selection. No extra writing is ever wasted. They are merely shards of rehearsal for another selection.

I hear myself say in my head what I read on the page seconds later.

The biggest problem in revising this morning is my itchy nose. I must be allergic to my own prose.

I have to keep stepping back, read a few pages of something else, keep my distance, or I'll be drawn into the

Students need help with the process of gaining distance. Teachers help through the writing conference. 'What story.

Sometimes I am drawn into my story. This is the reality, and I look back at the writer, at the desk, wondering who he is, why is he bent over, his nose almost touching his knuckles, making marks on paper, muttering to himself.

The story makes jagged unexpected moves. I laugh in surprise and chase after it.

After revising, I am much more observant when I walk to school, noticing the way women stalk in boots, how the three North African students gesture to each other. I see a man turn from a woman and I make up reasons, whole movies in my mind.

In revision, we are constantly adjusting distance, the distance between writer and experience, writer and meaning, writer and the writing, writer and reader, language and subject, text and reader.

I have only one reader while I am revising – myself. I am trying to make this page come clear. That's all.

did you have in mind here? Underline the one line that says more than any other what this selection is about.'

Stand back and watch an entire group of children in the process of writing. Some compose with their noses *on* the paper; others put their cheeks on the paper and look across at their pens writing; others squirm and jump in their chairs, place knees on the desk, whereas others lean far back, almost to the point of retreat.

Children do extensive reading when they reread and revise their own texts. Just how much reading is involved in the writing process is just beginning to dawn on our research team. Large amounts of time have been taken from formal reading instruction and given over to time for writing in rooms where the study is being conducted. Surprisingly, reading scores did not go down; they went up . . . and significantly. Since writing is the *making of reading*, children may decode for ideas differently than if they had never written at all.

The writer has a split brain – creator and critic – or competing forces – freedom and discipline.

There is no right or wrong, just what works within this situation.

Or, as one teacher in Scotland told me, 'I don't speak of the paper as right or wrong. It is only finished or unfinished. That's the way it is with art.'

Every change in the text affects the text fore and aft, sets off a chain reaction of new meanings.

At about the age of 8, with effective conferences, there is a growing group of advanced writers who recognise the effect that one change can have on an entire selection. Recognising the relationship of parts and wholes is an important developmental phenomenon.

The mad weaver keeps dozens of threads in his mind, weaving so hard he is only rarely aware of the weaving, and worried when he becomes aware of it. His weaving should appear natural, not contrived. He contrives to be natural.

How do you know what works? By the satisfying sound it makes when it clicks into place.

Why is it so hard to get working when it is so good to be lost within the experience, to lose all sense of time until there is a sudden coming to, and I stretch. My legs, arms, back, are stiff, as if I had been asleep or in a trance.

I think I have made no changes within a page, but I count 213 words put in and taken out.

What do I do when I revise? I read to add what is needed to be there, cut what isn't needed, reorder what must be moved.

Without knowing it, Murray has just listed the developmental order in which children learn to revise: (1) add material, (2) cut, (3) reorder.

I hear my writing as loud as if I speak it. Sometimes I do speak it. The final

How does it sound? Does it sound exciting, beautiful, funny? Children test is always, 'How does it sound?'

Yesterday I read some of the novel in Becky's class. It is helpful to read before an audience. I heard Frank's voice in my voice, clearer than I had ever heard it when I wrote it.

Each day I learn to write. No, each day I learn to see. If I can see clearly the writing will be easy.

Revision, or perhaps rehearsal for revision, goes on all the time — while I am in the car, walking to class, waiting for a meeting to start, eating, going to sleep, watching television. I constantly revise in my head, fitting things together to see if they work. I am convinced that what I know of this activity is only a small proportion of what goes on while I am awake and while I am asleep. My head is constantly writing.

The satisfaction of rearranging words is a physical satisfaction. Once you have the order right, you can thump a sentence the way a trucker thumps tires. The sentence will give off a satisfying sound.

The quality of the writing often comes from detail.

strive to put the sounds of speech back into their writing through prosodic markers (darkened letters, capitals for points of emphasis), the use of exclamation points, over-use of interjections, or conversation. Children are bothered by the silence of their words on the page. They like 'noisy' pages.

Rehearsal is an important act for all writers. Children are no exception. Rehearsal begins with drawing (when children need to *see* what they mean) just prior to the act of writing. Gradually, children rehearse farther from the actual act of writing. Or, the first draft becomes a rehearsal for the second. Rehearsals become more frequent and tentative. Daily writing leads to an increase in effective rehearsal. The most difficult writing of all, is that writing where rehearsal begins simultaneously to the assignment. When children write infrequently, this is precisely what happens, and is one of the major reasons why writing is the hated act. Indeed, unfamiliarity breeds contempt.

The piece of writing detaches itself from the writer. The writer can look at it as if it were a stranger — the daughter who comes to visit with a new husband. She — and the draft — is familiar and strange at the same time.

I like to revise by hand so that I can enter into the text the way a surgeon plunges his hands down into a body and messes around.

I hear the words as I use them. Revising is an act of talking to myself. I sound out the words, testing them by my ear, listening to how they sound in relation to each other.

Revision requires a special kind of reading. The reader/writer must keep all strands of the past writing in mind, and yet maintain a vision of what *may* come, of what is coming clear through the writing.

This is the same person who changes one sentence, yet sees the effect on the whole. But this person has a different pace, is a student of listening to the text. The teacher provides for this stance through a much slower pace for written selections as well as listening-type questions in the writing conference. Teachers who provide a slower pace do not lower demands or expectations. Actually, it is a much higher level of demand because the student must learn to listen to his/her voice rather than that of the teacher.

Writing is a puzzle with no one solution. There are always many right solutions. Any one you choose sets up new puzzles.

There is no such thing as free writing. The work takes over and establishes its own discipline. The piece of writing has momentum, energy — a river in flood. Learning to be a writer is learning to go with the flood.

The work can take over when the teacher consciously works for students to find their own voices and to be responsive to the effect of voice on information. Students must teach teachers about their subjects, whether it be grade one or a dissertation.

I knead language, pound it, stretch it, shape it, work it; I am up to my elbows in language.

Reading what isn't – yet – on the page is a special skill only distantly related to reading what is printed on the page.

Revising is, in part, a matter of making up reasons for what worked by accident, or at least what wasn't made consciously. It is the rational end of an irrational process. The intent often comes after the act.

The intent can come later if audience is not introduced too soon into the writing process. Too much store is put in knowing an audience before the writer begins. It may be that intent and audience are both discovered in the later stages of revision. To be responsive to oneself, my own voice, the information before me, demands the suspension of both intent and audience.

The surprise during writing of reading what you have written. You thought you knew what you were going to write, you thought you knew what you were writing, now you find out what you have written.

Reference

Calkins, L. (1980) 'Children Learn the Writer's Craft', *Language Arts*, 57, 567-3

9 ANALYSING STRUCTURE IN CHILDREN'S FICTIONAL NARRATIVES

Barry M. Kroll and Chris M. Anson

Interviewer: When you're writing a story, what things do you have to do to make it a good story?

Matthew: (9 years old) Well, this is the order we'd probably do it in: first of all we do it, how he begins, and then we go into the stage of what's the story about, and then we go into his adventures – if he has some – and then we go into the end. It's four parts.

The simplest story must have at least four propositions, representing a setting, beginning, development, and ending, if it is to be considered a story. (Jean M. Mandler and Nancy S. Johnson, cognitive psychologists)

Nine-year-old Matthew has a clear sense of the parts of a narrative, and he is able to articulate his four-part plan for a good story. Mandler and Johnson (1977) also propose that well-formed stories have four parts. In their work on comprehension and memory, these psychologists and others have proposed that individuals acquire a set of expectations about the structure of stories and that these expectations – or story schemata – guide both comprehension and recall. In order to find out what these idealised story schemata are like, psychologists have analysed folktales, myths and legends which stem from an oral tradition – on the assumption that these kinds of tales usually conform to an ideal (or 'canonical') story form – parsing these stories into units which have structural importance. The rules for parsing, or the 'story grammar', make it possible to represent narrative structure as a tree diagram. Because our major concern is with stories written by children, rather than with folktales, our interest in the story grammar focuses on its utility as a formal device for analysing the structure of children's written narratives. More specifically, we want to report on our efforts to use a story grammar to analyse a set of stories written by Matthew's peers, a group of 54 9-year-old schoolchildren from Bristol (England).

A word needs to be said about these children and the conditions under which they wrote their stories. The stories were collected under the auspices of the Bristol Longitudinal Language Development Pro-gramme (Wells, 1979), as part of a study of the writing attainment of children who had been participants in the longitudinal study, and who had also been selected for a detailed study of the acquisition of literacy during their first two years of schooling. A primary aim of the writing study was to examine relationships between such antecedent factors as early linguistic development, parental provisions for literacy, reading attainment in infant school, etc. and writing ability at age 9 (Kroll, Kroll and Wells, 1980). In addition to the 18 children from the longitudinal study (a group made up of children from deliberately diverse back-grounds and expected levels of educational attainment), a larger and more homogeneous group of children was needed to serve as a com-parison group of 'typical' 9-year-old writers. Hence, teachers in the fourteen junior schools which the 18 children attended were asked to select 4 additional children who were 'average to good' writers, but definitely not markedly weak or superior writers. Stories from the 54 children nominated by the teachers as 'typical writers' (and who com-pleted the narrative task) constitute the group of narratives that will be the focus for our consideration in this chapter.

The stories we will be discussing were elicited in the following man-ner. Each class teacher gave all the pupils in his or her class a cartoon-like picture of a hunter and his dog, both of whom were surrounded by a group of angry-looking animals (see Figure 9.1). Along the side of the picture which the children received was a list of all the names of the animals (giraffe, elephant, etc.), provided as an aid for spelling. In pre-paration for writing, the teacher led a discussion, following specific guide-lines, in which the children identified and described what was in the pic-ture. When the picture itself had been explored, the teacher asked each pupil to write a story to go along with the picture, a story that another child would like to read. In previous work on these stories, Kroll (in press) used a 'holistic' assessment procedure in which three raters assigned each story to one of six categories, ranging from poor to superior in overall quality. In addition to such ratings, however, a more detailed examination of specific aspects of children's narratives was planned.

Our aim in this chapter, therefore, is to consider more thoroughly the prospects and problems of analysing narrative structure in children's writing. While our thinking about children's narratives has been influ-enced by developmental studies of the structural complexity of stories told by young children (e.g. Applebee, 1978; Botvin and Sutton-Smith, 1977), even more influential have been those studies using 'story gram-mars' to represent the structure of simple narratives.

Figure 9.1: Bristol Longitudinal Language Development Programme: Subject for Children's Stories

Story Structure and Story Grammars

Recent story grammars have evolved from the two related fields of cognitive psychology and artificial intelligence. Although, as van Dijk (1980) points out, the methods and goals of these two branches of cognitive science are different, they are both interested in how language is understood, especially as it is organised in certain kinds of discourse. Story grammars, which represent a subset of the methods used in discourse analysis, show schematically the constituent structure of brief stories. In the terminology of one story grammar (Mandler's and Johnson's, 1977), the simplest complete story consists of a *setting* and an *event structure*, with the latter consisting of a single *episode*, with *beginning* causing a *development* causing an *ending*. Schematically, a simple story would appear as in Figure 9.2.

Figure 9.2: Mandler and Johnson's Story Grammar

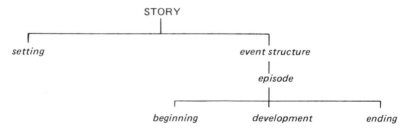

As Mandler and Johnson point out, the

> essential structure of a single episode story is that a protagonist is introduced in the setting; there follows an episode in which something happens, causing the protagonist to respond to it, which in turn brings about some event or state of affairs that ends the episode. The simplest story must have at least four propositions, representing a setting, beginning, development, and ending, if it is to be considered a story. (p. 119)

Many stories, of course, have more propositions.

Typically, researchers using story grammars have been interested in discovering what aspects of stories are remembered over time and what this can tell us about comprehension. Carefully chosen or designed stories are presented to subjects and comprehension is later measured by recall tasks. The conclusions of these studies are mixed, but suggest generally that a reader's 'story schema' (an idealised internal representation of the parts of a typical story and the relationships among those parts) facilitates story comprehension. In addition, memory for the details of stories tends to fade over time, but the gist or theme of the story remains. Inferred information consistent with the original story structure is then added to replace what is lost. Other conclusions describe a 'levels effect', which predicts that information high in the story structure will usually correspond to information in story summaries or recalls (Mandler and Johnson, 1977; Rumelhart, 1975, 1977; Stein and Glenn, 1979; Thorndyke, 1977).

The research using story grammars indicates that children acquire — through exposure to many stories — internalised expectations about story structure which guide their understanding and remembering of narratives. It seems plausible that these internalised story schemata would also guide children's production of stories. As Stein and Glenn (1979) suggest, one can assume 'that the structures that influence the comprehension of stories also influence the spontaneous generation of stories' (p. 118). This seems to be the case, for even a good many beginning writers can compose stories which reveal a basic sense of narrative, in that the stories have settings, characters, actions and outcomes (Gundlach, 1981; King and Rentel, 1981; Temple, Nathan and Burris, 1982). On the other hand, in their own stories children often omit details, focus on overt actions rather than internal responses and goals, and fail to relate story events in the logical way that episodes fit together in the prototypical narratives used in research on story comprehension.

Nevertheless, story grammars seem to have considerable potential as formal procedures for describing the completeness and complexity of children's written narratives. For example, in our informal reading of the 54 stories from the Bristol children, we noticed that the stories gave varying emphases to 'preparatory events' or descriptions setting the scene to the story, as well as to central episodes in the plot and to the results of characters' interactions. Some children chose to arrange their stories in such a way that the scene depicted in the cartoon appeared late in the plot, often as the climactic outcome of the hunter's attempt to stalk and kill the animals. In other stories, the cartoon became part of a single episode in a series of loosely structured events, and was not crucial to the plot and its outcome. Although we could describe these differences informally, we needed a formal procedure that could show simply and graphically how the stories were structured — a procedure that could be applied in the same way across the whole group of narratives. Because in many ways they meet these demands, story grammars seemed to us potentially useful for analysing the Bristol children's stories. In particular, we were interested in whether the story-grammar analysis would be useful (1) for providing generalisations about structural patterns in children's narratives, (2) for describing individual writers' stories, especially for pointing to flaws in narrative structure, and (3) for relating various types of structural organisation to the overall quality of children's stories.

Preliminary Analyses

Before applying the story grammar to our narratives, we eliminated a number of stories from consideration. Some stories (9 of the 54) did not make full use of the scene depicted in the stimulus picture. We called these 'associational' stories because they had a loose, associational link with some aspect of the picture: tales about hunters and hunting, tales set in Africa, or tales about animals — but none of which included the particular dilemma presented in the cartoon. The following story illustrates one of these tales.

> Once upon a time there lived a giraffe a snake an elephant some birds and monkeys a lion and some tortoieses and one rhinoceros they all lived in a jungle. One day the monkeys said they would go and get some food. So they went on there way to get some food as they walked on they thought they a rustle in a tree. So they started to climb the tree then they saw a man so they killed the man and carred him home they had him for supper and they all said it was good and they had seconds. Then they watched telly and then they went to bed.

We did not consider these stories further because their writers had avoided one of the central conceptual problems of our task: the problem of incorporating the depicted scene into the story line. The task required the writer to integrate the cartoon picture into a series of events without departing too much from its actual details, and to move beyond the cartoon by resolving the hunter's predicament, making this resolution plausible given the details in the picture.

We also eliminated from consideration those few stories (5) which were written in the first person. While several of these were complete and well written, it seemed prudent to restrict our structural analyses to stories which were all third-person narratives.

Another group of 'stories' (8) were not narratives at all, but rather descriptions of the details of the stimulus picture. Although some children began with formulaic narrative openings ('One day . . .' 'Once upon a time . . .'), they quickly became entangled in cataloguing the animals or describing the hunter, dog and situation. The following piece illustrates this predominant concern for describing rather than story-telling.

> This picture is a cartoon of a giraffe snake and a elephant and some birds and a monkey and a rhinoceros and a lion and some tortoises. There is a man whistling and he is steping over a dog and his foot is slipping down the cliff and he is hiding a gun by his back and there is a worm hanging out of the ground the man is frightened because he is being chased by animals.

On the most general level, story grammars specify that a narrative consists of at least one episode with beginning, development and ending. Seven of our stories did not meet this criterion for a complete narrative, usually because they lacked resolutions. While the number of incomplete narratives was small, there seemed to be several patterns to these unresolved stories. In one pattern, the writer provides a background and some events (usually brief) leading up to the scene in the picture, but then becomes so caught up in describing the picture that he remains centred on description. These incomplete narratives are a hybrid of description and narration. In a second pattern, the writer begins with background information but gets so involved in developing the character of the hunter that he never gets around to resolving the dilemma presented in the picture. In a third, related pattern, the writer becomes entangled in preceding events, dwelling on the details of these events (e.g. scheming among the animals) to such an extent that the central conflict remains unresolved. The simplest explanation for all of these unresolved narratives is that the writers did not have sufficient time to finish their work. While time constraints might account for some unfinished work, the conditions for writing were such that children were given as much time as they needed to produce their stories. A more plausible explanation, therefore, is that some children failed to plan what they were going to write, expending too much energy and time on a background for the story and then losing interest or becoming distracted when approaching the resolution. But some children seemed not to know *how* to end the story, using such devices as exclaiming about the hunter's state ('What a position'), giving a personal response ('I would jump off') or claiming ignorance of the outcome ('That's all

I know'). Below is an example of an incomplete narrative that begins as
a story but ends as a description.

> Once there was a man who liked to go hunting. One day the man
> dicided that he would go hunting in the jungle so he got a gun and
> took his dog with him. When he got into the jungle he was sur-
> rounded by feaus animals. There were three monkeys, one lion, one
> elephant, two birds, one giraffe, one rhinoceros, and two tortoises
> and a little worm. The man was whiling and he was nearly falling off
> a clift, with his dog hanging onto his foot.

Having eliminated associational and first-person stories, descriptions,
and incomplete narratives, we were left with 25 complete third-person
narratives which incorporated the scene in the cartoon into the story
line. These stories involved a problem or goal that motivates the characters' actions and gives the story its aura of conflict and resolution. In
this sense, they contain narrative structures rather than simple action
sequences (van Dijk, 1980); like fairy tales, they are about events and
actions which interfere with normal or expected events and actions, and
give rise to goals, complications and outcomes. By focusing on these
stories, we felt we could best assess the utility of the story grammar for
revealing structural features of children's narratives.

Initially, several story grammars appealed to us as ways to represent
the structures of the Bristol children's narratives. After analysing a few
stories using different grammars, however, we chose Mandler's and
Johnson's (1977) system for more detailed study. Stein's and Glenn's
grammar, like other 'finite state' grammars, is unable to handle self-
embedded stories (Black and Bower, 1980; Black and Wilensky, 1980).
Thorndyke's (1977) grammar allows the optional embedding of episodes, but has difficulty with stories in which the characters are relatively goal-less. Because many of the Bristol stories contained embedded
episodes or goal-less interactions, we rejected both these grammars as
candidates for our study. Rumelhart's (1975, 1977) pioneering work
seemed to us very useful, but since Mandler's and Johnson's version
refines some of Rumelhart's original insights, we found it the most
suitable for our purposes. (After nearly completing our analyses using
Mandler's and Johnson's 1977 grammar, we discovered the revised
version of that grammar in Johnson and Mandler (1980). The new
version consists of rewrite rules for the base structure of stories – rules
slightly modified from the 1977 version – and transformational rules
governing deletion and goal movement. We decided to continue to use

the 1977 grammar, in part because it was working fairly well for our purpose of parsing children's stories into major structural units, and in part because re-analysis of several stories using the revised grammar, while changing some terminology and altering slightly a few diagrams, did not contribute any major new insights into the structure of our children's stories. Work on story grammars continues, and there will undoubtedly be further refinements in the near future. From our perspective, these refinements are of greatest interest when they provide more adequate ways to appreciate structural features of children's narratives.)

The most important aspect of Mandler's and Johnson's grammar for story analysis is its delineation of an event structure based upon the characters' actions, reactions, goals and goal-reaching attempts. Essentially, the grammar is a series of 'rewrite rules' for stories and their constituents. As mentioned previously, a story consists of a *setting* and an *event structure*. The event structure contains one or more *episodes*. Each episode is made up of a *beginning*, *development* and *ending*. The development section can be of two principal types: (1) a *simple reaction* to the beginning on the part of the protagonist, usually in the form of an internal response or emotional state, which then causes an *action* or overt response; or (2) a *complex reaction* consisting of a *simple reaction* and a *goal* and appearing with a *goal path*. The goal path involves an *attempt* and the *outcome* of this attempt. The lowest statements in the grammatical hierarchy are either *states* or *events* according to whether they involve static or active descriptions. Also important are three 'between element' notations — *and*, *then* and *cause* (represented in the tree diagrams (Figures 9.3 – 9.9) as A, T and C respectively) — which indicate how the story constituents are related to each other.

Andrew's story below illustrates the grammar's various parts. First the story is broken down into numbered statements, units of text that express a state or event. (While Mandler and Johnson call these units 'propositions', we prefer to use the term 'statements', both to indicate that we are dealing with a surface-structure representation of the stories, and to avoid confusion with a different use of the term 'proposition' as developed by Kintsch and van Dijk, 1978.) The statements then appear linearly in the structural diagram, which also expresses the relationships between constituents. In our notation we have, for simplicity, omitted the terminal categories *event* and *state*, inserting statement numbers directly below the basic nodes to which they are attached (following the simplified notation in Mandler and Johnson (1977), p. 137).

Figure 9.3: Story-grammar Analysis: Andrew

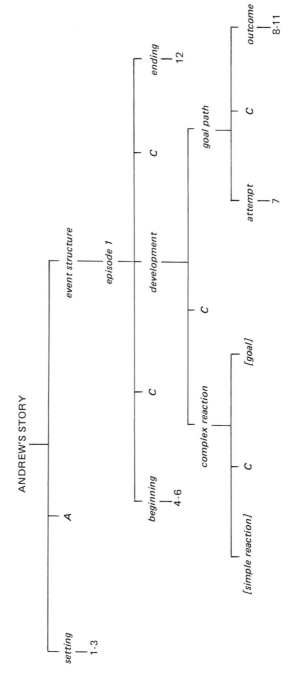

Andrew's Story
(1) One day Cedric Scrooge went to Zoomba Land
(2) where he lived
(3) his wife was Caboom Scrooge.
(4) When he got to his village, Zoombahdan the village was flat.
(5) One boy was left
(6) his son Zoobangdabong said that a tribe of electronic elephants attacked the village.
(7) So the hauter tracked down the elephants
(8) he was at the edge of the cliff
(9) when a herd of animals came out of the Jungle
(10) and he fell off the edge
(11) and land in sinking mud
(12) and Zoombahdan was not the same with out Cedric Scrooge.

This brief story contains the basic parts of a narrative as defined by the grammar: a *setting* and a single *episode*. Figure 9.3 shows all of the elements which should be present when a story conforms to the ideal structure specified by the grammar; elements missing from the story are placed in parentheses. Thus, we can see from Figure 9.3 that Cedric Scrooge's internal response is left unspecified (there are parentheses around the *simple reaction*), and that his *goal* (killing the elephants for revenge) is also unstated, although it is strongly implied in Statement 7 by his action of tracking down the elephants. When the protagonist's reactions can be inferred, a writer may choose not to state them explicitly in the story. As Mandler and Johnson comment, the

> surface structure of stories frequently omits both simple and complex reactions, leaving it to the listener to infer their nature from the surrounding context. That is, some reaction, either simple or complex, is assumed to exist in the underlying structure, although a well-formed story may allow its deletion. (p. 121)

However, as we will see in other example stories, consistent omission of the protagonist's reactions often results in weak characterisation and an underdeveloped plot.

Generalisations About Structural Patterns

One of our interests in applying the story grammar to our narratives was to see whether structural analyses revealed any general patterns of organisation among our stories. As will be clear from the following analyses, the process of diagramming children's stories is often fraught with decisions which are subjective to some extent. The more illogically arranged a story is, the more difficult it becomes to divide it into its structural constituents. However, most of the decisions we had to make in cases when a story element could be classified in either of two ways did not end up creating significantly different diagrams. Since we were mainly looking for general patterns and not minute details of story structure, such problems in applying the grammar did not trouble us a great deal.

Three main structural patterns appeared among the stories we studied. In the first type, the writer strings events together in a linear fashion, one after the other, with little causal connection between them. The result is a story in which each episode stands by itself in the plot. Because the characters' actions within a given episode do not cause new episodes, the resulting diagram is horizontal, as Justine's story illustrates.

(1) Once a man called Bruce.
(2) He was a hunter.
(3) He wore a blue jumper and black and white socks with grey trousers.
(4) On his head the hunter had a cap
(5) and he wore glasses.
(6) On particular day he decided he would go and find a freind.
(7) So he left the tree which he was sitting in
(8) and set off.
(9) He soon met a few brown monkeys.
(10) And a lion, a girraffe, a rhinoceros, and an elephant.
(11) But when ever he tried to talk to them
(12) they all hurried off.
(13) Once he saw a snake
(14) (he didn't want to make friends with him)
(15) So he ran off.
(16) The next day he was out walking
(17) when he saw all the animals he had seen the day before.
(18) They were all looking at him fiercely.
(19) He was so frightened
(20) that he walked back-wards whistling.
(21) As a result he fell over the edge
(22) and got hurt badly when he reached the bottom.

Figure 9.4: Story-grammar Analysis: Justine

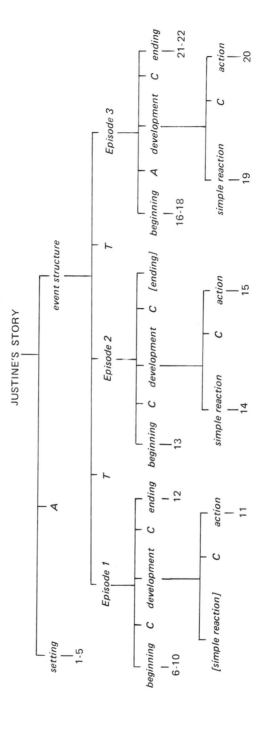

The episodes in Justine's story are all tied to Bruce's search for a friend. Bruce has three encounters with animals: in the first, the animals run away; in the second, Bruce rejects the thought of having a snake for a friend; in the third, the animals threaten Bruce and force him off the cliff. In our analysis the story has three separate episodes corresponding to these encounters, episodes which are linked sequentially but not causally, and which thus appear as isolated events strung together by *then*-relations. This analysis hinges, however, on our interpretation of the story. For example, an interpretive judgement is necessary in order to represent Statement 13, 'Once he saw a snake'. Is this encounter with the snake a continuation of the first day's adventure (in which case, *Episode 2* would be embedded in the ending of *Episode 1*)? We thought not. Our reading of the story emphasised the theme, typical in children's stories, of a search for friendship, a search involving the difficulties of rejection, revulsion and hostility. We therefore viewed Statement 13 as the beginning of a new episode exploring a new facet of this theme. Thus, decisions about structural representations could not, we found, always be made without consulting our intuitive judgements about the meaning of a story.

In the second type of story events are connected to each other by embedding. The *outcome* of an attempted *goal*, for instance, will lead to a new episode or series of episodes. Stories in this category began with a single episode which then developed into further episodes, but the tendency was to embed rather than to link them sequentially. James's story illustrates this pattern:

(1) One day a Jungle hunter called Doctor Jack was camping in the East-african Jungle.
(2) When he got up
(3) he decided to go elephant hunting
(4) so he got his gun
(5) and set off.
(6) He had'nt gone very far
(7) when he spotted an elephant
(8) (he did'nt no that this elephant was King of all the animals in the Jungle)
(9) so he aimed his gun
(10) and shot the elephant
(11) the smallest monkey had been watching this
(12) so the monkey went back to tell all the animals.
(13) The hunter had taken the tusks to his tent with the help of his

super dog fred.
(14) Then they started to walk to the cliff
(15) the animals had been following the hunter
(16) they followed him to the cliff.
(17) Then they started to charge at him
(18) until he was all most off the cliff
(19) then an earthquake came
(20) and freds tail started to wagle
(21) the earthquake shuke them both off the cliff.

Figure 9.5: Story-grammar Analysis: James

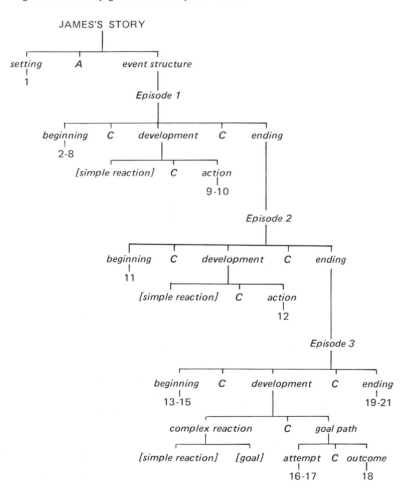

Unlike the episodes in Justine's story, those in James's story build a plot in which one action leads into or causes another. There are three main episodes in James's story: in the first a hunter shoots an elephant; this leads directly to a second episode, in which a monkey reports the incident to the other animals; in the last episode the animals respond to the report by hunting down the hunter. While James's story illustrates well a narrative with embedded episodes, the story presented us with some difficulties of analysis. A major problem is what to do with Statements 13 and 14. In the surface structure of the story, these statements come between *Episodes 2* and *3* — between the monkey's report and the animals' quest for the hunter. Semantically, however, the statements belong, at least partly, to *Episode 1*, since they conclude the episode of shooting the elephant. On the other hand, the beginning of the walk to the cliff does set the scene for the animals to follow the hunter in *Episode 3*. Moreover, the monkey's involvement (Statement 11) is most effective when it follows directly from the shooting (Statement 10), so that we cannot fault the writer for not placing Statements 13-14 after Statement 10. In the end, therefore, we decided to include the statements as part of the *beginning* of *Episode 3*.

The diagram of this story points quite clearly to the lack of internal (psychological) reactions and explicitly stated goals (note the consistently empty nodes in *complex* and *simple reactions*). James's story would be considerably more effective were he to include the characters' feelings, responses and plans. Thus, the grammar shows us an area where the story could use some further development. The ending of the story also needs reconsideration. The earthquake which ends the tale is not causally related to any events in the story. Its presence may have come from the writer's desire to include some explanation for the dog's wagging tail, a detail which James accounts for in a way unrelated to the dog's emotions.

Stories in the third group combined structural features of the first two groups: that is, they had linearly arranged episodes, one or more of which contained some further embedded episodes complicating the plot. (Since this pattern is a combination of the two already illustrated, we will not examine it in any detail.) Stories with this mixed linear-embedded pattern tended to be longer and more detailed than the others, although this was certainly not true in all cases.

Given the amount of intuition and interpretation involved in our application of the grammar, we want to be very tentative about our findings. Nevertheless, it is interesting to note the proportions of stories conforming to the three structural types, as long as these proportions are regarded as approximate rather than exact. Ten of the 25 narratives were structured in a linear, episodic fashion. (Included in this category are several stories with only a single episode, which may not in itself suggest structural linearity. But because the stories lacked the kinds of causal links expressed in the other structural types, we placed them in this first category.) Nine stories were structured around embedded episodes, and 6 of the stories had a mixed linear-embedded pattern.

In addition to noting the occurrence of three principal structural patterns in the narratives, we examined the proportion of the two permissible development types: (1) *simple reaction* followed by *action*, or (2) *complex reaction* leading to *goal* and *outcome*. In the first type of development, for instance, the animals may frighten the hunter (*simple reaction* in the form of an *internal event*) so that he runs to the cliff (*action*). In the second type of development the animals may become angered by the hunter (*simple reaction*), so they plan to attack him (*goal*). In their *attempt* they drive him to the cliff edge, whereupon the *outcome* may end the story (the hunter falls off and dies), or it may lead to a further *episode*. This further *episode* may be embedded in the previous episode (in the *outcome* the hunter yells for help, which then becomes the *beginning* of the new episode) or it may stand on its own (the hunter escapes, and the story continues with a new episode).

Results of our analysis showed that, in general, the narratives contained more Type-1 developments (simple reactions followed by actions) than Type-2 developments (complex reactions leading to goals and goal paths). This finding is consonant with the observations of other researchers that children tend to focus on overt actions in their stories, leaving out the internal responses and psychological dimensions of central characters, and particularly omitting the protagonist's goals (Temple, Nathan and Burris, 1982). Indeed, we found that structural complexity tended to be related to the complexity of the motivations, reactions and goals of a story's characters. The deeper these qualities of characterisation become, the greater is the need to structure the story in a complex way. However, this tendency did not hold true for all the stories. For example, one particular story begins with a psychological description of the man in the cartoon (he is jealous of his father, a famous game hunter), yet this initial characterisation does not lead to the expected use of complex reactions and goal paths.

In general, then, we found the story grammar useful for describing structural patterns and types of development in the children's narratives. Although the Mandler and Johnson grammar is designed to represent a canonical folktale form, most of the children's stories conformed fairly well to the structures predicated by the grammar. Of the deviations from the grammar, two kinds of 'gaps' showed up from time to time in the children's narratives and deserve some consideration. The first kind occurred when an element was deleted from the surface form of a story, but was inferable given the surrounding context. As we mentioned previously when discussing Andrew's story, in development sections the protagonist's internal response can sometimes be left out but still 'understood' from his subsequent actions, as in the following excerpt from John's story:

(4) Won day gorge had a letter saying Would you like to go to wone of Africas Jungles tomorrow

(5) so gorge phonde up

(6) and said yes

Figure 9.6: Story-grammar Analysis: John

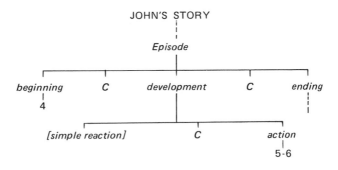

As Mandler and Johnson point out, this kind of omission is usually acceptable — though not always stylistically appealing, as in cases of abrupt or deleted *endings* following the *outcome* of a *goal path*. Additionally, some structural manipulations such as flashbacks, simultaneous actions by two characters, and between-episode retrospections require representations not specified by the grammar (but see Johnson and Mandler, 1980, for a discussion of some transformational rules).

A second kind of 'gap' results from under-development of an episode. In those stories that we called 'incomplete narratives', omissions sometimes created major gaps which would tax the reader's inferential abilities and create frustration or confusion. Such gaps in development were not so severe in our complete narratives. Gary's story illustrates some relatively minor problems arising from under-development.

(1) Once there was a hunter.
(2) His name was the great O'Roin.
(3) One day he was hunting animal's as always.
(4) When he herd the animals having a meeting.
(5) He herd them say this hunting will have to stop
(6) here here they all said.
(7) But when they saw him
(8) they walk toward him
(9) When he all most fell of the cliff
(10) they stopped.
(11) The Lion said you will have to stop hunting
(12) if you do not we will eat you for dinner.
(13) The snake sssed
(14) and the rhino grunted
(15) and the Lion growled.
(16) he tryed to excape
(17) when the Lion aet him up

While some things in this story impressed and amused us (such as the series of animal noises reinforcing the lion's threat in Statements 11-12), the story lacks the kind of structural development that would make it a successful narrative. One problem illustrated by the structural diagram of Gary's story is that the first episode gives us none of the hunter's reactions to the animal's meeting — the first episode is quite undeveloped. A second problem is that Gary does not elaborate the circumstances under which the animals catch sight of the hunter (in Statement 7). We can imagine, for example, a fuller narrative in which the eavesdropping hunter reacts to the animals' discussion, perhaps dropping his gun in fright, leading to his discovery and a chase to the cliff edge. Thus, the grammatical diagram can clearly illustrate gaps in the story's structural development and point to specific events which the writer might consider developing further.

On the whole, acceptable gaps occurred much more often in the full narratives than gaps which weakened the story structure, and many of the gaps (such as those in Gary's story) affected a story's texture more than its meaning. Judging from these results, it appears that most of the 9-year-olds we studied were able to make sophisticated decisions about what the reader can infer and what needs to be supplied in the episodes' development. In other words, the children knew intuitively that successful story-writing requires a careful balance of supplied and expected information. Too much of the first ends up boring the reader by weaving

Figure 9.7: Story-grammar Analysis: Gary

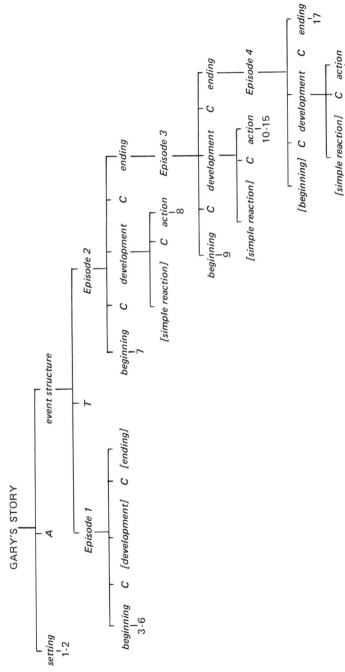

an overly simplistic tale (or one that sounds that way); too much of the second taxes the reader's ability to put the pieces together, unless clues are artfully provided in other ways.

A few more observations could be made about the body of narratives we studied, but inevitably these lead to individual differences between stories and not to conclusions about 9-year-olds' writing in general. Consequently, we will shift our focus to the second of our major interests in the story grammar: its usefulness for describing some of the key features of individual stories.

Describing Individual Stories

Since we have already used the grammar to analyse the strengths and weaknesses of several writers' stories, we will focus here on a pair of stories, both good examples of fully developed third-person narratives, which make an interesting comparison. Both contain multiple episodes, simple and complex developments, and omissions of inferable information. Yet the stories are structured quite differently, and the scene from the cartoon appears in quite different places in the two stories. (The broken lines around constituents indicate where in the structure the cartoon scene appears.) These stories also presented us with some interesting difficulties in our grammatical analysis.

Jane's Story
(1) One day in the jungle there were a lot of animals hearld up together
(2) there were monkeys rhinoceros birds elephants and lions a snake tortoises and last of all a giraffe
(3) well a few meters away from the animals was a man who was whistling and looking abit afraid of them
(4) he had a dog at his feet
(5) the dog looked certainly frightend
(6) the man had a gun behind his back
(7) the animals did not see the gun
(8) and just stared at the man
(9) and the man just stared back at the animals
(10) the man wanted to kill the animals for there skin
(11) so he could stuff them
(12) and sell them
(13) and then he said all be rich

(14) he waited until dark came
(15) the animals went to sleep
(16) the man was not a sleep
(17) he was waiting to kill the animals
(18) and then the man was just about to shoot
(19) when the animals all woke up
(20) and the man hid
(21) so they went back to sleep
(22) the morning came
(23) and all the animals woke up
(24) and the animals all snift the air
(25) and there was a strange smell in the air
(26) the day past
(27) the sun went down on the water
(28) and the man went to try and kill the animals
(29) and he was just about to shoot
(30) when just the lion woke up
(31) and the man did not see the lion
(32) and the lion pounced on to the man
(33) and in a minute he was dead
(34) in the morning the lion told the animals
(35) and the animals said it is good that we have such a brave king
(36) and the sleeped happy of all the nights after.

Jane begins her story with a lengthy description of the scene in the cartoon, a situation from which we can gather that the hunter has made up his mind to kill some animals prior to this opening scene, so that the exchange of stares in Statements 8 and 9 seems more properly part of the setting than the beginning of an episode. The stand-off between hunter and animals provides a transition into the first episode, and the reader can infer a *beginning* for this episode even though it starts with a *goal* statement in Statement 10. Jane's story consists of four episodes. The story is predominantly linear, structured around a temporal sequence of events. The first episode tells the story of the hunter's attempt to kill the animals during the first night, an attempt foiled when the animals wake up. The second episode advances the story through the next day, although nothing much happens except that the animals notice a strange smell (a detail which appears to have little connection to the plot). The third episode recounts the hunter's attempt to shoot the animals on the second night, an attempt which backfires and results in the hunter being killed by the lion. The fourth episode takes place

Figure 9.8 Story-grammar Analysis: Jane

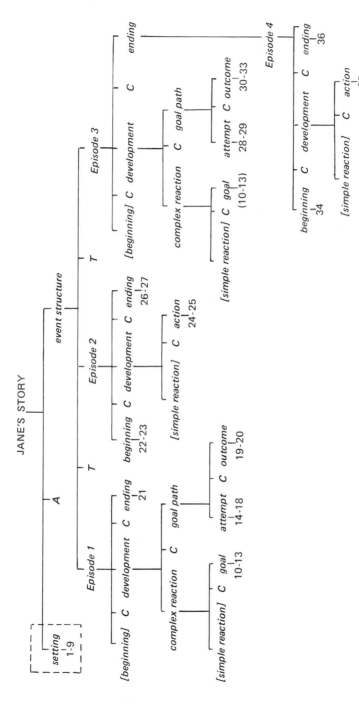

the next morning, and thus might be considered another parallel event; but because the lion's report seems a result or outcome of the death of the hunter, we have chosen to embed this last episode. Even so, the story remains episodic. Jane seems to have composed the story 'thought by thought', which may explain the linear structure, the shifts in point of view, and the absence of internal reactions to previous events — all features highlighted by analysing Jane's narrative with a story grammar.

Francis's story provides an interesting contrast in terms of structure.

    (1) One day a huntsman was walking through the jungle
    (2) when he thought something was creeping up behind him.
    (3) So he ran up a tree with fright.
    (4) He looked down
    (5) and it was a tortoise.
    (6) He loaded his gun
    (7) and tryed to shoot it.
    (8) But its shell was bullet proof.
    (9) The animals didn't like being disturbed.
  (10) The hunter was really frighted
  (11) so he jumped down from the tree
  (12) and ran off.
  (13) The tortoises shell was hurtting
  (14) so he went on his way to the other animals.
  (15) The tortoise told the other animals all about it.
  (16) They made up a plan.
  (17) Next day they all got up in a bunch
  (18) and started walking.
  (19) The hunter was looking down a cliff.
  (20) While the animals were coming
  (21) he looked around.
  (22) He was so frighted.
  (23) The animals started coming towards him.
  (24) He started walking backwards.
  (25) He forgot about the cliff.
  (26) He was whistling.
  (27) Then he fell down the cliff.
  (28) And that was the end of him.

The structural diagram shows clearly the embedded nature of this story's development. However, our efforts to analyse the story led us to consider two problems in applying the grammar. One problem arises

Figure 9.9: Story-grammar Analysis: Francis

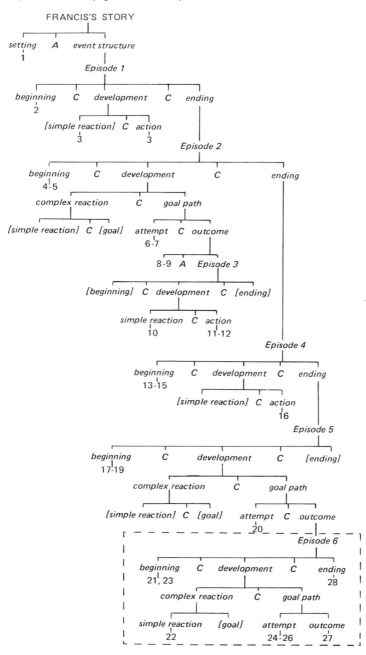

when a single statement contains two grammatical functions. For example, Statement 3 ('So he ran up a tree with fright') seems to contain both a *simple reaction* (fright) and an *action* (ran up a tree). We solved the problem of where to place Statement 3 by putting it under both nodes. (One might need to consider whether statements should be defined in a more semantically primitive way, perhaps along the lines of those developed by Kintsch and van Dijk, 1978.)

A second problem arises when the writer shifts focus in the middle of an episode. This is what appears to happen after Statement 9. In our reading of the story, the second episode involves the hunter shooting the tortoise (in Statements 6-7). The outcome (in 8) is that the tortoise is saved by his protective shell, and (in 9) that the animals are disturbed (presumably by the noise of the shot). In Statement 10, however, Francis shifts to the hunter's response – jumping down and running off. Then, in Statements 13 and 14, the focus shifts back to the hurt tortoise and the beginning of a new episode involving the tortoise's report to the other animals and their formulation of a plan. The problem, then, is what to make of Statements 10-12, statements which seem to be a separate episode. Since the grammar is not designed to handle an episode which interrupts another, we had to be creative. One option is to bracket Statements 10-12 and treat them as parenthetical. But a more logical choice is to call the statements *Episode 3*, and to treat this episode as an outcome of the shooting of the tortoise in *Episode 2*. This gives us a rather unwieldy outcome node for the second episode, but this solution manages to account for the problematic structure of this part of the story.

The more interpretive aspects of the story grammar remind us that story structure is to some extent in the eye of the beholder. Our primary concern is not, of course, with the technical details of story grammars designed to parse ideal narratives, but rather with the imperfect structural features of the kinds of stories that children write. There are problematic aspects of applying story-grammar analysis to children's narratives, but on the whole we have found that diagramming stories has been a very useful aid for appreciating the strengths and weaknesses of children's stories. As we have tried to demonstrate, the story-grammar diagrams give us insights into the way a child has developed a story, and the formal structural analysis can help us discover which alternative structures and types of development a young writer might profitably explore.

Relationships Between Story Structure and Overall Quality

Finally, we want to consider whether structural analyses of the kind we have been discussing can be used to assess the overall quality of a child's narrative (or the developmental level of the writer). In this case, structural analyses seem to offer us little. To be sure, the incomplete stories are less satisfying than those with the full features of complete narratives. But beyond this simplistic observation, it becomes quite difficult to equate story quality with particular kinds of story structure. For example, within each of our three structural patterns – linear, embedded and mixed – we found about the same proportions of stories of high and mediocre quality, based on our own judgements as well as on the results of the holistic ratings of other judges. Perhaps it should seem self-evident that a simply structured, linear narrative can be quite effective, while a complex structure with multiple embeddings does not guarantee good character development, effective description and so on. Although complex structure can contribute to effectiveness, especially when the complexity is the result of a fully developed character's involvement in an engaging quest, good stories entail the use of many other elements and story-telling devices.

In concluding, then, we want to examine briefly some elements other than structure that made some of the stories stand out as particularly effective. One element that we have touched on several times already is good characterisation – the creation of a central protagonist with individual motives, traits and dispositions. In quite a few stories the writer assigned the hunter a motive for his actions in the jungle. These motives could be grouped in three broad categories: monetary rewards (in 4 stories), personal rewards (e.g. curiosity, pleasure, desire to rule – in 7 stories), and the fulfilment of a mission (e.g. revenge, to capture animals, search for a friend – in 5 stories). Of the 25 complete third-person narratives, 16 (or 64 per cent) provided an explicit motive for the hunter. In the remaining 9 stories the motive is implicit, often part of the hunting routine (e.g. 'one day he was hunting animals as always').

Beyond simply providing a motive for the hunter, several children gave special attention to creating a rich and interesting central character. Most often the protagonist depicted in these stories fits the role of 'silly hunter', a bungler who brings on problems through his own ineptness, cowardice or some comic foible. In several stories the hunter's name is a clue to his comic character. For example, the hunter in Sharon's story is named 'Sir Improper', a name which indicates the hunter's propensity for megalomaniacal schemes. The story begins:

The hunter sir improper as he was so Improper. Thought to himself
I will rule the jungle. They shall be at my feet he said. I shall be their
king. Well I did tell you he was improper.

At the end of the tale, after the hunter falls from the cliff, Sharon comments: 'that was the end of the Angry Silly hunter'.

In another story, Christine effectively uses the detail of the hunter's
checked socks to create a 'silly hunter' character.

Along time ago there was a hunter called Henry Fread John Check.
Do you want to know why his surname was Check because he always
wore check socks he had a thousand of them.

Henry turns out to be a coward, but his love of socks is stronger than
his fear of the jungle, as we see in the following excerpt.

'I I I am not going' said Henry picking up cougrae. 'It's worth a
thousand pounds' said Sir Roberts 'let me see I could bye another
thousand pairs of socks I take it.' Said Henry 'You leave at 6:00
p.m.' said Henry's boss. Henry went home got a suit case and started
packing. We all know what he packed checked socks.

The passage above also illustrates the way some children – a relatively small number – were able to use dialogue to create the central
character, most often a comic characterisation. In Alan's story, for
example, the hunter arrives on a paddle steamer, jumps to shore, and
exclaims: 'By jove! I've made it Ah, what?' – a fine job of mimicking
the language of the colonial-aristocratic type of character which will
figure in the story. Another writer, Claire, begins her story with dialogue – quite an unusual opening, since the great majority of stories
(22 of the 25 complete third-person narratives) began with formulaic
story openings: 'Once (upon a time),' 'One day', or a similar opening.
While the more conventional openings demonstrate a widespread familiarity with the story genre, Claire, who began with dialogue, seems
to have a more sophisticated sense of story, for she is able to begin in
the stream of action, move back to provide background, and then com-
mence the main events of the narrative.

'Have you got your sandwhiches Henry'? 'yes Katey'. Henry was a
English expoler who was going to a Country called jumble land which
was right at the end of the world and he wanted to go there because

he had heard about all the strange animals there so on Monday morning he got all his things packed and set off and thats when his wife called out Have you got your sandwhiches? Now then heres where our story begins.

Use of special linguistic devices set several stories apart. A few writers used syntactic options to achieve particular effects. The best example of this is a story told in the first person, an unusual story in this respect and others, but chiefly of interest for the manipulation of sentence length and structure. Short sentences seem to be used quite deliberately to achieve the effect of suspense: 'I stepped back. My left foot slid of the edge. "Oh, no." I moved forward. The sun was shining hard. I grew hot and tired.' In places, Neela also inverts normal word order to give the story a special, perhaps sinister, tone: 'Nearer the cliff edge I got'; 'Closer and closer the animals came.' This is the voice of someone telling a frightening tale, not a narration of everyday events.

Diction is a key feature of several stories. One writer in particular, Andrea, seemed to be experimenting with word choice. At the beginning of this tale the hunter decides to go on an expedition 'on a Sunday when all the animals would be hanging around *boringly*' (our italics here, and later). The hunter and his companions '*slung* their guns on their backs and set off'. When the hunter faces the animals on the cliff,

he started walking backwards to the edge of the cliff and with an *enormouse howling noise* he fell of the edge. And then a *faint plop* could be heard followed by a help. All the animals were terribly surprised at what had happened. But secretly some of them thought it rather funny.

Finally a couple of writers used a device common in animal tales: use of alliterative names for the animals. Claire described the gathering of the animals as follows:

Then a whole set of animals came up Larry the loin, molly the monkey, george the giraffe, edward the elephant, and the bird family, and Sammy Snake, and lots more but lets get on with the story.

Alan describes the chain reaction of the animals to the arrival of the hunter.

Eric the elephant heard him come. Gillian and Gerald the giraffes saw him come. Eric told Edith his wife. Gillian and Gerald told Melvin and Mavis the monkeys, Melvin told Stanley and Sylvia the snakes and soon it reached the king of the jungle.

Later in the story, 'Andrew the ardvark', 'Miles the mole' and 'Seargent Walter worm' play important roles.

By examining a few features of inventive and effective stories, we hope to have underscored the point that structural analyses will not tell us everything of importance about children's narratives. Despite our preoccupation with story grammars in this chapter, we would argue for viewing structural analysis for what it is: one method among several for describing the kinds of choices writers make in constructing texts. Sometimes structural analysis is illuminating, and sometimes it is not; but always it is only a single band in the full spectrum of elements that make up a child's story.

References

Applebee, A.N. (1978) *The Child's Concept of Story*, University of Chicago Press, Chicago

Black, J.B. and Bower, G.H. (1980) 'Story Understanding as Problem-Solving', *Poetics, 9*, 223-50

— and Wilensky, R. (1980) 'An Evaluation of Story Grammars', *Cognitive Science, 3*, 213-30

Botvin, G.H. and Sutton-Smith, B. (1977) 'The Development of Structural Complexity in Children's Fantasy Narratives', *Developmental Psychology, 13*, 377-88

Dijk, T.A. van (1980) 'Story Comprehension: An Introduction', *Poetics, 9*, 1-21

Gundlach, R.A. (1981) 'On the Nature and Development of Children's Writing' in C.H. Frederiksen and J.F. Dominic (eds), *Writing: The Nature, Development, and Teaching of Written Communication*, vol. 2, Erlbaum, Hillsdale, NJ, pp. 133-51

Johnson, N.S. and Mandler, J.M. (1980) 'A Tale of Two Structures: Underlying and Surface Forms in Stories', *Poetics, 9*, 51-86

King, M.L. and Rentel, V.M. (1981) *How Children Learn to Write: A Longitudinal Study*, The Ohio State University Research Foundation, Columbus

Kintsch, W. and Dijk, T.A. van (1978) 'Towards a Model of Text Comprehension and Production', *Psychological Review, 85*, 363-94

Kroll, B.M. (in press) 'Antecedents of Individual Differences in Children's Writing Attainment' in B.M. Kroll and G. Wells (eds), *Explorations in the Development of Writing: Theory, Research, Practice*, John Wiley, Chichester

—, Kroll, D.L. and Wells, G. (1980) 'Assessing Children's Writing Development: The "Children Learning to Write" Project', *Language for Learning, 2*, 53-80

Mandler, J.M. and Johnson, N.C. (1977) 'Remembrance of Things Parsed: Story Structure and Recall', *Cognitive Psychology, 9*, 111-51

Rumelhart, D.E. (1975) 'Notes on a Schema for Stories' in D. Bobrow and A. Collins (eds), *Representation and Understanding: Studies in Cognitive Science*, Academic Press, New York, pp. 211-36

— (1977) 'Understanding and Summarizing Brief Stories' in D. LaBerge and S.J. Samuels (eds), *Basic Processes in Reading: Perception and Comprehension*, Erlbaum, Hillsdale, NJ, pp. 265-303

Stein, N.C. and Glenn, C.G. (1979) 'An Analysis of Story Comprehension in Elementary School Children' in R.O. Freedle (ed.), *New Directions in Discourse Processing*, vol. 2, Ablex, Norwood, NJ, pp. 53-120

Temple, C.A., Nathan, R.G. and Burris, N.A. (1982) *The Beginnings of Writing*, Allyn & Bacon, Boston

Thorndyke, P.W. (1977) 'Cognitive Structures in Comprehension and Memory of Narrative Discourse', *Cognitive Psychology*, 9, 77-110

Wells, C.G. (1979) 'Describing Children's Linguistic Development at Home and at School', *British Educational Research Journal*, 5, 75-98

Part Four: WRITERS AND AUDIENCE

INTRODUCTION

Helen Cowie

The final section of this book concerns the young writer in relation to other people, whether these are a potential audience or fellow-authors in a writing community. Joan Tamburrini, James Willig and Clive Butler discuss the responses of forty 11-year-olds to individual interviews about the purposes of writing, the development of a sense of audience and the role of reflection in writing as part of the move from egocentric thinking. They discuss the importance of making explicit to children what the purposes of writing might be since, in their particular sample of pupils, this is often far from clear. Their results suggest to me the strong influence which the teacher has on children's concepts of story, their views on the imagination and the extent to which they take the opportunity of using writing as part of the decentring process.

The issue is explored further in the chapter by Heather Hanrott and me, where we present a case study of the setting up of a writing community in a class of 7 and 8-year-olds. We show how the teacher can devise strategies for helping children to overcome writing difficulties. In addition, we argue that one way of allowing effective and authentic writing to emerge grows from the teacher's ability to share in the young writers' experiences by developing a sense of trust in the audience. We present a variety of methods for achieving this aim.

The last word goes to Donald Graves, who believes passionately that it is the child's voice which underlies each part of the writing process — choosing the information, selecting the right words, organising the theme. When this is well done, he says, the reader enters in imagination into the theme of the writing. But it is ultimately upon the responsiveness of the teacher that the emergence of this voice depends in classroom contexts.

10 CHILDREN'S CONCEPTIONS OF WRITING

Joan Tamburrini, James Willig and Clive Butler

Introduction

There is impressive and growing evidence of the importance of intentions in human learning. For instance, McShane (1980) argues that intentional communication with another person is central to language development in its earliest stages, and Donaldson (1978) has shown that children's understanding of what a task entails determines how they set about completing that task.

Turning directly to the language curriculum, the Southgate, Arnold and Johnson (1981) study of children's understanding of the purposes of reading suggested that the majority of their sample of 7 to 9-year-olds regarded reading as a means to further learning, to help with spelling, and to obtain information — all firmly utilitarian functions. Only 4 of the 50 children interviewed indicated that they enjoyed reading for its own sake; and 13 children either could not answer the question, or admitted to seeing no reason at all for reading.

Our belief that effective learning depends in large measure on clarity of intentions prompted us to examine children's conceptions of writing, about which little is known. As a basis for the investigation we decided to use the Britton, Burgess, Martin, McLeod and Rosen (1975) model of language development, partly because it conveniently identifies the various functions of writers and their audiences, and partly because it is widely referred to in the literature and is probably the most influential model among teachers.

One of Britton's major hypotheses is that in the early stages young children write in the expressive mode, a form of written-down expressive speech that stays close to the self of the writer or speaker, revealing his thoughts and feelings, and fully comprehensible only if one knows him and his context. As children progress, their writing, according to Britton, will move from this starting point into three broadly differentiated categories: the transactional, when the writer wishes to inform, report or record; the expressive; and the poetic, when the writing is intended to achieve an aesthetic effect.

Another aspect of writing development examined by Britton and his

188

colleagues is concerned with the pupil's sense of audience, the growth of his ability to make adjustments and choices in writing that take account of the audience for whom the writing is intended. Britton and his associates propose six main audience categories, ranging from writing for self to writing for an unknown or public audience.

Thus, progress in writing may be appraised in terms of the pupil's ability increasingly to differentiate in terms of both function and audience. The two are related, since writing expresses a relationship with the reader in respect to the writer's purpose.

The development of the power to differentiate is a characteristic of cognitive development in general. A model that relates aspects of linguistic development including the development of writing closely to cognitive development is that of Moffett (1968). A central characteristic of cognitive development, he argues, is increasing powers of abstraction, and closely associated with abstracting is 'decentring', a movement from the self outward. Moffett lists several specific aspects of decentring, but for the purposes of the present study only one need concern us, since it is related to the sense of audience. There is progressive decentring, Moffett argues, when a child moves from formulating his own thoughts in order to clarify them, which is required when addressing a small known audience like oneself, to writing them down for an unknown audience. This kind of decentring points up the role of reflection in writing, reflection before, during and after writing.

These considerations provided the conceptual basis for the interview schedule we designed to explore children's notions of writing, our primary objective. What we shall also be doing, however, is to provide some indirect information on teachers' strategies in promoting and assessing children's writing, since children's understanding of the purposes of writing will have been influenced by the teaching they have experienced.

The Investigation

The first and second objectives of this study were concerned with children's understanding of the different forms of writing and their sense of audience, aspects central to Britton's model discussed above. The first objective was to examine children's conceptions of the purposes and characteristics of different categories of writing; and the second was to determine the extent of children's awareness of audience in writing.

The subject matter of the third objective was the function of reflection in writing, a process referred to in the earlier discussion.

The sample consisted of 40 10 and 11-year-old children (20 boys and 20 girls) selected by their teachers on the basis of their above-average ability in written expression. No formal assessment of socioeconomic status was made, but the children were drawn from five schools, all of which were located in relatively prosperous suburban areas.

We interviewed the children individually so that we could go beyond surface responses and question children more closely about the attitudes they were expressing. After a number of pilot studies the following interview schedule was agreed.

The first objective was to examine children's conceptions of the purposes and characteristics of different categories of writing. To this end we asked:

Why do you think you write stories?
Why do you think you write poems?
Why do you think you write in your project work?

We asked additional probe questions where necessary, one of which we used in every interview because it was particularly useful in helping children to make the distinctions asked for. This was:

Suppose your teacher said to you, I want you to help a boy/girl new to the school to write a really good story/poem/project, how would you go about helping him to make it the best story possible?

The responses were categorised under six headings, the first three of which were concerned with learning. Children told us that writing educated them or promoted their learning in three main ways: by helping them to develop their imagination, to extend their knowledge and to acquire language skills. Accordingly, our first category was 'Learning – imagination' as illustrated by the response 'writing helps me use my imagination'. Category 2 was 'Learning – facts' as indicated by the response 'we learn about things; it helps us to remember things'. Category 3 was 'Learning – skills', which concerns the use of writing in improving grammar, spelling, punctuation and handwriting as in the response 'to help improve my spelling'. Category 4 was 'Record purposes', where the emphasis was on recording as an aid to memory (for example, 'to help remind me'). Category 5 'Enjoyment' (for example, 'it's fun') and Category 6 'Reason unknown' are self-explanatory.

The second objective was to determine the extent of the children's awareness of audience in writing. To this end we asked:

Whom do you write stories for? Anyone else?
Whom do you write poems for? Anyone else?
Whom do you write projects for? Anyone else?

The responses were categorised according to the following audiences children named: 'self', 'teacher', 'trusted adult', 'peer group' and 'universal audience' (for example, 'anyone who wants to read it').

The third objective was to examine the role of reflection in children's writing. To this end the following questions were asked:

When you have been asked to write what do you think about
a) before you actually put pen to paper?
b) when you are actually writing?
c) just after you have finished writing?

In this analysis the following four categories were used. Category 1 was 'Vocabulary' (for example, 'I search for words that are interesting'). Category 2 was 'Story line' (for example, 'I think of what's going to be first and last'). Category 3 was 'Mechanical features' such as spelling, grammar, punctuation and handwriting (for example, 'I look over for spelling'). Category 4 was 'Audience' (for example, 'I think of what the teacher would approve of').

Analysis of Results

We set out first to examine children's conceptions of the purposes and characteristics of different categories of writing. The responses are given in Table 10.1 below.

Table 10.1: Reasons Given for Writing Stories, Poems and Projects

	Learning – imagination	Learning – facts	Learning – skills	Record purposes	Enjoyment	Reason unknown
Stories	25	–	26	–	8	6
Poems	7	–	9	–	3	22
Projects	–	32	5	25	2	3

Stories

Over half the sample told us that writing stories facilitated learning in the sense of developing their imagination. Time and time again we were told that writing stories 'helps your imagination', 'widens your imagination' or 'gets you to use your imagination and helps you express what you think about things'.

Whenever children spontaneously mentioned 'imagination' we asked further questions, and requested examples of imagination so that we could better understand their conception of the term. In our view imagination is a process that involves a reconstruction and reinterpretation of first-hand experiences and feelings associated with them, and it should result in increased insights into the world of external reality and into the nature of human feeling. There are other senses to which the word 'imagination' is sometimes applied, and one of these is fantasy in the sense of the unreal, the impossible and the 'fantastic'. Our probes revealed that the children's dominant conception of imagination was in terms of this sense of fantasy, all children except three describing it in such terms as 'making up stories that are not real like animals that talk, witches and wizards', 'things that couldn't really happen like ghost stories', 'space ships, something that doesn't exist, green men'. More than half the children strongly denied that imagination could involve events that had occurred or could occur. 'Imagination — it's things that pop out of your head like a light bulb . . . not things that could happen.' 'If you use your imagination you can't write about people like you and me.' 'You don't use your imagination when you write about everyday things.' Most of those children who did concede, when pressed, that imagination could involve the world of external reality, did so somewhat reluctantly, like the child who initially said 'It's not a true thing, it isn't something that really happened', then when asked if she were sure, said 'Well — you can use your imagination for something that is reasonably likely to happen — exaggeration is a better word — something about science which isn't exactly true.' Two children, having first firmly described imagination in terms of fantasy, then conceded that it could involve the real world, but only if the events described had not happened to them. 'You can write about something that might happen to you but it's not imaginative if you know what happened.' And: 'You could write about things that could happen because they might not have happened to you.' There were only three responses that did not emphasise fantasy and two of these were, incidentally, the most sophisticated in that a sense of audience was introduced. The first of these was:

> Imagination — a good story near to true life. It need not be near to true life. It's unimaginative if it's very like real life — very boring.

When a story is imaginative the people who read it can visualise what the characters are like, what they feel.

And the second:

Something I would make up and like to happen — you can write about something that did or didn't happen, like getting lost or going to another school — vicarious (*sic*) experience — some stories would give [the reader] experiences if you were in the same position — gives you more imagination.

As might be expected, the acquisition of language skills featured strongly as a reason for writing stories, with 26 children suggesting that it helped to improve their grammar, spelling, punctuation or handwriting. Eight children specifically mentioned enjoyment as a justification for story writing, while only 6 pupils were unable to reply to our question.

Poems

The dominant finding here is that just over half the children we talked to could give no reason at all for writing poems. Typical replies were: 'I don't know.' 'I've no idea.' 'Haven't the faintest really.' 'Not sure actually.'

We then tried to explore children's conceptions of poetry more closely. Many pointed out that poems rhyme, but when pressed would quickly agree that they need not do so. Several children told us that poems were usually shorter than stories and a few 'that they ought to have short lines'. One girl commented that 'you need more concentration to write a poem and to choose words more carefully', but not surprisingly she could not elaborate the distinction further. According to our children, the principal subject matter of poetry seemed to be nature. Thus: 'Poems are about the seasons, summer, flowers and birds.' 'They are all about spring; we write about blossoms and the breeding of animals, etc.' But here again, when questioned further most acknowledged that poetry covers a much wider range of subject matter than that. Here and there we came across children groping for greater insights into this art form as they talked with us. One boy had reached the conclusion that poems could be 'about ugly as well as beautiful things, like living in slums'. He continued: 'It seems to me I'm very sorry for people living like that [in slums] and because I'm so lucky myself.' That same boy thought that 'you can put exactly what you like and how you feel in a poem', and when he was asked how he might best help another boy to write a poem he replied 'I would try to help him put his heart in it and get involved.' The engagement of feelings was also mentioned by a girl who revealed that she 'sometimes thinks up a poem without writing it down, about for example, how the day went, whether I'm lonely or whether I'm playing with lots of friends'. But such sensitivity was rare.

A dislike of poetry sometimes emerged incidentally. One child commented: 'Just grown-ups like poems; children aren't interested really.' And another: 'I don't think that many children are interested in poetry.'

The other findings in this section are straightforward and need no comment. A minority of children gave development of the imagination and language skills and providing enjoyment as reasons for writing poetry.

Projects

Over three-quarters of our sample unequivocally and for the most part without hesitation stressed that project-writing helped them to acquire facts. Of about equal importance was the record-keeping and reference function as illustrated in the comment: 'If you've just learned about it in class by being talked to, after a while you'd probably forget it, but if you've got it down on paper, then you can just look over it again.' One other point of interest emerged in the discussions. Children frequently emphasised the importance of reference books in this form of writing, not to copy from, but to use in writing an account of their own words. However, only occasionally was the possibility of direct observation suggested as in the comment: 'In projects you can find things out for yourself, not just read books.'

The other findings in this section indicated that enjoyment and the development of writing skills did not feature prominently as reasons for project writing.

In general, it is clear from the analysis in Table 10.1 that children do make distinctions between writing stories and project-writing. In broad terms, stories are concerned with imagination and topics with knowledge and the recording of that knowledge. The learning of skills as a reason for writing was given more often in respect to stories than project-writing, while for all forms the enjoyment aspect was specifically mentioned only infrequently. This analysis also showed that writing poetry was construed as a separate activity, although for the most part children were quite unclear as to its purpose.

The second objective of this study was to determine the extent of children's awareness of audience in writing. Children's responses to our questions about whom they wrote for are set out in Table 10.2.

Table 10.2: Children's Awareness of a Sense of Audience in Writing

	Self	Teacher	Trusted adult	Peer group	Universal audience
Stories	20	37	15	19	4
Poems	10	37	13	3	5
Projects	12	37	11	8	4

Undoubtedly, teachers are seen as the main audience for all forms of writing considered in this study. Responses to our probe questions such as 'Whom do you write for mainly?' made it clear that the vast output of writing in schools was written almost entirely for teachers. Writing for oneself comes next in order of frequency. Here we gained the impression from our probes and such spontaneous comments as 'I write stories for myself at home out of interest' that children do write stories in their spare time simply for enjoyment, but that poetry writing outside school was a rare practice. Almost a quarter of the children wrote for themselves in projects, and what they seemed to be telling us was that they were intrinsically interested in the subject matter, like the boy who said 'I can get a lot of research out of it and learn about things that interest me.' For all three forms of writing which children did at home adults in the family usually served as the audience. Although many stories were written with the peer group in mind, this finding was explained by the occasional practice in one school of asking children to write for younger age groups. Writing for other children occurred only rarely in poems and topics.

Although we found it impossible to quantify frequency of writing for the various audiences, we formed the strong impression that children wrote mostly for teachers, and for teachers in their role as examiners. One girl summed up the position thus: 'She gets it, she reads it and she says it's good or bad.' They wrote occasionally for themselves (particularly stories), their parents and their peers, but as far as we could judge the children we talked to did not vary their style markedly according to the different audiences they were writing for, except when writing stories for much younger age groups.

The third objective was to examine the role of reflection in children's writing by asking them what they thought about before, during and after writing. The results are given in Table 10.3.

Table 10.3: The Role of Reflection in Children's Writing

	Vocabulary	Story line	Mechanical features	Audience
Before	5	37	8	2
During	10	33	10	2
After	7	6	28	15

This analysis showed that before they began writing children thought of the broad outline of the story although not necessarily to the end. Typical comments were: 'I think of who is going to be in it and what's going to happen.' 'I think roughly through the whole story at the beginning.' When pressed, a good many children admitted to 'working out the first bit and then starting to write'. At this stage very little attention was given to features like grammar and spelling, and the audience was hardly considered at all.

Once writing had begun the major preoccupation continued to be with the story line, but some concern with vocabulary and mechanical aspects was evident. Once the work was finished, however, the focus of attention was then on grammar, spelling and punctuation and to a lesser extent vocabulary. Common responses were: 'I read it over in case there's any wrong spelling or anything, like words I've missed out.' 'I check for spelling, grammar mistakes and put in better words sometimes.'

The same pattern applied to audience awareness. During writing, there was little mention of possible audiences. One boy commented: 'I don't think about who's going to read it, I think about the story.' However, once the work was finished, 15 children indicated that they then began to consider what the teachers would think of it. Thus: 'I hope that when I give it to my teacher − well − I hope she likes it.' A very few children referred to a slightly wider readership like the girl who told us 'I wonder whether anyone would like to hear it.'

Overall, we found little evidence of children deliberately setting out to write with a given audience in mind, and our impression was that once a piece of work was finished, it was usually checked simply for spelling and grammatical errors. Very rarely indeed was there any suggestion that the writing was reworked and polished.

Discussion

Two main factors need to be taken into account in considering the results of this study. First, the size of the sample (40 subjects) is relatively

small, and as a result only a simple quantitative analysis has been undertaken. The study is therefore essentially impressionistic, but we believe
the children's comments have yielded interesting insights. Secondly,
most of the subjects were drawn from a middle-class socioeconomic
grouping, and were selected by their teachers on the basis of being
above average in written expression. Our object was to question children most likely to produce more sophisticated responses. If their constructs of writing are shown to be inadequate, then those of the general
population are likely to be even more so. With these limitations in mind
the following conclusions can be drawn.

Findings in respect to the first objective showed that children in this
sample had clearly progressed from the undifferentiated stage of early
writing confined to the expressive mode. In terms of Britton's functional categories it was the transactional that the children seemed to
be most clear about. The recording and reference, reporting and inform-
ing purposes were given with confidence by over three-quarters of the
sample. Instrumental reasons concerned with the mechanics of writing
– spelling, punctuation and grammar – were given very infrequently
for writing projects. This was in sharp contrast to the reasons given
for writing stories where the highest number of responses were in the
instrumental category. However, an almost equal number of responses
were given to the development or use of the imagination as reasons for
writing stories. At first glance this seemed a highly satisfactory state of
affairs, but our probe questions revealed that the children had an inadequate notion of 'imagination' conceiving of it predominantly in terms
of fantasy which was concerned with the unreal rather than the world
of external reality. Very few children believed that imagination could be
concerned with plausible everyday events and the feelings of the participants in those events; and even fewer children understood imagination
as a process in which aspects of one's own first-hand experience were
reconstructed. Whether or not this reflects an over-exposure to the fantasy genre of literature one can only speculate. Whatever the reason it
is important that teachers help children to understand that imagination
is rooted in personal experience and that, in the words of Wilkinson,
Barnsley, Hanna and Swan (1980) it 'offers insights into motives and
relationships in such a way as to increase the awareness of the inter-
preter and those to whom he is interpreting'. A particularly disturbing
finding was the children's lack of knowledge as to the reasons for
writing poetry. This is perhaps hardly surprising when one notes their
limited conception of what poetry is. For the majority of them poetry
should rhyme (even though when pressed many conceded that it need

not), consist of short lines ('it's like a cut-up story'), and consist of a description of some aspect of nature.

Findings from the second objective of this study suggest that the children wrote mostly for the teacher as audience, as did the survey of Britton *et al.* (1975) of 11 to 16-year-old pupils. Moreover the teacher was conceived largely as examiner. Even when, infrequently, they wrote for other audiences, their responses suggest that they did not attempt to vary their style accordingly — except when writing for much younger children. The children's replies to questions about what they thought about before, during and after writing, the subject matter of the third objective, were particularly revealing in this respect. A sense of audience entails a two-stage process of reflection before and during the act of writing. The first stage involves the writer in formulating and clarifying his thoughts, whereas the second stage involves a decentring to the point of view of the audience and adjustments made with this in mind. A similar decentring should be involved in appraising, reworking and polishing the first draft to achieve a final draft that the writer is satisfied is appropriate to his audience. The children in our sample confined their thinking before and during writing to the first stage, to formulating and clarifying their thoughts. Neither was there evidence of decentring to the point of view of audience as part of a revision process; any working over when the writing was first completed seemed to be mainly concerned with checking for correctness of spelling, punctuation and grammar, though occasionally children mentioned a reappraisal of vocabulary. In sum, there was little evidence of decentring with a given audience in mind. What we do not know is the extent to which this state of affairs reflects inadequate time allocated to specific pieces of writing. Some children mentioned the time factor. One child said: 'I think we should be allowed to think for ten minutes before we start.' Another child said:

> I don't think we get enough time to write because say we've got half an hour for poetry, then I have to think fast, but if I do one at home I may only write five lines in half an hour and I can go over it again and scratch it out and use only two lines of the poem and then carry on.

It is, of course, impossible to know to what extent the children's responses in this study are an aspect of their cognitive development. Nevertheless, teachers' own conceptions of the purposes and forms of writing are bound to be reflected to some extent in pupils' work and attitudes. The first essential, then, is that teachers should clearly understand the functions and characteristics of various kinds of writing, and the second essential is that these are made quite explicit to their pupils. By doing this children can be made sensitive to the various criteria governing good writing in all its forms, and thus be helped to place greater emphasis on qualitative aspects of writing in contrast to mechanical skills. Our subjects were willing to think deeply in response to our questions, and most of them struggled intellectually with the nature of qualitative characteristics, particularly 'imagination'. Their thoughtfulness suggested that their understanding of the quality of their writing could have benefited from discussions in which meanings of, for example, 'imagination' and 'poetic' were made explicit, and exemplified in published literature and in their own writing. Thus, children need adequate time to reflect before they begin writing, and to revise when it is completed, but time alone is insufficient. Children need to be helped to understand the purposes of rehearsal and revision including the consideration of audience. Above all, our findings confirm the evidence cited earlier of the importance of clarity of intention in human learning. They support Harpin's (1976) claim that children are 'too often left in the dark about what the business is for. The purposes of writing . . . remain unexplained'. Classroom time and explicitness are necessary to rectify this state of affairs.

References

Britton, J.N., Burgess, T., Martin, N., McLeod, A. and Rosen, H. (1975) *The Development of Writing Abilities*, Macmillan Education, London

Donaldson, M. (1978) *Children's Minds*, Fontana/Collins, London

Harpin, W.S. (1976) *The Second 'R': Writing Development in the Junior School*, Allen & Unwin, London

McShane, J. (1980) *Learning to Talk*, Cambridge University Press, Cambridge

Moffett, J. (1968) *Teaching the Universe of Discourse*, Houghton, Mifflin Co., Boston

Southgate, V., Arnold, H. and Johnson, S. (1981) *Extending Beginning Reading*, Heinemann Educational Books, London

Wilkinson, A., Barnsley, G., Hanna, P. and Swan, M. (1980) *Assessing Language Development*, Oxford University Press, Oxford

11 THE WRITING COMMUNITY: A CASE STUDY OF ONE JUNIOR SCHOOL CLASS

Helen Cowie and Heather Hanrott

Writing Blocks

'Once a person went for a walk at home, her name was Lizzie isn't she silly?' Natasha, aged 7, sits moodily at her table. 'I can't write stories', she says. 'Mine are stupid.' To herself she adds, 'This is boring!'

Natasha is experiencing a writing block. Around her, children are absorbed in writing. Susanne is already on to her second page; William is illustrating his war story; Joanne is discussing a good beginning with the teacher. Natasha's sense of failure increases; yet what is happening to her is neither wrong nor unusual. The problem of writing block at times confronts most, if not all, writers when they come to put their ideas down on paper. Smith (1982) identifies three main types of writing block which he terms procedural, psychological and physical. Procedural blocks arise when the writer's mind has gone blank and it is not clear what should be written next. When the writing task appears too difficult, or the audience is perceived as a threatening one, the block may be psychological. Finally, the sheer physical demands of the writing process can inhibit the young writer from completing the task. However, with the aid of a sensitive teacher, writing blocks can be overcome. In this case, Natasha can cope with the physical task of writing, but she cannot keep the flow of ideas going. The longer she stares at the blank page, the more discouraged she becomes. Yet what Graves (1983) in his New Hampshire work calls a 'conference' can lead Natasha to value her two-line story, and to see it as the stepping-stone to a new draft. Far from being a worthless piece to be quickly discarded, it is an important part of an ongoing process.

For this conference the teacher decided to discuss a number of possible openings and entered them in Natasha's book in the form of a flow chart:

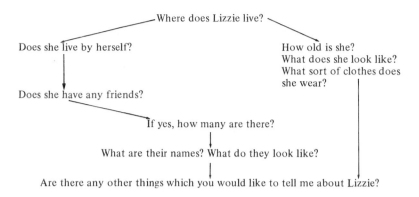

These simple leads enabled Natasha to write:

> Once a person went for a walk at home. Her name was Lizzie. Isn't she silly? She's babyish. She does not want to learn things. She wears clothes too big for her. Every day she wears party shoes.

The story still did not satisfy her. Two days later she produced a third draft entitled *The Cat and the Dog*.

> One day there was a cat and a dog. The cat's name was Lizzie the dog's name was Tom. The cat is 2 and the dog is 3. The dog lives in a kennel the cat lives in a basket. The dog's house is in the garden and the cat's house is inside. The dog had minced morsals the cat had Delicat. But the dog had the cat's food and started to turn into a cat. The cat laughed and the cat started to sing. 'Oh you are a little cat sitting on a mat a cat sat on a mat!' and the dog started to laugh as well and started to meow! so the cat ate the dog's food but nothing happened. The End.

It is interesting to note that Natasha had not been told how to use exclamation marks, but had overheard a discussion about punctuation between the teacher and Susanne at the next table. Although at the time she gave no sign that she was attending to the conversation, later she used the new technique to enhance her own story. Natasha's confidence in herself had grown, and the next day she wrote *The Magic Blanket* without any help from her teacher. Again she experimented with punctuation, using double exclamation marks for emphasis. Sentences like 'Can you guess what Frizzo gave her? A magic blanket!!' indicated a developing trust in her audience.

> There was once a little girl. She was 7 years old. Her name was Claire.
> It was Christmas time. She knew a wizard called Frizzo. It was Christ-
> mas day!! Can you guess what Frizzo gave her? A magic blanket!!
> She loved it so much that she went on it every day. Then one day
> her mother said 'why don't you go outside on your magic blanket,
> its a hot day.' 'O.K. mother' and she went out on her magic blanket.
> The rug went up very gently. the police came to see what was the
> matter . . .

Natasha was beginning to find her own voice.

By contrast, children may know what they want to write, but feel
that they lack the sheer physical skills of putting their ideas down
coherently. Such perceptual and motor difficulties can soon lead to
anxiety about the writing process itself and lowered self-esteem. For
7-year-old Archie story-writing is usually a discouraging experience.
Diagnosed as having minimal brain damage, he is incapable of writing
more than four lines in the course of a lesson.

One day he approached the teacher saying that he wanted to write
a story about the Second World War based on one of his father's books.
Noticing his frustration over the mechanics of writing his ideas down,
the teacher asked him a few questions about his theme and, after this
conference, suggested that he might like to dictate it to her. For Archie
the creation of this story was a tremendous achievement, and he was
not content until four pages had been written. Even breaktimes were
seen as an interruption to his writing. Archie's attitude to himself
changed as he dictated the story since for the first time he saw himself
as a successful member of the class who could produce stories as well
as the others. Again the conference had revealed the possibilities which
can lie beneath the most unpromising lines of writing. *The War of
World War Two* was for Archie an important milestone in his writing
development.

> The Germans used to be very destructive to our men, not to our
> prison camps. This is in the middle of the war and not after. Our
> men had to only run twenty yards for the enemies. This is how long
> to get airborne sixty minutes. The hospitals were full up at Christ-
> mas time and the prison camps too. But it's hard to fight in the
> snow and it's hard for the planes to fight in the air. It's bad for the
> guns to operate in the snow. The guns had to be cleaned out by the

Red Cross men. we started to finish the Germans off but they still fought back. We still kept the end of our share of England. We moved in the chaps from the R.C.2. They went up in the Spitfires trying to dodge them and shoot them down, but they had two bigger bombers. The Americans kept sending in bombers so we could shoot down enemy bombers. The Germans were coming in to England too strongly . . .

These two examples illustrate how both procedural and physical writing blocks can have psychological effects on the child's self-confidence and can inhibit the expression of voice. Both Natasha and Archie found that through a conference with their responsive teacher they were able to develop strategies for overcoming blocks. They began to understand that writing blocks are natural occurrences, just one aspect of the much wider writing process.

Strategies for Overcoming Writing Blocks

If children are encouraged literally to visualise the scene which they are trying to describe, this can sometimes help deal with a writing block. Frequently the drawing which accompanies a story is as important to the young child as the writing. For 7-year-old Mark his space picture is alive. As a rocket blows up, he shouts, 'Aaaargh!!!' and red felt pen swirls over the page to indicate flames and blood. When he becomes blocked the drawing of a picture can act as a release which stimulates further writing. During writing lessons he draws and writes alternately, one activity sparking off the other. For 8-year-old Ashley too the drawings are an integral part of the story. The margin becomes a cave wall round which peers a sinister dinosaur; a victim's blood drips down to the foot of the page. In addition, Ashley's exclamation marks literally represent the increasing loudness of his hero's shouts. When asked to explain why he uses punctuation he says, 'You know, in a cave there's an echo and you really have to shout things like IT'S ALL RIGHT DOWN THERE!!!' Later on he will tone down his punctuation, but for the present it is serving a useful function and is giving him a visual device for producing effective writing. His friend Richard later asks the teacher, 'Can I have some of those big things that make words sound louder?'

Figure 11.1: Ashley Gives Expression to his Hero's Shouts

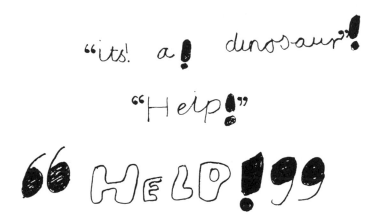

Blank cartoon squares can provide a secure structure for the reluctant writer, since the words can be added as each picture is completed.
The writing task is less threatening for the child and the results are
likely to be pleasing to both writer and reader. In addition, the rudi-
ments of narrative form are being mastered as the central character
progresses from one episode to the next.

Later on, story charts in the form of flow diagrams can provide a
useful reference for children when they cannot think what to write, or
when they need help with the development of themes and characters.
The charts may be supplied by the teacher or children can be encouraged to devise their own.

It is often difficult for the child to have a mental plan of the story
before it is written down. More commonly, ideas grow out of the process itself. Ideas need time to incubate, and if the child is encouraged
to note down thoughts and episodes as they occur she is more likely to
have a store of ideas from which to draw. These rudimentary sketches
can be kept in a folder for future use. It is important to realise that the
time lag may be quite long. Nicky, who was very moved by *Charlotte's
Web* when it was read in class, made notes on the characters with the
intention of using them some day. However, it was *seven months* before
she wrote a story based on the novel into which she wove her own dialogue and narrative.

Figure 11.2: Cartoon Squares Used as Structure for Reluctant Writer

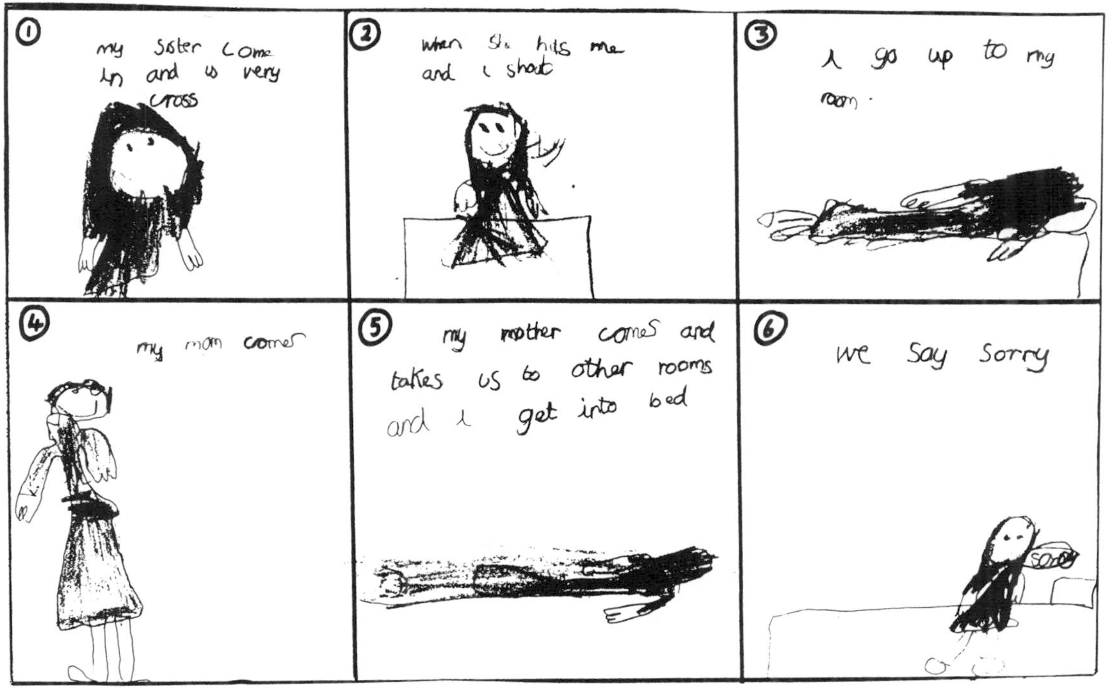

① my sister come in and is very cross

② when sh hits me and i shot

③ I go up to my room.

④ my mum comes

⑤ my mother comes and takes us to other rooms and I get into bed

⑥ We Say Sorry

Figure 11.3: Make-a-story Chart

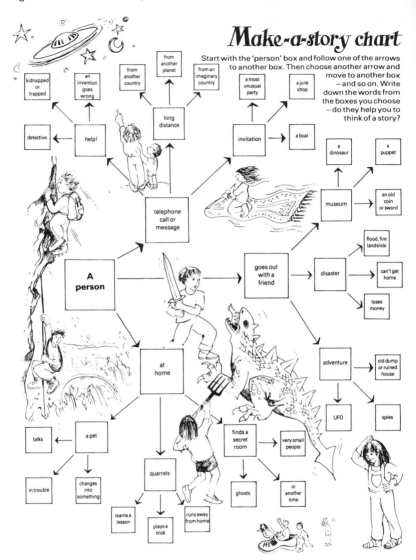

Make-a-story chart

Start with the 'person' box and follow one of the arrows to another box. Then choose another arrow and move to another box — and so on. Write down the words from the boxes you choose — do they help you to think of a story?

Nicky's Story

'Where is Dad going with the axe?' said Fern to her mother.
'Down to the pigsty because some baby pigs were born.'
'But I still don't see why Dad needs an axe?' 'One of the pigs was a weakling and your father's going to kill it.' 'No!' said Fern 'I will not let him do it!' Fern said as she rushed out the door. 'No you will not kill it!' 'Darling he's a weakling.' 'But it's cruel I want to keep him.' 'But he's your responsibility.' 'O.K. Dad.' Several years had gone, the pig died, Fern was very old.
Another year went by Fern died.

Of course, such a folder of ideas can just as well be based on the child's own experiences. Short episodes can be noted while they are fresh in the writer's mind and incorporated into later stories.

One effective method of resolving writing difficulties is for young writers to help one another view blocks as natural occurrences to be discussed with a sympathetic older person, rather than as shameful, solitary experiences. Take Grant's story, for example. The crossing-out indicates that some revision has already taken place, but while the author is aware that the story could be improved, he cannot see how to do it. A conference with Ashley clarifies some points.

Figure 11.4: Grant's Story

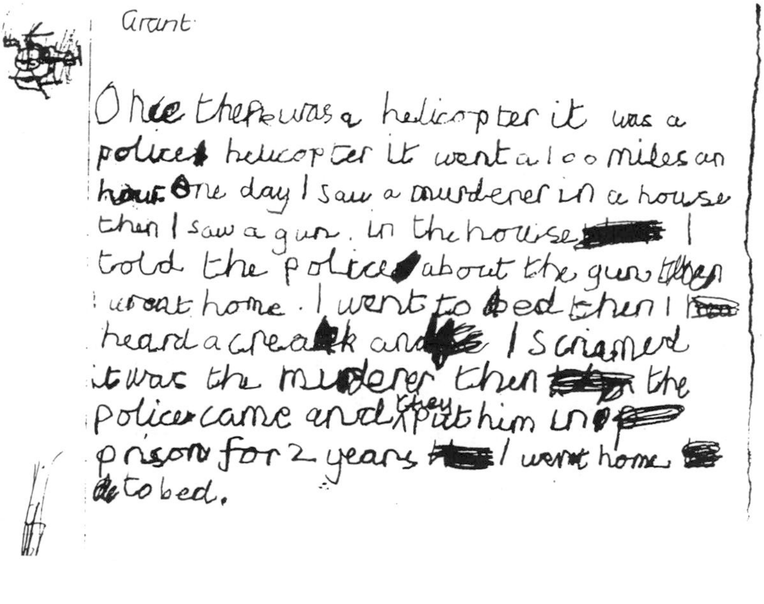

Ashley: I think I would change 'I saw a murderer in a house' to 'Then I saw a gun in the house.'

Grant: Yes, I think that would be better. I've put the gun afterwards.

Ashley: And *then* put, 'I told the police about the gun.' How do the police know about the murder?

Grant: I phoned them up.

Ashley: You don't say that!

Grant knows that the situation will be reversed when he comments on Ashley's story. He may change his piece or he may simply note that there are some ambiguities in the sequence of events and that some essential episodes have been omitted. Yet what these two children are also learning from short conferences like these is that they have control over their own writing processes, that when problems arise they can consult another person, and that they in turn can have some influence over the writing of others. As Smith (1982, p. 202) points out, too often we underestimate the ability which children have to evaluate a piece of writing or to infer the words which the author intended. With guidance from the teacher, conferences between child and child can break down some of the barriers to good writing.

The Teacher as Writer

Observations in this particular classroom indicate the crucial part which the teacher plays in creating an environment where writing will flourish. One aspect which is often overlooked is the use which teachers can make of their own experiences as authors. Graves (1983, p. 19) suggests that teachers should share their writing with children, and even at times invite criticism. The teachers need not be especially accomplished as writers; in fact it may actually be an advantage to share in the difficulties which young writers have. If the teacher takes the risk of revealing her own writing, then she is more likely to respond with sensitivity to the child's writing, however short or ungrammatical the latter may be. By writing with the children, teachers will also experience the great variability which occurs in the process. Some days writing flows and there is hardly time to get all the ideas down; on other days the words emerge as stilted and incoherent. In this way the teacher may come to realise that finding what to say and how to say it well continues to be a problem, even for the mature writer. She too must develop strategies for overcoming writing blocks, for finding words to capture an event, for expressing herself with an authentic voice. In addition, by knowing at first hand the 'ebb and flow' of the composing process, she will have greater understanding of what to observe in young writers and how to respond to them. As Graves (1983, p. 51) argues:

> Writing becomes a process of sharing what we know about our experiences. The class becomes a community because we possess a growing fund of facts about each other's experiences. Strangers don't work well alone. When a class becomes a community, its members learn to help and model for each other.

The Value of the Conference

The teacher as receptive audience can also develop ways of responding which allow the ideas of young writers to emerge in their own way. Here is Emma, for example, who cannot find the right word.

Emma: What word could you make if someone had just put a knife through you? (makes a noise)
Teacher: What do you think? What could it begin with?
Emma: It could begin with 'H'. . . hussh . . . hoh . . . hoc. . . (keeps experimenting with words) . . . You should ask a Chinese person. They would know. Hoh . . . Huch . . .?
Teacher: Could you use a 'K'?
Emma: How could you spell it? (Makes a sound) Hoeek! Now can I read it to you?
Teacher: Yes.
Emma: Title — *Hammer House of Horror.* 'Once upon a time there lived a family and their names are Bryony, Marc, Janina and Serena. (I changed my name!) and their father's and mother's names are Diana and Caspian. One fine day it was Janina's birthday. Her brothers came and her sisters came too. Her friend brought her a rusty knife.
"O no! Not that rusty knife!" said Diana and Caspian.
In the morning a knock at the door — knock, knock.
The mother said, "Come in!"
HOEEK!!"
Now that is the end of the story. THE END.'
Teacher: Aaah! What happened to her then?

Emma:　She died.
Teacher:　How do I know that if I didn't know the story?
Emma:　O dear!
Teacher:　How could you make it so the reader could know that had happened in the story?
Emma:　Rub that out and add more?
Teacher:　Perhaps you could use brackets as you did in your *Aslan* story when you said, 'This is a sad ending'.

It is clearly important to Emma to get the right sound for the knife attack, and the teacher rightly gave time for the making of sounds. It would be easy to overlook the importance of this for Emma if the teacher only looked at the end product, the written piece, but by talking to Emma in conference she shares in the imaginative enactment of the killing. The reader of course would still be confused. Who does knock at the door? Is it an accident or a deliberate murder? The teacher in this conference simply points to one possible source of ambiguity — the fate of Diana. In addition, she refers to another piece of writing, the *Aslan* story, in which Emma had already solved the problem of an ending, and responds to the father's name, Caspian, with its source in the C.S. Lewis *Narnia* stories, which are Emma's favourite reading. The story — short and incomplete as it might appear to a casual reader — is rich in meaning for Emma, and is treated with sensitivity by the teacher. Yet at the same time Emma probably senses that there are links between past and present writing, and that she can draw on ideas from other pieces for the solution of problems in the future. Perhaps most importantly of all, she has shared with her teacher the sheer delight in playing with words and ideas, which is an essential part of the writing process. She is discovering for herself what Polanyi (1958) has called 'the indwelling of reader in writer', and sharing with a responsive audience her pleasure in the imaginative process.

Comments by a group of children can also be illuminating. Here the teacher reads part of Matthew's story and asks the children to devise their own conclusions.

Flight and Eagle Man with the Dragon by Matthew 12
One day there was a man his name was John Macan he worked in a laboratory he at the moment was working on a strange thing in eagle's blood once he by mistake put his hand on it but told no-one one day he was on the cliff then he went too near it and fell down down and when he was at about 30 metres he found himself flying

then he saw a dragon then out of his eyes came water and it died. The

Figure 11.5: Matthew's Story

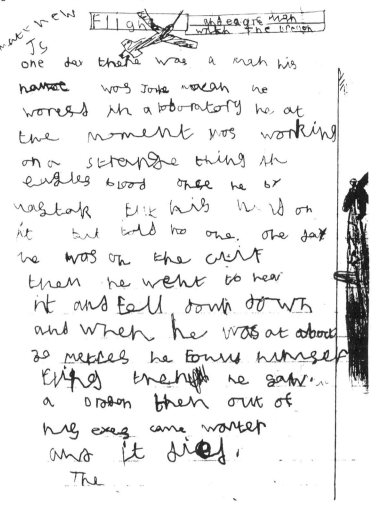

Teacher: . . . then he saw a dragon. What happened next?
Emma: The dragon tried to eat him but the dragon was so fat and the wings were so small and he couldn't lift himself up because he was so heavy and the dragon decided to blow some hot air and fire on the wings and he burnt his wings and he found himself falling

down and down . . .

Matthew: Who did?

Emma: Eagle man. And he fell to the bottom of the cliff and by mistake the dragon tripped over him and he fell tumbling down and he tried and tried to fly but he couldn't and he landed — voom — like that!

Nathan: I'd make it that he brought him back to his cave and put him in a room and he found a plank and it was in a room of gold and pearls and then he went to the other end and he fell down the cliff and was killed.

Marloes: Well, if he was 30 metres off the ground I think if I saw a dragon I would scream, but if he suddenly started flying, I would fly away from the dragon and then I'd let myself fall into a chimney pot and then I saw my mother and father and then I was all right . . .

Matthew: The way I ended it was water came out of the eagle man's eyes and blew up the dragon and it died.

Teacher: What do you think of that one?

All: It's a good one.

Emma: Yes, but it says 'THE . . .'

Matthew: I think probably the bell rang and I didn't get round to writing '. . . END'.

Teacher: What do you think of the ending?

Marloes: Nathan's is best because it's a very clever way of doing it.

Teacher: Why?

Emma: Because sometimes if something *lands* you can get killed or stay alive but if he gets killed it's as if it's a real story — that it was really true because if you fall off a cliff you can't really fly; you don't normally stay alive. You fall down to the ground — splat!

As the children explore different ways of ending they have the opportunity to learn aspects of the writer's craft and the control which an author can have over a piece. They are also learning about the beginnings of critical reading as they talk about the credibility of the various suggestions. Although the story is imaginary, these 8-year-olds are quite aware that, within its conventions, the story still has to make sense, otherwise the plot becomes unsatisfying to the reader. Emma raises this issue in her questioning of the whole idea that Eagle man could magically fly just at the crucial moment. The dragon is still killed, but in a more 'realistic' way, according to Nathan's version, by being lured into a cave and then falling over the edge of the cliff.

The author, of course, reserves the right to retain his ending in spite of what his readers say. In fact, Matthew considers the story to be one of his best, but would still have changed the ending, as he himself explains.

> *Teacher:* Are there any ways in which you might change it?
> *Matthew:* There could have been more on to the end. When it says, '. . . and then he died' it could have been more exciting, like 'he exploded but two days later they saw the *ghost* of the dragon but instead of breathing fire he was breathing water'. That would have made it more exciting. Actually it was fun!

The source of the story comes from comics and television but he has recreated the Spiderman idea in his own imaginative way.

> *Teacher:* What gave you the idea for the story?
> *Matthew:* Part came from Spiderman, like the bit where he touched the strange thing in the eagle's blood. Spiderman was bitten by a spider which had got something to do with a strange chemical. Then Spiderman could climb up walls. Instead of being able to climb up walls, Eagle man is able to fly. He didn't know *how* he could fly, he just found he *could* fly. That's a bit like Spiderman. He didn't know that was why he could climb up walls. I thought why not make it partly super-hero and partly imagination to make it quite exciting.

Again, the conference has given insights into Matthew's writing process, including some of the influences on the themes in his stories. He has been made aware of the response of his readers, and has learned how to justify a particular way of organising his story. He is becoming open to the idea that different endings are possible, and that ideas can be changed and developed.

The Child's Sense of Audience

In this class the children help to develop in one another a sense of audience. Writing is shared in groups or with the whole class, and children take a great deal of interest in stories written by others in the class. By responding to one another's stories they also learn about the sources of imagination and the ways in which ideas from reading or real experience may be integrated into a piece of writing. Here a group of children relate *The Flying Horse* to two books which have been recently read aloud in class.

Figure 11.6: The Flying Horse

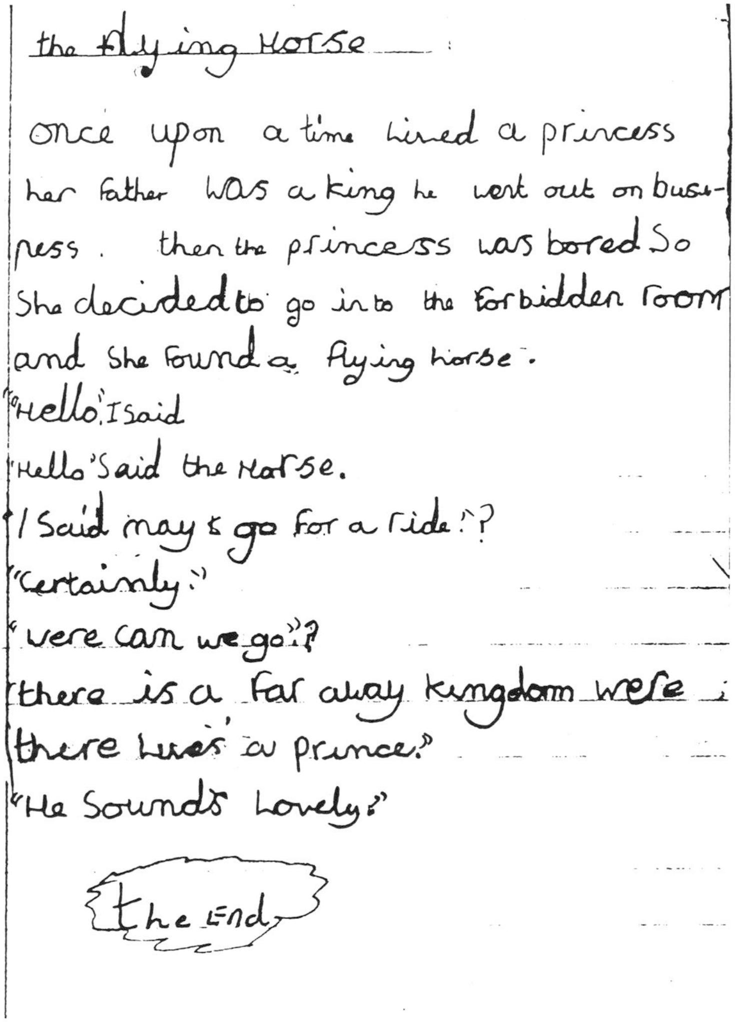

the flying Horse

once upon a time lived a princess
her father was a king he went out on business. then the princess was bored so
she decided to go into the forbidden room
and she found a flying horse.
'Hello' I said
'Hello' said the Horse.
'I said may I go for a ride'?
'Certainly'
'were can we go'?
'there is a far away kingdom were
there lives a prince.'
'He sounds Lovely?'

the End

The Flying Horse
Once upon a time lived a princess her father was a king he went out
on business. then the princess was bored so she decided to go in to
the forbidden room and she found a flying horse.
'Hello', I said
'Hello' said the horse.
'I said may I go for a ride?'

'Certainly'.
'Were can we go?'
'there is a far away kingdom were there lives' a prince'.
'He sounds lovely'.
The End.

Ashley: Oh! I think that's a good one because they don't come back, but I think she got the horse bit from the story we read. Remember the bit where this man took the golden leaf?
All: Oh yes!
Ashley: I think she got it from there — the kingdom far away and all that.
Neil: Except there was a prince. She got a handsome prince.
Ashley: They usually have happy endings like this . . . (thinks for a moment) . . . though *Charlotte's Web* didn't have a happy ending. That had a sad ending. The spider dies.
Neil: But that was a good story.
Ashley: It was good before the spider dies.
Teacher: You like stories to have a happy ending?
All: Yes!
*Catherine:*It makes it feel nicer.
*Charlotte:*Our friend Vanessa — she's in Canada now — she cried at the end.

The children thoughtfully consider the story and reflect on issues which arise out of it. If this is nurtured, then it can grow into a sensitive awareness of others' thoughts and feelings. The author herself admits one source of inspiration to have been C.S. Lewis, as Ashley noticed, but the other children did not guess. She says, 'It came from *The Magician's Nephew*, from the cover. There's a flying horse. The forbidden room comes from Bluebeard.' This information in turn can lead to further imaginative thinking in the minds of her audience. Some of it may never be expressed in writing, but these brief glimpses into the writing processes of other children indicate the wealth of thinking which goes into the shortest piece, and which is waiting to be tapped if the right kind of encouragement is given. As the same writer says, 'If I write a tiny one *that* long it gives me ideas for another story.'

The children are in addition learning to have trust in an audience, and to understand that their readers have needs which have to be met. In turn, they are discovering how to be that effective audience by listening and commenting in a constructive way. This growing perceptiveness in children both as readers and as writers can be one of the most power-ful ways of finding a voice. The children learn that what they write matters, that their experiences and their thoughts are of interest to others. They learn to identify with the other and to take on another's role; they grow in their sensitivity to feelings; they learn about them-selves; and they learn to value what they know. This sharing of writing in a community which is based on trust, interest and involvement helps each child to find a unique way of expressing the ideas which matter. Graves, in fact, argues that when this writer's voice is absent the child has lost control of the writing process, and the results are hollow echoes of what other people say.

Not only do children, in this kind of environment, increase their sensitivity to one another's personal development, but also they show a growing awareness of the technical aspects of the writer's craft which concern any person who attempts to put words down on paper. They can, for example, help one another with ideas on how to improve the structure of a story through effective revision strategies. Their comments on content can be invaluable in helping the author to move beyond egocentric patterns of thought. Here, Ashley, so quick to comment on other children's stories, reacts to Grant's criticism of the first line of his story which goes, 'One day John and Jane found a crack in a wall. It was just big enough for the two of them . . .

Grant: You could put this, 'Once there was two children called John and Jane.'
Ashley: It's good to say 'John and Jane' as if you say, 'One day *they* found a crack in the wall' and you don't know who's found it . . .
Grant: How about this? 'Once . . . once . . . once there was two children called John and Jane.'
Ashley: You couldn't say, 'Once, once, once.'
Grant: You could say for 'once' 'one day'.
Ashley: I've put 'one day' before in another story. I wouldn't like to put 'once'. 'Once' is like a very long time ago. 'Once'! You prob-ably get that from fairy tales . . . 'once upon a time'.
Teacher: Grant means you should explain who John and Jane are.
Grant: Yes!
Ashley: But they're children. Of course they're children!
Grant: But they might not be. They might be husband and wife.
Ashley: OK you could say, 'One day two children found a crack in the wall' and you wouldn't know who their names were.

Teacher: . . . two children called John and Jane?
Ashley: Oh!
Grant: Or you could have, 'Hullo' said the two children . . .'

The problem of finding an effective lead can be as time consuming for these 8-year-olds as it is for the accomplished author. Thinking aloud, trying out different beginnings, listening to how it sounds, sharpening the words, eliminating those which are not essential — these are only some of the problems which face the writer, and in this kind of writing community the children can help one another resolve them.

Conclusion

This chapter indicates how one teacher has tried to create the kind of environment which facilitates the writing process. Participation by children in activities which involve both reader and writer can, it is suggested, develop a heightened awareness of the needs of the audience. In addition, mastery over their own writing processes encourages children to devise new strategies for dealing with problems of style and content. But these are only guidelines which do no more than indicate the wide range of individual differences which exist. There is no one way to good writing; teachers and children change together in the process. As Graves (1983) argues:

> Because the teacher is sensitive to what she sees in folders, to whole-class observation, to the children while writing, as well as to their statements about writing, she can make knowledgeable adjustments. Observation and revision go hand in hand. (p. 293)

It is unlikely that all children will be inspired by the same topic or that writing will flow equally well at all times. Physical requirements vary. Some children prefer to face a wall when they write and cut themselves off, as far as possible, from the rest of the class; some find the presence of others stimulating. Some like to think about a topic for days before setting pen to paper; others need the security of structures from the teacher.

Yet some common themes emerge. In order to write well, it does seem to be necessary to acquire the habit of writing regularly, and this is more likely to happen in a context where personal writing is a daily occurrence, where experiences and thoughts are frequently jotted down in notebooks, where variations in standard are accepted as part of the process, and where experimenting may be tried for fun. A sense of trust in an audience seems to be essential. Young writers need to feel sure that their tentative first drafts can be shared without fear of ridicule. They need space for experimental explorations and time for ideas to incubate. In a similar way, they need to develop sensitivity to the needs of their readers.

In short, it is argued that the conditions for establishing a writing community are most suitable where teachers foster reciprocity and trust in a playful atmosphere, share with children the enjoyment of happy writing experiences, and support them through writing difficulties. Perhaps, then, the essential task for the teacher is to help young writers increase their sense of control over writing processes in order not only that they may understand their own experiences and thoughts, but also that they may convey this meaning more effectively to other people. In this chapter we have outlined some ways in which the teacher can establish an environment in which this process is likely to happen. We can conclude with Gundlach (1982) that:

> we who teach must become intelligent readers of children's written language. We must learn to hear the coherent voices that often speak in fragmented and uncontrolled written forms; we must learn to recognise the merging of several functions in individual composition; and we must learn to detect evidence of learning in progress in the errors and immaturities in children's written texts. (p. 145)

References

Graves, D.H. (1983) *Writing: Teachers and Children at Work*, Heinemann, Exeter, New Hampshire
Gundlach, R.A. (1982) 'Children as Writers' in M. Nystrand (ed.), *What Writers Know*, Academic Press, New York
Polanyi, M. (1958) *Personal Knowledge*, Routledge & Kegan Paul, London
Smith, F. (1982) *Writing and the Writer*, Heinemann, London

12 PATTERNS OF CHILD CONTROL OF THE WRITING PROCESS

Donald H. Graves

Children want to write. For years we have underestimated their urge to make marks on paper. We have underestimated that urge because of a lack of understanding of the writing process, and what children do in order to control it. Without realising it we wrest control away from the children and place road blocks that thwart their intentions. Then we say, 'They don't want to write. What is a good way to motivate them?'

Children show us how they seek to control writing when they go about composing. They show us their stumbling blocks and the orders in which they grow in the writing process. They do not show with any one behaviour, nor in an antiseptic laboratory setting. Rather, they show us their growth patterns over a long period of time and in the setting where they normally function, the classroom. If we are going to help children, and not stand in the way of their gaining control of their own writing, we need to become familiar with what they do when they write. I will report on two areas of data from our two-year study of how children gain control of the writing process, 'Children's Transitions from Oral to Written Discourse' and 'Children's Development in Revision'.

Three researchers, Susan Sowers, Lucy Calkins and I, have just completed two years observing 16 children in a small rural school in New Hampshire, USA. The 16 children were chosen because of their differences in ability. Some hardly knew how to hold a pencil in first grade, whereas some third graders were capable of writing eight to ten pages of a story. The children were followed in two clusters: (1) grades one and two and (2) grades three and four. In this way we were able to map how children grew in control of the writing process over the first four years of school.

The 16 children were observed directly in the classroom. That is, we did not gather information unless the teacher asked the children to write or the child chose to write. Information was gathered by hand-recording or video-taping child behaviours during the writing process. We also used interviews, structured interventions, and the analysis of children's writings. Everything that the children wrote in any subject area was xeroxed during the two years. In the main, the researchers attempted to gain information with the least interference to the children.

Still, we bear no illusions. The presence of the researchers had great influence. It is impossible to have three guests in a home for two years, every day, and not have an effect on the owners or residents. We had a specific policy of not conducting workshops with staff, or consciously seeking to change teacher direction. We had this policy because we wanted to be good guests. If teachers, administrators or parents wanted to ask about what we were doing, we would be happy to answer, or share our data on request. My suspicion is, that because we took this stance, we had many more professional-type questions than might ordinarily be expected. In a way, we ended up having more influence on environment than might be expected.

In spite of this influence we did not feel our objectives would be lost — that is, determining how children would grow in their control of the writing process. Our theory (and I believe the data hold us up) was that if teachers were comfortable with the teaching of writing, knew more about it, and responded effectively to the children, a wider range of development would ensue. In turn, we would gather more information. Furthermore, the *order of development would not be changed*, the order of problems solved would be basically unchanged, even though the rate of solution might be accelerated.

Since our research was designed to find out 'what' was involved in the growth of children's control of the writing process, more than 'why', we felt secure with this arrangement. One other very helpful outcome of this approach to research was that teachers themselves became collaborators in the research project. Since they maintained control of their teaching they became quite aggressive in stating their opinions about writing and the research data. Major contributions were made by the teachers. On countless occasions they had indispensable observations and records on the children.

Making the Transition from Speech to Print

There is much for children to learn to control in writing that is very different from speech. They must supply the context, write in a certain direction, learn to control the space–time dimensions of writing on a flat surface, understand what the medium of writing can do, know the relation between sound and symbols, know how to make the symbols, learn to put symbols in a particular order, and while composing one operation understand its relation to the entire order of what has been and will be in the message, and compose in a medium where the audience is not usually present.

When children first write they are fearless. Egocentricity has its own protective cloak. Children are merely concerned with getting the marks on the paper and usually getting it down for themselves. Children are quite pleased with their own competence, and they experiment fearlessly with the new medium given a small amount of encouragement. Although children share work with others, this work is usually done for themselves. The behaviours displayed during writing are very similar to other play behaviours. Fortunately, children are not aware of all the transition steps they are making from speech to print. The child is a delightful pragmatist and seems to be saying, 'I want to get this writing down. I'm doing it because I want to, and what I am putting down is not only interesting to me but to others as well.'

Children's attempts to control the conventions of writing are marked by many holdovers from speech. For example, in speaking the context is usually supplied by the parties to the communication. Charles and Edward are working in the block area and Charles wants Edward's curved block. Charles merely points to the curved block and says, 'Give me that one.' But when Charles writes he must provide the setting through the words he supplies. Charles does not know how to provide the setting, the context for his writing. Instinctively he does much of this through drawing before he writes. The drawing provides double duty. On the one hand it provides the setting for the text, on the other it serves as a rehearsal for what he will write.

Although speech is directional, compared to the specifics of letter following letter on the printed page, it is non-directional. When children first write, their messages go in many directions. They may start in the middle, lower right, or upper left of the page and proceed in column form or diagonally, depending on the whim of the writer. If the child is aware of word separation, words may follow in column form, looping diagonals, even in a circle. In either case the child is aware that letters follow letters. Breaks for words are done by more advanced writers, again reflecting a written feature, since most words are run together in conversation — as do most words first written by the children.

Teachers permit most of the first-grade children in our study to learn spelling via spelling inventions. That is, the child spells the word the way it sounds. Thus, from the first day children are able to use whatever sound-symbol relationships they know to produce messages. At this point it appears that a child who knows six sound-symbol relationships (usually consonants) can begin to write. And they do. This year on the first day of school Mrs Giacobbe, one of the first-grade teachers, passed out bound, hard-covered books with the child's name in embossed letters on the outside. She merely said, 'Write'. Even though 30 per cent of the children had had no preschool experience they all wrote in their fashion. Some drew, others wrote their names, some put down numbers and letters, and about five wrote in sentences. The important thing is that none of the children believed they could not write.

Spelling inventions make it possible for children to control their messages from the first day of school. In addition, our data show that the words evolve from crude spellings to greater refinement. Susan Sowers, research associate on the project, has taken all words used by different cases, traced and dated their spelling evolutions during their first year in the study. The following is an example of a word tracing:

Toni's Pattern			*Sarah's Pattern*		
11/10 – LC	– like		11/20 – FLLAOWZ	– flowers	
LAT	– liked		FLLAWRZ		
12/8 – LOCT	– liked		FLLAWR	– flower	
12/19 – L	– like		1/11 – FLAWRS		
4/10 – LICT	– liked		6/1 – FLOWERS		
KLIC	– like				
5/14 – LIKE					
5/21 – LIKE					

At first the children feel little control since they know too few sound-symbol relationships to provide enough cues to recognise it again. Toni's 'LC' or 'L' above for *like* may be difficult to read at a later time. On the other hand 'LICT' gives more cues. It is an important moment when the child is able to compose, and read back his information from the page. In several instances we were able to be present with our video cameras when the child first realised he had the power to read his own message. 'I don't know how I do-ed that', one child said.

Putting symbols in order is a difficult task for many children. The ordering of symbols is quite dependent on the speed with which a child recognises sound-symbol relationships from his own speech, and the speed with which the letter is written. Sometimes the process is so slowed down by the difficulty the child has in retrieving the letter unit from his own speech that the full context of the message is lost. In Figure 12.1, notice how Jamie makes sounds to produce the correct sound-symbol relationship, yet must continually reorient himself to where he is in the message. Jamie produces the message so slowly that the text is obliterated by the next sound-symbol he encounters. He then must reread from the beginning each time in order to add the new letter in a word. The first line in Figure 12.1 indicates the point at which the letter was written in relation to the second line, the sounds produced by the child.

Figure 12.1: Jamie's Composing

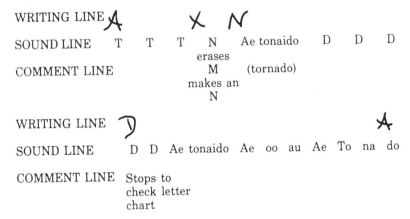

WRITING LINE ↔

SOUND LINE   T   T   T   N   Ae tonaido   D   D   D
                                                     erases
COMMENT LINE   M   (tornado)
                                             makes an
                                                N

WRITING LINE ↗   ↔

SOUND LINE   D   D   Ae tonaido   Ae   oo   au   Ae   To   na   do

COMMENT LINE   Stops to
                check letter
                chart

Figure 12.1 shows just how much language and sound Jamie must produce to sequence the letters for his message, 'A tornado went by here now.' It took him fifteen minutes to write his *unassigned* message. How easy it is to assume that Jamie struggles because he must produce a product. Jamie does not know he is supposed to be having difficulty. Jamie has just seen an account of a tornado's destruction on television and wanted to write about it. Jamie wrote this message in December at the bottom of a drawing he had already composed on tornadoes. Note how few cues are in this message for Jamie to read. In fact, he could not read the sentence, only 'tornado'.

Most young writers who make the transition from oral to written discourse must produce language and sound when they write. The following are some of the different types recorded thus far from our video transcripts:

1) *Sounding* to probe for sound-symbol relation.
2) *Sounding* to 'break off' a phonemic unit from the word under attack.
3) *Rereading language* for reorientation in the composing unit. The

child must hear where he is in the text. The difficulty or length of time spent on the composing operation determines how much the writer must reread.

4) *Conversations with friends:* 'This monster is going to eat up all the good guys.'

5) *Procedural language:* 'Now what am I going to do? No, this isn't right. I need to change it.' Procedural language is a more advanced form of transition from speech to print.

6) *Advanced statement of the text:* The child says the text in order to sense the appropriateness of the current word. 'He *cast* the line into the stream.' The child is now writing 'cast' but wants to make sure it fits correctly into the rest of the sentence. This is very different from Jamie, who has to say everything *before* the current operation. 'A tornado come *by*.' 'By' is the word under draft, but is determined syntactically by all that has preceded it, not by what may lie ahead.

7) *Conversations before and after the composing:* Not only is the child speaking during the composing, but language surrounds the entire written event. *Before:* 'I'm going to write about monsters today. And you know what, the good guys are going to lose.' *After:* 'I'm finished, Mrs Giacobbe, and everybody's killed. Look at 'em here, all burned up. See, this ray gun (pointing to the picture, not the text) cooked every one of 'em.'

In summary, the amount of language a child must produce before, during and after the written event is paramount. Beginning writers show through voice alone that writing is much more of a *speech* event than a writing event. A careful assessment of the nature of language the child supplies also gives us a picture of where the child is in his control of the writing process. These are data that make it possible for the teacher to help the child gain, and maintain control of his own writing.

As children gain more distance on the writing process they deal with new issues in making the transition from speech to print. Children speak less, make fewer vocalisations, and show more prosodics in their writing. That is, more speech forms appear in the writing. Ask the child to read while you observe his paper. The child will show with his voice how he uses prosodics. Examples of some of the prosodics are the following:

capitalisation of important words — 'Jumped'
capitalisation of the entire word — 'The fish BIT!'
blackening in important words, capitalisations
underlining important words.

Children also place more sound in their text through the use of inter-jections, dialogue and exclamation marks.

These features enter texts toward the end of the first grade. They come at a point when children grow in audience sense, gain skill in read-ing, and become interested in conventions. All three of these factors seem to occur simultaneously. They are accompanied by child state-ments that show distance, yet show a disturbance about their new lack of control in composing: 'This is stupid. This isn't what I want. I used to be able to write good, but I can't anymore. I don't like the sound of this.'

Later, as children gain more control of their information, realise that the data are strong enough to support themselves without prosodic markers, the markers fade. At this point children have usually moved into much more advanced uses of revision, sustaining a single selection over several weeks. New levels of control have been reached. The child writes to find out more what he means. The writing, as we shall see in Lucy Calkins's data on revision, becomes clay, is malleable, and does not need such explicit speech markers.

Summary of Principles

A number of principles emerge in reviewing how children gain control of making the transition from speaking to writing:

- At first children need to hear and see what they mean. They con-trol their writing through drawing and speaking as they write, and in discussing the writing with friends and the teacher. Writing is more speech than writing.
- As children gain distance on the process of relating sounds to symbols, and handwriting issues are put behind them, they become more dissatisfied with their text and look for new ways to insert speech features.
- At first writing is a highly egocentric exercise. Later, as the child gains more distance on the text and other children provide different responses, he realises the message needs to be changed.

Children's Development in Revision

When children revise they demonstrate their changing visions of inform-ation, levels of thinking, what problems they are solving, and their level of control over the writing process. Revision is not only an important tool in a writer's repertoire, but is one of the best indices of how children change as writers. For this reason, the data on revision have been one of the most important aspects of our study of children's writing.

Consistent with transitions from speech to print, children first revise their drawings because the drawings are more important. If children feel their drawings are accurate, the texts are seldom changed. Simple changes in syntactical accuracy, changing words because of the way they are formed on the page, or the addition of words for the sake of feeling are typical of first revisions.

At first children write for the sake of writing. They enjoy putting marks on paper. Their composing behaviours are play-like. The decision to write, the composing and completion of a selection may all occur in the space of ten to fifteen minutes. The child does not look back. Attempts to 'revise' the completed work with the child are sometimes met with diffidence or polite participation. The concept of the work as a message, usable at another place and time, is not necessarily understood by the child.

For this reason it is all the more important for the teacher to 'revisit' the writing through the give-and-take of an oral conference. The conference becomes the bridge between past and present, in which the child gains distance on the content and the concept of what writing can do. Furthermore, the conference is an invaluable source of information for both the teacher and child. Conferences run from three to twenty minutes. Transcripts of hundreds of teacher–child conferences over the two-year period have given us a valuable profile of the child's control of the writing process. Barbara Kamler (1980) of Riverina College at Wagga Wagga, who just spent six months with us at the research site, has written a very important article for the September issue of *Language Arts* (NCTE), in which she documents myriads of influences on one child's written selection as it developed over a two to three-week period. Her work closely documents the many functions of the language conference through actual transcripts between teacher and child and the child with other children.

The language conference that focuses on the child's paper is the cornerstone of children's revision. As the teacher revisits the child's paper, listens to the voice of the child as the paper is read, or notices the child's uneasiness about some information, the seeds of the child's desire to revise are observed.

Children wish the new information were in the text when they have chosen a topic that they feel is an important one in their own lives, one worth publishing, one containing information of interest to other children, or one that is of great length. When these first-grade children 'revise', the revision is usually in the form of adding information at the beginning or end of the selection. Seldom does it occur in the interior of the text. Disturbing the interior of the text is much more sophisticated than dealing with initial and final states.

Even though the strength of the topic is a strong determinant in the child's interest in revision, several other factors are involved. First, the child needs to spell and write comfortably, having enough speed so that extra writing does not become a penalty. Secondly, the child must have help in dealing with some of the effects of his first experiences with audience. Thirdly, the child gets help in dealing with spatial–aesthetic issues of changing the text.

When children have sufficient speed in the motor, sound-symbol components, and the general ordering of these on the page, the child can attend more to the text. No longer is the child losing sense of syntax because of the demands of spelling and letter formation. Now when the child is asked, 'And then what will happen?', the child is able to answer several sentences ahead, whereas before, the child was unable to think beyond the next word. In short, the child is now operating in a much broader space–time frame on the text, and can have greater distance on the information.

With distance the child does not find freedom. New problems of control arise. The child can usually read well enough now to recognise the discrepancy between intentions and what, in fact, has occurred in the text. The child does not necessarily like what he sees. Up to this time egocentricity has provided a protective mask, pushing the child into playful activity when writing. Audiences may have responded negatively to what he has done, but the child does not hear. He believes the audience has major problems. *He* does not.

At the end of their first formal year of schooling, many children shed their egocentric masks. When they do, they are not unlike the butterfly emerging from the chrysalis: weak, floppy, grotesque in movement, yet full of promise. They begin to hear the comments of classmates and teachers. They are aware of a discrepancy between their intentions and what is on the paper. 'It doesn't sound good', says the child. The child wants to change the selection, but often doesn't know how. Children may cease to write, avoid writing, or turn to the stronger suit of reading. For many young writers this is a highly vulnerable time, one that calls for an understanding teacher in conferences, a teacher who has helped the class to become a good audience. More than ever, a teacher's comments need to be specific, carefully listening to the child's voice as the paper is discussed.

A third element that stands in the way of children's control of revision at this time is the spatial–aesthetic issue. Children simply do not know how to fit in the new information. The teacher may say, 'Show me where you want to put what you have just said.' The child may not be able to locate where the information should go. If the child can locate it, he may still not know the mechanics of inserting information. Writing up margins, drawing arrows, putting in a caret are not tools that are part of the child's repertoire. Up to this point most of the children have erased words or several sentences when changes were made. But looking through the child's eyes, this question arises, 'How do you put something in when you don't want to change what's already there?' Splicing is new territory. The child needs help.

Revision presents an aesthetic barrier. The reason most children erase is to preserve the appearance of the paper. This occurs even in rooms where teachers stress lining out, or drawing arrows as a revising procedure. Children erase because they want the next to be right first time.

Have you ever observed children during the moment of their first encounter with a new piece of blank paper? Note how many times they 'clean' it before writing on it. They stroke, brush, even blow away imaginary dust. The cleaning continues during and after writing as well.

The following writing conference demonstrates a child in transition and how the teacher helped him deal with the spatial–aesthetic issues:

Teacher: I see that you were able to put in the word 'may' to show that 'Brontosaurus *may* travel in families'. (Chris had been able to sandwich in the small word without erasing.) But you didn't say why they travel in families.
Chris: They travel in families to protect the young.
Teacher: Do you think that is important information?
Chris: Yes, but there isn't any place to put it. (Chris's writing goes from left to right over to the right hand margin at the bottom of the paper. Above this writing is a picture of a brontosaurus.)
Teacher: Look the paper over and show me where you could write it in.
Chris: There isn't any . . . (voice rising)
Teacher: Look the entire paper over and put your hand on any space where there isn't writing or drawing. (There is a space above the drawing.)
Chris: Well, I could put it up here (motions to the top of the paper) but it would look stupid. The other part is down here.

Teacher: How could you show they were connected?
Chris: I could put an arrow down here pointing to the part that's at the top.
Teacher: Good, but you'll need to connect the arrow with the top. This is what writers do when they are getting their books ready for the publisher.

What does not show in the dialogue is Chris's concern about drawing the line connecting the information from the bottom to the top. Although he came up with the solution for the placement of information, he was not satisfied with the appearance of the product. He was pleased to know what professional writers would do when they wrote, but still may wish to recopy the text.

Revision in the Upper Primary Grades

Lucy Calkins, research associate on this study, has completed a major work on revision practices of third-grade children. She has identified four kinds of revisers from observation of child behaviours during writing, the analysis of their drafts, and data gathered from their attempts to revise a text written by Calkins about a common classroom experience. In the last of these the children were directed to revise a text filled with informational inaccuracies. They first told the researcher what they felt should be changed, then they changed the text on the page they had just critiqued.

Calkins (1980) has particularly attended to how children change their use of information when revising. She asks such questions as: 'How does the information change between first and last drafts? When children move from one draft to another, how do they use the last draft when they compose the new one? What are the changing strategies that children use as they advance in the writing process?'

Calkins found that children's strategies followed time–space development in a very consistent way. The degree to which they were able to control revision was dependent on their ability to use the draft from one page to the next, their ability to infuse information into the text, then to manipulate information from one page to another. These abilities show in the practices of the four types of revisers:

Type I. These children write successive drafts without looking back to earlier drafts. Because they do not reread and reconsider what they have written, there is no comparison or weighing of options. Changes between drafts seem arbitrary. Rewriting appears to be a random, undirected process of continually moving on. In their own writing they have many unfinished writing selections. They learn little from draft to draft. On the common classroom exercise they might come up with new information, but could only add it on to the end of selections.

Type II. These children keep refining earlier work, but the refinement is of minor consequence. The content and structure of their writing does not change. Some spelling, punctuation, or a word or two might be changed, but that is all. On the common classroom exercise these children, unlike *Type I* children, would look back at the text and come up with new information, but could not insert the data in the text.

Type III. These children move between periods when they refine drafts and periods when they are continually abandoning them and beginning new ones. At times they appear to be like *Type I* children, but they are closer to being *Type II* children. Moreover, their periods of restless discontent with their drafts indicate that they are in transition to the next level, *Type IV*. On the common classroom exercise they are able to insert the information convincingly into the text. Their restlessness seems to come from the higher standards they have set themselves.

Type IV. For these children, revision results from interaction between writer and draft, between writer and internalised audience, between writer and evolving subject. They reread to see what they have said, and to discover what they want to say. There is a constant vying between intended meaning and discovered meaning, between the forward motion of making and the backward motion of assessing. On the common classroom exercise these children immediately asked if they could change parts of it. One change led to another. Arrows, lines, stars and carets were used to change and insert the information.

Most writers seem to go through these four stages of development in revision. More data will be added, findings of the first year checked from another entire year of information on revision. Without extensive review of the data, many children have advanced in stages of revision. Many of the *Type IV* children from the third grade have changed drafting habits – that is, they no longer do as many drafts, and more information appears in final draft form from the first draft. They also do more rehearsing of writing when they are not in class. They think about revision strategies when they are with friends or reading or watching television.

Lest all of these revision data sound too cut and dried, it is important to mention one child, Amy, who does not fit this pattern of development. Amy was a good writer from the start of the study, but did not revise. She was the kind of child who would sit down to write and produce the following lead about cheetahs: 'A cheetah would make a sports car look like a turtle.' Her first drafts were better than most of the *Type IV* children who did extensive revisions. For a year and a half Amy baffled us both with the quality of her writing and her lack of revisions. Amy could tell by our questions that we did not understand how she went about composing. I think she enjoyed our perplexity.

In April of this year she informed Lucy Calkins:

> I think I know how I write. The other night I was lying in bed and I couldn't get to sleep. I was thinking, 'I wonder how I will start my fox piece in the morning.' It was 9.30 at night and Sidney my cat was next to me on the bed. I thought and thought and couldn't figure how to start it. Finally, about 10.30, my sister came home and she turned on the hall light. Now my door has a round hole where there ought to be a lock. A beam of light came through the hole and struck Sidney in the face. Sidney went 'squint'. Then I knew how I would start my fox piece: 'There was a fox who lived in a den and over the den was a stump and in the stump was a crack and a beam of light came through the crack and struck the fox full in the face.'

Amy is an excellent artist with an eye for detail and the language to go with what she sees. She does many off-stage rehearsals of what she will write. From this incident we merely get a glimpse of what she must do as she goes her own way in composing. Fortunately, she has a teacher who does not assign revisions just for the sake of revision.

Final Reflection

These data on children's transition from speech to print and on the process of revision provide a base for observing children as they change in the writing process. These data are not cast in concrete; they must be viewed within the limitation of the setting in which they were gathered. I think the data show us *what ingredients* are significant in observing children's growth as writers.

I am frequently asked, 'What can I do to speed up children's growth as writers? What can I do as a teacher to move the child from a *Type I* to a *Type IV* writer?' It is natural to want children to progress. But our anxieties about child growth lead us to take control of the writing away from the children. We want to produce materials, or come up with methods that unfortunately convince children that the source of control of their writing lies outside of themselves. When children feel in control of their writing their dedication is such that they violate the child-labour laws. We could never assign what they choose to do.

The teachers at our site have taught me a great deal in these two years of inservice training for researchers. They have slowed the process of teaching down in such a way that children have begun to catch up to what they already know. They listen for children's intentions to emerge, observe where they are in their development, and then find ways to provide the appointment for the child to control what he is doing.

Children will continually surprise us if we let them. As in Amy's case, when everyone seems to fit a pattern, if we look carefully, many do not. This may seem to lessen the importance of growth patterns across children. I think it heightens their importance. They are a solid base from which we can see the important differences in each child. And every child has them. As the study has gone on, we have become more fascinated with the differences in children than in their similarities. This is what happens when we slow down, listen, and let the children lead. That is the joy of both research and teaching.

References

Calkins, L. (1980) 'Children Learn the Writer's Craft', *Language Arts*, *57*, no. 2.
Kamler, B. (1980) 'Case-study of One Young Writer', *Language Arts*, *57*, no. 2.

AUTHOR INDEX

233

SUBJECT INDEX